Dear
Ross—
Merry 2001
Christmas!
Enjoy!
Love, Brenda

Charles Erskine Scott Wood
photograph by Ansel Adams, circa 1933

Wood Works

~~∂

The Life and Writings of
Charles Erskine Scott Wood

Edwin Bingham and Tim Barnes

Oregon State University Press
Corvallis

Substantial gifts from the following foundations and individuals helped make publication of this book possible. The Oregon State University Press is grateful for their support.

The Adams Foundation
Rose E. Tucker Charitable Trust
University of Oregon Humanities Center
Robert and Rebecca K. Burt
Noyes Family Ltd. Partnership
Mrs. Erskine Wood
Kirkham B. Wood

The paper used in this publication meets the guidelines for permanence and durability of the Committee for Production Guidelines for Book Longevity of the Council on Library Resources and the minimum requirements of the American National Standard for Permanence of Paper for Printed Library Materials, ANSI Z39.48-1984

Library of Congress Cataloging in Publication Data
Wood, Charles Erskine Scott, 1852-1944.
    [Selections. 1997]
    Wood works : the life and writings of Charles Erskine Scott Wood / [edited by] Edwin Bingham and Tim Barnes.
        p. cm.
    Includes bibliographical references and index.
    ISBN 0-87071-397-3 (cloth : alk. paper)
    I. Bingham, Edwin, 1920- . II. Barnes, Tim, 1946- . III. Title.
    PS3545.0465A6   1997
    811'.52—dc21
    [B]   97-25047
                                                                         CIP

 Oregon State University Press
101 Waldo Hall
Corvallis OR 97331-6407
541-737-3166

Series Editor's Preface

In 1990 the Oregon State University Press issued its first two books in the Northwest Reprint Series, *Oregon Detour* by Nard Jones, and *Nehalem Tillamook Tales,* edited by Melville Jacobs. Since then, the series has reissued a range of books by Northwest writers, both fiction and nonfiction, making available again works of well-known and lesser-known writers.

As the series developed, we realized that we did not always want to reissue a complete work; instead we wanted to present selections from the works of a single author or selections from a number of writers organized around a unifying theme. Oregon State University Press, then, has decided to start a new series, the Northwest Readers Series.

The reasons for the Northwest Readers Series are the same as for the Northwest Reprint Series: "In works by Northwest writers, we get to know about the place where we live, about each other, about our history and culture, and about our flora and fauna."

RJF

PREFACE

FOR MANY YEARS AFTER HIS DEATH in 1944, Charles Erskine Scott
Wood and his writing were known to but a handful of the faithful,
most of them on the Pacific or Atlantic coasts. This book is
designed to give its readers a vital sense of Wood's writing and
life. His contribution to American literature and his participation
in his epoch make him a figure whose legacy invites
reconsideration and deserves recognition. A well-known figure in
the early part of this century, his fame has faded since the 1950s.
It has not, though, vanished. Since his death and the last reprint of
Heavenly Discourse in 1946, writers, historians, and free spirits
have been rediscovering him and working to restore honor to this
prophet in his own country.

One of the editors of this collection first came across Wood in
the late 1950s, and published an essay in *Northwest Review* in 1958
called "Charles Erskine Scott Wood: 'An Era and a Realm.'" This
was followed by other essays and a pamphlet on Wood published
by Boise State University's Western Writers Series in 1990. In the
early 1980s, John Miller and Katherine O'Neil, both associated
with the Portland law firm of Wood Tatum Mosser Brook and
Holden, launched a series of Round Tables at the Oregon
Historical Center that sought to rekindle interest in Wood. This
law firm, of which Wood's grandson Erskine B. Wood was a senior
partner, joined with the Oregon Historical Society and the
Portland Art Museum to stage an impressive exhibit entitled "The
Legacy of C. E. S. Wood," timed to celebrate the centennial of his
entering the practice of law in Portland.

The other editor of this collection has published several essays
on Wood and between 1984 and 1989 produced three different
adaptations of *Heavenly Discourse* for the stage; he also organized
a group of players called The Heavenly Discoursers who
performed readers' theater versions of *Heavenly Discourse* in cafes
and taverns around Portland. In the early 1990s, photographer
Ron Cronin combined his photographs of eastern Oregon with
passages from *The Poet in the Desert*, presenting exhibitions at the
Oregon High Desert Museum and the Oregon Historical Center.
More recently, a New York firm has reprinted three of Wood's
works: *A Book of Tales, Too Much Government,* and *The Poet in the
Desert*, all of them selling at collectors' prices.

These activities and publications attest to a continuing interest in C. E. S. Wood. Indeed his works, especially *Heavenly Discourse*, have been an underground secret for years. It is not an uncommon experience for either of the editors to hear that someone has read a tattered copy of *Heavenly Discourse* or of *The Poet in the Desert* and felt enlightened and liberated. In his book, *The Sixties: Years of Hope, Days of Rage*, sixties radical Todd Gitlin remembers finding a copy of *Heavenly Discourse* in a Bronx bookstore and calls Wood, "My old inspiration." Wood's life and writing seem to have this effect on certain people. They feel enlarged and encouraged by learning how he lived and how he saw the world. The editors hope to give the reader a sense of Wood's scope and power and influence by providing a coherent, concise, and affordable way to read his work.

We have drawn almost completely from Wood's published writing and there is plenty from which to choose. Wood was frequently in print over a long period. Without a doubt another anthology or two lies within his unpublished manuscripts but we have made our selections with the idea of producing an introductory text. We tried to choose the best and most representative of his work. We decided not to include letters even though Wood was a superb and prolific correspondent.

Looking down at Wood's literary career from the vantage of the present, his life as a writer falls into four stages. In the first stage (1877-1901), he calls on his frontier experiences, especially his encounters with American Indians. The second phase (1899-1911), his real apprenticeship as a writer, revolves around his frequent contributions to *Pacific Monthly*, for which he wrote (sometimes under pseudonyms) poetry, short stories, essays, satire, reviews, and a regular column, "Impressions," that always carried his real name. The second decade of the twentieth century marks his third stage and his literary flowering. His late fifties and early sixties were Wood's most productive and profound period as a writer. His fourth stage (1920-1944), in which he won his greatest recognition as an important literary figure, was spent in California with Sara Bard Field, his second wife, and was devoted to writing. He published a good deal in these years, some of it reprints and revisions of previous work, but the outpouring that marked his third phase, spurred by Sara's sharing his life and by his passionate opposition to World War I, could not be matched.

As much as possible we have presented Wood's work within each stage in chronological order. We have also provided several layers of introductions. Each stage has a biographical/historical introduction. There are introductions to specific pieces and to specific books. Also, introductions to some of the genres in which Wood wrote are placed throughout to help the reader appreciate his achievement. Readers with questions about characters mentioned in the text may consult the end notes.

In addition to John Miller, Katherine O'Neil, and Erskine B. Wood, the editors would like to thank these people for their enthusiasm for this project and their support in achieving it: Jo Alexander, Brian Booth, Tom Booth, Kay Caldwell, Walt Curtis, Marian Kolisch, and Terence O'Donnell. Also to be thanked are: Virginia Bingham, Bill Deverell, Robert Hamburger, Marcia Hart, John Henley, Larry Johnson, Louie Levy, Bruce Livingston, Dan Lucas, Karen Reyes, Charles Seluzicki, Phil Wikelund, the Oregon Cultural Heritage Commission, and The Heavenly Discoursers. We are also grateful for help from these institutions: The Bancroft Library, The Huntington Library, The Multnomah County Library, the Oregon Collection of the University of Oregon's Knight Library, the Portland Art Museum, and the Oregon Historical Society.

As their last word, the editors would like to thank their insightful and enthusiastic partners, Ruth South and Ilka Kuznik, without whom this book would not have been possible.

Contents

Introduction

C harles Erskine Scott Wood led an extraordinary life, long, varied, and vital. Soldier, poet, attorney, satirist, philosophical anarchist, reformer, bon vivant, boon companion, painter, art patron, bibliophile, and pacifist—C. E. S. Wood was all of these. Approaching the Renaissance ideal of the universal man, he packed into nearly 92 years of living three distinct careers and a remarkable variety of experiences, exhibiting a rare capacity for savoring life and a stunning diversity of talent, including a protean, at times profound, facility for the literary arts.

An early impression derives from a large camera study of Lieutenant C. E. Scott Wood in his mid-twenties. He wears the uniform of an infantryman in the United States Army. He is seated on a rough-hewn chair, casting a level gaze at whatever crosses his line of vision, a revolver held loosely on his thigh. The youthful face is handsome—straight nose, resolute mouth, strong jaw.

In his later years, Colonel Wood (a militia title conferred by an Oregon governor years after Wood left the military) looked like an old testament prophet, with long snowy hair and full-flowing beard, but still the level gaze, the deep-set blue eyes. In a portrait by Ansel Adams, he looks far into the camera's eye, his face remarkably unwrinkled, except around the eyes where the lines seem etched by wisdom.

Between the handsome lieutenant and the snowy-haired sage lies almost a century of U. S. history, from the Wild West to the Second World War. Wood's life and writing chronicle and interpret many aspects of American life: westward expansion, the Progressive movement, women's fight for suffrage, isolationism and the Anti-imperialist League, the "Wobblies," Victorianism, Christian Socialists, the anarchist movement, Social Darwinism, and others that are faint in our cultural memory. Literature professor James Caldwell summed it up in a single phrase when he described his father-in-law as an "era and a realm." In the sparkle of Wood's exceptional character and vision lies a literature

1

Lieutenant C. E. Scott Wood during the Bannock-Paiute campaign.

of some distinction, capable of grace, wit, delight, and righteous fire.

C. E. S. Wood lived intensely, often extravagantly, in terms of money, emotion, and engagement in the arts. He drew friends from contrasting corners of society: Mark Twain and Chief Joseph; anarchist Emma Goldman and James J. Hill, builder of the Great Northern Railroad; Robinson Jeffers, California poet, and Clarence Darrow, prominent defense lawyer; Bill Hanley, Harney County cattleman, and Childe Hassam, American impressionist painter; Margaret Sanger and Mark Van Doren; Corinne Roosevelt Robinson, Teddy Roosevelt's sister, and Langston Hughes, Black poet; John Reed and John Steinbeck—to name a few. Described by a contemporary as a man of "vitality, magnetism, charm, wit, and teasing irreverence," Wood was a complex, contradictory, and unique man who forged a distinctive and refreshing lifestyle and projected, as well, a vision that illuminates the American West. His life and work can be seen as taking Jeffersonian values—that "all men are created equal . . . endowed by their creator with certain unalienable rights, that among these are life, liberty, and the pursuit of happiness"—and passing them through the crucible of what the historian of the American West Frederick Jackson Turner called, "the ennobling experience . . . the fierce love of freedom . . . furnished to the pioneer."

There was a rugged dimension to Wood's character and vision, the result, no doubt, of his frontier experience and his years on the Pacific slope. He put it bluntly in 1902 at the Manhattan Club when he spoke to a large gathering of Eastern Democrats:

I come from the West where the illimitable mountains lift up their heads to the very silence of God. Where the vast wilderness sits in silent brooding on the truth. I come from the West, where in a civilization founded on the mine and the camp, we believe that

*the saloon and the theater has as good a right to be open on
Sunday as the church and the school. I come from where we think
that it is the right of every American to go to hell and be damned
if he wants to. That is not humor—it is the truth.*

The rangy defiance ringing in that statement, coupled with the
conviction that freedom salted with knowledge will solve society's
problems, ran through most of his life. In addition, Wood had an
aesthetic side, a deep love of beauty and a sensuous appreciation
of the good things in life—fine wines, pungent cheeses, exotic
stones, and rare art objects. This, as well as his reading in
classical literature, tempered his broad-shouldered western
individualism, lending an urbane and learned flavor to his western
verse and anarchist sallies.

The overall impression of Charles Erskine Scott Wood is of an
expansive and singular man of engaging personality, warmly
human and in love with life, capable of profound personal growth,
deeply and articulately responsive to both the world of nature and
the injustice of the world, with a rare capacity for moving easily
and without affectation between the sophisticated spheres of
business, the professions, and high society, and the simpler
circles of workers and artisans.

C. E. S. Wood was born February 20, 1852, in Erie,
Pennsylvania, the second son of seven children (six boys and a
girl) of Rosemary Carson and William Maxwell Wood, a navy
surgeon, a Whig, and a friend of Zachary Taylor. Erskine, the
name Wood preferred, remembered a stern father who imposed
naval discipline upon his sons and a loving mother with deep
violet eyes who insisted on strict observance of the Sabbath—no
whistling, laughing, or "kicking down the leaves." Though
descended from Ralph and Ebenezer Erskine, founders of the
"New Kirk" movement, a religious rebellion in Scotland aimed at
liberalizing church doctrine, Rose was deeply aware of her
subordinate role in the Wood ménage.

Surgeon Wood was on active duty for much of his career. In
1846, speaking fluent Spanish, he traveled incognito across
Mexico delivering to Commodore Robert Stockton long-awaited
word of the outbreak of war between the United States and
Mexico, news that facilitated the acquisition of California. A few
years later, serving with the Asiatic Squadron, he was on hand at
the opening of Japan. He wrote several popular books about his

experiences. Surgeon Wood had a substantial library of Spanish, French, and English classics. Here Erskine first read Cervantes (one of his father's favorites), Voltaire, and Swift. In his autobiographical notes, Wood writes that his father's "taste for classical literature, his ideas upon culture and manhood, his contempt for wealth as an object of sole pursuit in life, had an influence on my own character." Wood's literary imagination was also clearly affected by the romantic tales of adventure and exotic objects his father brought home from his voyages.

With the close of the Civil War, William Maxwell Wood, now Surgeon General of the Navy in recognition of his service with the North Atlantic Blockading Squadron, took his family from Erie to Rosewood Glen, a small farm in the rolling hill country on the outskirts of Baltimore and within convenient reach of his office in Washington.

In his manuscript autobiography (begun in 1913 but never completed), much of which reads like passages from Mark Twain, Erskine sees himself as a mix of Huckleberry Finn and Tom Sawyer with the Erie Canal serving as his Mississippi River. Erskine pictures his teen years on the Maryland farm in lyrical tones. The prevailing atmosphere in the Wood home was upper-middle-class conservative with order, duty, and propriety as cardinal virtues. But the beauty of the surroundings seems to have helped offset some of the harshness at home. A clear, swift-flowing stream threaded stands of oak, hickory, maple, and red gum hung with clusters of purple fox grapes. Spring brought trailing arbutus with its scatter of pink stars, and laurel, wild honeysuckle, and azaleas sweetened the woods. At Rosewood Glen, Erskine learned to ride horseback, swing the scythe and cradle, and to hunt possum and raccoon.

Erskine received his early education in private and public schools. In the fall of 1868, he enrolled as a day scholar in the St. Thomas School for Boys. He remembers most vividly the snuff-taking, cane-wielding "Old Murray" who taught English and Latin grammar, geography, history, and composition through a combination of intimidation and drill. Increasingly the teen-ager indulged his appetite for good reading in his father's library. He was also an avid reader of Mayne Reid's frontier stories and those, together with the sprawling pink expanse of the "Great American Desert" depicted in school geographies, set visions of the Wild West pulsing in his mind.

In the late spring of 1869, much to his surprise, Erskine's life took a dramatic turn. Surgeon Wood arranged an interview for his son with President U. S. Grant. Erskine remembers nothing of what transpired during his talk with the President except that Grant lit a new cigar from the glowing stump of an old one. Erskine marked this in his mind as a bad habit. The interview combined with his father's influence resulted in Erskine's appointment-at-large to the United States Military Academy.

There is nothing to suggest that C. E. Scott Wood, as he was invariably listed on the military rolls, coveted the career of a professional soldier. Except for top marks in military drawing and creditable performance in ethics and law, he was a mediocre student and his military record bordered on disgrace. Piling up demerits just short of dismissal, the young cadet spent most weekends walking off punishment tours. In four years he never held a cadet rank. Years later, in New York, Erskine wrote in his journal: "I never pass West Point without thinking of my cadet days. . . . I hate the memory of it even now."

C. E. Scott Wood's class was unique in that it enrolled James Webster Smith of North Carolina, the first Black to enter the Academy. Erskine joined his classmates in consigning Smith to "Coventry," the silent treatment. That action drew a sharp reprimand from Erskine's father. Smith eventually was found deficient in natural and experimental philosophy and dismissed. Nearly forty years later, in 1912, Wood resigned from the Oregon Bar because it refused to admit a Black, one of many stands demonstrating Erskine's departure from his youthful conformity.

Cadet Wood resented what he considered to be undue emphasis on scientific and technical subjects in the West Point curriculum. Seeking relief, he did an unusual amount of extracurricular reading, checking out works by Shakespeare, Spenser, Milton, and Sir Walter Scott, among others. He also found stimulation in the Academy's social scene, such as it

C. E. Scott Wood as a plebe at West Point, 1871.

Nanny Moale Smith

was. He was an enthusiastic and graceful dancer and he often "led the German," a popular dance of the day. He was very handsome, quite the charmer, and amid the hops, cotillions, and flirtations he met and fell in love with Nanny Moale Smith, a Washington belle, who lived with her stepfather, Dr. Nathan Lincoln, a prominent Washington physician.

Casting desperately about for a way out of West Point, Erskine wrote letters home full of plans to resign and offer his services to the Mexican or Egyptian army or to go to Florida to grow oranges or, most frequently, to turn to a writing career. In a typical letter written to his son in the cadet's fourth year, William Maxwell Wood expressed his disapproval of Erskine's restlessness in flat, measured, elegant prose: "It is this unreasonable desire to escape from the present to an unknown and uncertain future, which has from the beginning been one of the causes of your demerits. . . . My earnest and final advice to you is to abandon all feverish desire after change and address yourself with honest and unceasing vigilance to the labor, the claims and obligations of the present around you—and of the place and position to which you are called." The elder Wood's counsel prevailed, for when the class of 1874 was graduated, reduced from an entering strength of sixty-seven to forty-four, C. E. Scott Wood stood academically squarely in the middle.

Along with other Academy graduates of indifferent record, Wood was assigned to infantry duty on the frontier in the Department of the Pacific. In his late autobiographical notes he remembers inaccurately: "I tried to change into Custer's cavalry but the Adjutant General refused and thus saved my life." Actually, correspondence in the Huntington Library's Wood collection shows he tried to trade with another new officer who had a cavalry assignment but met with refusal.

The young "shavetail" reported first to Fort Bidwell, an outpost
in the northeast corner of California. En route to Fort Vancouver,
Washington Territory, his permanent post, Lt. Wood marched
with his company along the lonely stretches of southeastern
Oregon. The journey through the Harney Desert worked a
profound influence on the 23-year-old lieutenant. The world of his
youth had been green and wooded, with water ever close at hand.
Now Wood was learning a new conception of space and scale. The
human figure was minuscule and much of the land lay stark and
brooding all the way to the horizon. The line of march took the
soldiers to the west of Steens Mountain, an extended ridge-like
uplift, its upper reaches patched with perpetual snow, rising to
nearly ten thousand feet, forming on the east a jagged escarpment
with over a thousand feet of free fall. The high desert is gray with
sagebrush, greasewood, and rabbit brush, mottled with tough,
twisted juniper and mountain mahogany, broken and uplifted by
ramparts of rimrock. There are alkali flats that glare under the
sun or float like puddles of pewter beneath the desert moon.
Steens Mountain is more than a dramatic landmark, for snowmelt
and springs cascading down glacier-cut gorges along its flanks
produce marshland and meadow in the Harney Basin. Wherever
there is water—along the narrow valley of the Donner and Blitzen
River, for example—there are natural meadows of wild hay, rich
browse for cattle and sheep and wild horses. When Lt. Wood and
his companions were passing through, early settlers such as John
Devine and Pete French were developing an impressive range
cattle industry in the region.

As they approached "P" Ranch, home place of Pete French, the
troops camped at the southern tip of a long marsh that stretched
north to Malheur and Harney lakes. Here tules, pondweed,
cattails, reeds, and grasses of all kinds grew rank and high,
providing perfect cover as well as food and nest material for more
than two hundred species of waterfowl and wild birds. Lt. Wood
rambled along the marsh's edge, wide-eyed at the teeming bird
life on every side. The tules were hung with blackbirds, some of
them red-epauletted, others with brilliant yellow heads. In a
clearing where the matted sedge thinned out he counted more
than thirty sandhill crane feeding quietly in the shallow water. The
marsh fluttered with movement and rang with song—the sibilant
notes of the blackbirds like air forced through a dusty flute, the
muffled pile-driver boom of the bittern, the mewing cry of curlew

7

and gull, the cacophony of countless ducks, the plaintive, monotonous shrill of killdeer and other sounds more or less musical but too muted or confused or unfamiliar for the young officer to sort out and identify. One species of wader caught Wood's fancy with its curved bill and its gleaming plumage of iridescent green and purple and bronze. He shot two of them, stretching the skins to dry in the sun, intending to send them to decorate the summer hats of Nanny Moale Smith, his sweetheart back east.

Years later, in his first effort at autobiography, Erskine recalls with sensitive precision that night on the Harney Desert when he lay sleepless, feeling keenly "the isolation, the beauty, the solitude and hush and above all the vastness of the desert and the breathtaking sweep of the dark dome above with its bursts of stars." As the camp noises subsided, "a small owl, puffed up and mottled like a partridge, mounted a badger mound and stood solemn and still on legs long enough to seem borrowed. For some time the owl was mute and then it began its song, a tremulous, high, mellow coo-co-hoo, much like a dove but higher, fainter, incredibly soft."

The entire journey across the high desert of eastern Oregon affirmed the sense of freedom and expansiveness that the West had symbolized in Wood's boyhood. In a letter to Max Hayek, translator of *The Poet in the Desert*, Erskine explains his love for eastern Oregon:

> *It means youth to me and the smell of sagebrush is the most delicious fragrance on earth; especially after a rain. Its blinding light, dazzling wide stretches—pale far purple mountain peaks— and the glorious skies are beautiful to my eyes—intoxicating beyond green mountains or sapphire sea.*

Wood welcomed his new assignment. Vancouver was just across the Columbia River from Portland, a metropolis compared to Fort Bidwell. Yet Erskine did not forget the days and nights in the Harney Desert and he was drawn back to what he called, in *The Poet in the Desert,* "that lean and stricken land" many times until he knew its contours, its diversity, and its moods in intimate detail. In fact, the region was to run as a kind of theme through most of his life, and before he was done with the desert it would help turn him toward poetry, painting, and rebellion.

Stationed at Fort Vancouver, Wood grew restless. He had begun to keep a journal, a practice he would continue for much of his life. He also hoped to publish some of his writing back east. In the spring of 1877, he took a leave from his duties to escort a small expedition intent on climbing Mt. St. Elias. The party failed to reach the mountain but Wood collected stories and artifacts that would become the basis for an 1882 piece in *Century Magazine* called "Among the Thlinkits in Alaska." Noteworthy for its careful description and ethnographic detail, this article and *A Book of Tales* mark the beginning and ending of the first stage of Wood's writing career.

Lt. Wood had hoped to continue to explore Alaska, but in early June 1877 he was recalled to join his company that had taken the field in pursuit of Nez Perce Indians moving toward Canada to avoid confinement on the reservation at Lapwai, Idaho Territory. Lt. Wood served creditably in this campaign, his baptism in fire, being one of only two white men to pursue the Nez Perce for the entire anabasis. As aide to General O. O. Howard, he was closely involved with the surrender negotiations on the morning of October 5th, gathering, through an interpreter, the gist of Joseph's sentiments regarding surrender. It is very likely that the young officer's literary bent moved him to shape the surrender speech, since become so famous, that he understood to have come from Joseph's lips. In fact, Lt. Wood's gift for phrasing goes far to explain the renown the speech has attained. The whole episode opened Wood's eyes to the power of the state to subdue a desperate and dignified people who were guilty simply of being in the way. Wood also bitterly resented Colonel Nelson Miles, who had entered the campaign only in its final stage, taking full credit for the Nez Perce surrender when it was Wood's commander, General O. O. Howard, who had given chase to the Indians for nearly 2,000 miles. An indignant Wood released an account to the Chicago papers that corrected the false impression, thereby arousing Miles's ire and setting up a tension between lieutenant and general that became a factor in Wood's resignation seven years later. At any rate, from the time of the surrender, Erskine and Joseph became friends and later, during his teens, Wood's eldest son, Erskine, spent parts of two summers in Joseph's camp at Nespelem, Washington.

In 1878, Wood served with Howard in the campaign against the Bannocks. In November, after the defeat of the Bannocks led by

Chief Moses, Wood, now a first lieutenant, returned east to marry Nanny Moale Smith, his sweetheart of cadet days. He brought her back with him to Fort Vancouver. In February of 1879, Wood served as Howard's emissary to Chief Moses, handling the peace negotiations. That fall the Wood's first son Erskine was born at Vancouver Barracks.

With the Pacific Northwest secure, General Howard was appointed superintendent of the United States Military Academy and Erskine returned with him to the scene of his unhappy cadet experiences, this time as adjutant. A second child, Nan, who was to become Oregon's first congresswoman, was born at West Point in 1881.

When Mark Twain made several visits to West Point to talk to the cadets, Erskine, as his host, delighted Twain by making a secret printing on the Academy Press of Twain's *"1601," or Conversation as it was by the Social Fireside in the Time of the Tudors*, the humorist's racy, rough-and-tumble reconstruction of talk in the time of Queen Elizabeth. Participants, including Elizabeth, Sir Walter Raleigh, the Duchess of Bilgewater, Ben Jonson, and others, gathered in the Queen's private chambers, discuss such bawdy topics as who has broken wind. Adjutant Wood put together a small but sumptuous edition of the unsigned scatological piece on deckle-edged vellum, stained in mild coffee to suggest age and using old English-style type to give a touch of elegance to the four-letter words. The Academy printing of *"1601"* circulated among the military "brass" and one copy went to John Hay and another to the Bishop of London. For a time Wood and Twain exchanged letters and the latter's influence on much of Wood's writing is apparent, especially in his satire. This publishing adventure affirms Wood's rebel soul, his literary leanings, and his interest in fine press printing, something he would retain all his life.

By 1882, Wood was considering the law as an escape from the army. Citing earlier duty as judge advocate in the Department of the Columbia and arguing that formal training in law would improve his military efficiency, he secured a leave of absence to enroll in Columbia University, where he earned a B. S. and an LL. B. in 1883.

While in New York, Erskine formed what would become an abiding friendship with the painter J. Alden Weir, son of Wood's instructor in military drawing at West Point. Weir brought the lieutenant-on-leave into a small bohemian circle of artists and agents, including sculptor Olin Warner; A. W. Drake, art editor of *Century*; the impressionist painters Wyatt Eaton and Childe Hassam; and the eccentric and mystic, Albert Pinkham Ryder. Wood reveled in the company of this creative crew that gathered in a French restaurant on the south side of Washington Square or at a saloon on the corner of 14th and 4th to talk of European art trends or to deride the Hudson River School and denounce the sterility and inhibitions of the artistic establishment. Here, Erskine's penchant for rebellion took on another dimension.

In March 1883, law degree in hand, Lt. Wood was relieved of duty on Howard's staff and sent to Boise Barracks, Idaho Territory, to join his regiment. Nanny, with the two children Erskine and Nan and a third child, William Maxwell, about to arrive, were in Fort Vancouver. Erskine tried desperately for assignment to Vancouver. Extended military correspondence, in which Wood skirted insubordination, earned the insistent lieutenant what amounted to a reprimand from commanding General Miles; whereupon Erskine submitted a resignation that was promptly accepted, effective September 22, 1884. At 32, C. E. S. Wood turned to life in Portland and the practice of law.

In 1884, Portland was a prosperous shipping town of over 20,000 population, known as the Boston of the West. Located in a temperate, green region west of the Cascade Range, the city lies along the shores of the Willamette River close to its juncture with the Columbia. To the west are the Coast Range and the Pacific Ocean about 100 miles away. The Willamette Valley spreads to the south.

On a clear day several white mountain tops glisten to the east— Mt. Hood the most prominent. Portland was and is a wet, grey-green, blossomy town, especially beautiful in the spring and fall. As the century turned, the city became famous for Helen Corbett's cow that grazed in the backyard of her mansion in the downtown district. Portland was on the edge of explosive economic and population growth. A deep-water harbor combined with the completion of the Northern Pacific railroad the year before to provide rich opportunities for the expansion of shipping and transportion. It was logical that the fledgling attorney on the brink of a new career would specialize at first in maritime law. In 1893, Judge Matthew Deady jotted this estimate in his diary: "Mr. CES Wood (too many initials) has delivered a couple of briefs this week that show a good deal of original thought and much care, research and taste. He ought to succeed at the bar." This praise from "Oregon's Justinian" augured well for Wood's future. In fact, by the turn of the century, Colonel Wood was recognized as an effective trial lawyer with a substantial practice in maritime and corporation law. He also came to represent the international banking firm of Lazard Freres as land agent for a sprawling military wagon road grant winding across Oregon from Albany in the Willamette Valley to Ontario at the Idaho line.

When the Woods arrived, they were welcomed into the homes of the Portland aristocracy, with whom they had become acquainted while stationed in Vancouver. The first years were difficult financially. In his memoir of his father, Erskine Wood recalls a family story that illustrates their early life in Portland:

> We lived in a little house on what was then Tenth Street, and the Failings, one of Portland's most prominent families, were giving a fancy-dress ball, and my mother had no dress. So she took down some muslin curtains, white with black and red spots, and made a dress out of them; and since my parents naturally had no carriage, my father took a box, lined it with furs which he had brought back from Alaska, and tucked my mother in it and pulled her through the snow down to the large and luxurious Failing house where the party was going on.

The unconventional, resourceful joie de vivre this story reveals is vital in understanding C. E. S. Wood as both writer and man.

In 1887, Wood was taken into Oregon's first law firm—Durham & Ball—that became Williams Ach & Wood when he joined. George Williams, U. S. senator for Oregon from 1864 to 1871, was also a member of the firm. Clients included the Port of Portland, the Great Northern Railroad, the Ladd & Tilton Bank, Henry Weinhard, Portland Flouring Mills, and the Ladd, Corbett, Flanders, and Meade families.

In an essential way, "Ces" Wood, as he was known downtown, was a very solid citizen, demonstrating pervasive and persistent leadership in Portland's cultural development. When Stephen Skidmore, early Portland druggist and councilman, bequeathed the city $5,000 for the design and construction of a fountain, Wood arranged for the work to be done by his friend of New York days, Olin Warner, sculptor of the doors of the Library of Congress. The Skidmore Fountain, that still graces the intersection of First and

Ankeny, was dedicated in September 1888, and stands today as one of Portland's premier cultural landmarks. Erskine also wrote the slogan inscribed on the fountain's base: "Good citizens are the riches of a city." He was a founding trustee of the Portland Art Museum and one of the early directors of the Portland Library Association. As early as 1889, Wood proposed holding an annual rose show in May or June, an event Portlanders know as Rose Festival. He was a charter member of the exclusive Arlington Club and was in demand all over town as after-dinner speaker. He moved easily within the select circle of Portland's patrician families, both

Painting of Wood by his good friend J. Alden Weir.

as legal advisor and friend. He and his socially prominent wife and their five children (Lisa and Berwick were the last two born) lived in a house with five fireplaces and a large garden on "the Heights," a lovely residential section of the city's west side. The children were being educated in the east. Surely, here was the image of a proper Oregonian.

But there was quite another side to the attorney and man of affairs, an artistic, romantic, and rebellious side. In dress and appearance "Ces" Wood suggested the poet or bohemian rather than the professional man. Sporting a full beard and longish hair, he worked in loose, tweed suits and soft shirts and if his pants were not always creased, he paid no mind. In the summer, he wore sandals. His evening costume included ruffled silk shirts with opal cuff links that set off to full advantage the heavy, handsome beard he had worn since his army days. With his curly hair, his wide-set, luminous eyes, a soft, broad-brimmed Stetson, and a flaring, black military cape to turn the Oregon rain, he made a commanding and dramatic figure.

The household C. E. S. Wood established on Ford Street (now Vista Drive), like the man himself, was a fascinating blend of contradictions. Along with other prominent Portland families—the Henry Failings, the W. B. Ayers, the Charles Ladds, the H. W. Corbetts—the Woods presided over a large house that expressed hospitality, comfort, and dignity. Nanny Wood was a handsome and cultivated woman with a passion for flowers and music, an unerring sense of the social graces, and a firm belief in the responsibility of the well-off to ease the plight of the less fortunate. Barbara Hartwell, a neighbor and friend of the family, remembers her as completely charming, "a combination of the utterly natural and the woman of the world." Yet the Wood home set itself apart from other distinctive Portland residences. It was, in Mrs. Hartwell's words: "Bohemia without shabbiness; unconventional, but shot through with conventionality like changeable silk. . . . . [it was] the world of art, music, literature, and also the world of 'who's who' and society Bluebook and the I. W. W."

The furnishings expressed a love of rare, exotic, and original things. Rich tapestries hung from the walls along with paintings by Albert Pinkham Ryder, Weir, Childe Hassam, A. L. Brennan, and Wood himself. There were tall shelves crammed with books, many of them redolent of hand-tooled leather, some of them unexpurgated translations of Petronius, Boccaccio, and Rabelais. Tall-backed Spanish chairs, Persian handicrafts, brass urns, Olin Warner's medallions of members of the Wood family and of Indian chiefs, oriental rugs and vases, figurines in porcelain and glass, statuary, and Indian masks filled the house with such an overflow of precious things that guests were startled by plunging horses from the Parthenon threatening them in the shower. If the taste revealed was eclectic, it was nonetheless sound.

The Woods made an art of entertaining, serving venison haunch or hams stuffed with honey or canvasbacks couched in cress and served with wild rice and spiced huckleberries or the Colonel's famous possum stew. The dining room, gleaming in candlelight, was heavy with fragrance of spices and wine. The conversation crackled with wit and irreverence, encouraged by the host, who would often enthrall the assembled with a tale from his Indian-fighting days. He was a superb storyteller. Holidays and birthdays called for family and neighborhood festivals with the reading of poetry and the presentation of masques written by the head of the house. At the Woods' one might meet bankers, painters, labor radicals, Northwest Indians, anarchists, editors, railroad magnates, or poets. There were parties where signs such as "Gamble for God's sake" shocked or shamed guests into contributions to a current cause. Erskine delighted in sending subscriptions of *The Masses* to "hide-bound conservatives." The overriding impression was one of elegance and ease but there was enough of the incongruous and mildly improper in the home to lend originality and pungency.

As the unconventionality of his dress and home suggest, Colonel Wood had not lost his creative impulse. The journals and notebooks of his military years are packed with perceptive, graceful descriptions of his surroundings—the streaming forests, the twisted canyons and white waters of northern Idaho and western Montana, the harbor at Sitka, and above all, the rimrock, rabbit brush and sage stretches of southeastern Oregon. He drew on these materials in his writing and he continued the notebook habit as his legal and business dealings kept him on the move to St. Paul, to Washington, D. C., and out into the Harney Desert to check on the vast land grant for Lazard Freres. Armed with a battery of sturdy, thick-barreled fountain pens clipped to his vest, he wrote on trains, in depots, alongside irrigation ditches, and around campfires, recording bits of dialogue with a Twainian ear for speech patterns, ideas for stories, sketches of situations for later development, songs, sonnets, occasional poems, vignettes, aphorisms, philosophical musings, and nature notes. All through Erskine's notebooks shine his love of beauty and his aesthetic relish of the world.

Inseparable from his literary urge was a growing radicalism that stood in stark contradiction to the conservative core of his legal work. As his practice grew, he came to feel that too often in the clash between property rights and human rights the latter were sacrificed. The Indian wars provided glaring examples and he found the pattern repeated as he represented private utilities, shipping interests, railroads, banks, and other powerful financial agencies. In a letter to Helena Kay, author of a 1937 Master's thesis on his writing, he explains the development of his ideas concerning the economic and social order:

> *I saw that the trouble was we were living in a feudal system, and by the old feudal fee simple deed, we were giving to a few shrewd forerunners the people's heritage and creating a small group of feudal barons who owned all and who were willing the people*

should multiply to become fighters and industrial serfs. Even when as a young lieutenant I was campaigning against the wild men of the desert, the desert had got into my blood [and] I saw this going in fee simple to cattle and sheep men, the water all seized, no place for hopeful settlement, and the great forests also stolen by the fee simple deed, a corrupt or ignorant congress, and some organized perjury. I saw everything of value taken usually by some form of fraud—water power, oil, iron, coal, copper— everything.

Wood's libertarian views were shaped in part from reading in Jefferson, Thoreau, Marx, the French anarchist Proudhon, the Russian anarchist Kropotkin, and single-taxer Henry George. Wood subscribed to Benjamin Tucker's *Liberty*, an organ of American anarchism that served, after the turn of the century, as an outlet for his increasing literary flow, playing an important part in his apprenticeship as a writer and a social thinker. Wood came to believe in the doctrine of right and beneficial use, the concept that land and water should be owned by those who use it productively, not by the grantees and their heirs and assigns, in perpetuity. Privilege and class distinctions violated Wood's sense of justice.

Erskine's broad philosophy of freedom that he called philosophical anarchism, the belief that the best way to assure one's own freedom was to insure the freedom of others, carried over into aspects of his personal life. There it involved their children, who were given the maximum amount of freedom consistent with their own safety. Barbara Hartwell writes of them: "They were utterly uninhibited before anyone even heard the word; their personalities were allowed to ramble richly at will . . . " When he was criticized for excessive permissiveness, Erskine responded: "Doubtless I made many mistakes, but I preferred to err on the side of minimum restraint, having been subjected to its maximum operation in my childhood."

The turn of the century marks a serious shift in Wood's life in Portland. His interest in the law waned and his urge to write intensified; his passion for his wife subsided into affection, and his philosophical anarchism cohered, strengthening his radical stance.

The most crucial aspect of Erskine's personal rebellion was his rejection of the institution of marriage. He saw monogamy as a kind of tyranny that stifled freedom. He could not accept the idea that two people sign a piece of paper that binds them together no matter how they change or what is in their hearts. In his own case, the marriage ties were not holding. Nanny's health was uncertain. She suffered from chronic headaches and in 1891 and for several years after she spent a great deal of time at a spa in Colorado Springs. Husband and wife grew apart, taking vacations alone and sleeping in separate rooms. Moreover, Erskine was a handsome, articulate, charming, and romantic figure. Beautiful women found him most attractive and he in turn was attracted to them. Sometime around the turn of the century, his secretary for the Lazard Freres account, Kitty Beck, a sensitive and appealing woman with radical sympathies, became his lover. The gap separating him from Nanny widened, although his affection for her remained strong.

Between 1900 and the entry of the United States into World War I, "Ces" Wood was in full stride, shifting the focus of his interests and spreading his energies in an ever-widening arc. His law practice was varied, demanding, and lucrative, although he tended to live beyond his means. He was increasingly intrigued with a life in literature and art and at the same time he was committed to progressive and radical social reform. He was for years on the edge of negotiating the sale of the wagon road grant for his employer Lazard Freres, and that took him out to the Harney Desert summer after summer where he stayed with his friend Bill Hanley at either the Flying O or the P Ranch. As was true from his early days in Portland, he continued to play a leading role in community affairs, especially in the cultural sphere, and with burgeoning interest, he continued to write.

Colonel Wood's first book came in response to a request by his 14-year-old son, Maxwell, and his friend Lewis A. McArthur, the future compiler of *Oregon Geographic Names,* for a manuscript to print on a small hand press that the boys called the Attic Press. Wood drew on his army notebooks to produce *A Book of Tales*, a collection of Indian myths of Alaska and the Pacific Northwest retold by Wood, plus one tale of his own devising. Published in 1901, it brings Wood's first stage as a writer to a close.

Three years earlier, Lischen Miller, Eugene poet, dramatist, amateur actress, and sister-in-law of Joaquin Miller, "the Poet of the Sierras," had solicited Erskine's help with a new promotional and literary magazine, *Pacific Monthly*, that was to be for more

"Ces" Wood in his fifties.

than a decade the foremost literary journal in the Pacific Northwest; Wood was a shareholder and his good friend Charlie Ladd was, for a time, the primary financial backer. Wood served his apprenticeship as a writer with *Pacific Monthly.* He was by far its most frequent contributor, writing often under outlandish pseudonyms—Felix Benguiat, Gustave Korter, Orrin Seaman—and providing verse, short stories, book reviews, art criticism, and a monthly commentary, "Impressions," under his own name where he unloaded unorthodox opinions on contemporary topics with a bold and vigorous independence. Wood was in good company in *Pacific Monthly,* appearing with national and regional writers such as Jack London, Ella Higginson, George Sterling, Mary Austin, John Muir, Charles Warren Stoddard, and John Reed. Erskine was also publishing fiction, verse, and social protest in Benjamin Tucker's *Liberty,* in New York; Marion Reedy's *Mirror,* in St. Louis; and Louis Post's *Public,* in Chicago.

Wood's radicalism was not confined to print. When Emma Goldman was denied a podium in Portland, Erskine came to her rescue, gave her legal representation, and appeared defiantly upon the public platform to introduce her to audiences in the city. In like manner, he defended Margaret Sanger and her right to disseminate birth control information. During her trial Erskine called Portland a "backwoods town." He made it known that he supported the Industrial Workers of the World, the I.W.W., and he helped defend the "Wobblies," as they were called, arrested in Everett, Washington, in 1916. Wood wrote an appellate brief, "Free Speech and the Constitution in the War," defending Marie Equi, an Oregon physician imprisoned for speaking against World War I; she called it, among other things, "the big barbecue." Wood's brief, an eloquent defense of free speech in time of war, was read into the Congressional Record. He also took the case of Floyd Ramp, a Eugene socialist farmer arrested when he asked soldiers on a troop transport train if they knew what they were fighting for.

Although "Ces" Wood was a lifelong Democrat and, in 1904, ran for the U. S. Senate, he was too much an individualist ever to be considered a party man. For a time, Henry George's single tax intrigued him, as did direct legislation (initiative, referendum, recall, and direct election of senators), and he had a hand in forging the instruments of Progressive reform as C. C. Chapman, founder and editor of the *Oregon Voter*, pointed out: "Colonel Wood was consulted by Bre'r U'Ren . . . and the effect of his advice was to simplify into an orderly arrangement much that was complicated and confusing." On other political issues, Erskine supported Abigail Scott Duniway in her drawn-out struggle to win women the vote, backed Harry Lane's fight for municipal reform, and campaigned for Woodrow Wilson because he promised to keep the United States out of war.

Throughout his years in Oregon, Wood was in demand as a public speaker. Representative speaking engagements in 1913 included: toastmaster for the Portland Press Club; an address on land monopoly to the Mutualists, a cooperative body; a Robert Burns birthday banquet oration; a lecture before a chapter of the American Institute of Banking on the responsibilities of bankers to society; a Portland Library talk on "What is Art?"; and a speech at a Universalist church on "The Value of the Beautiful in Life." In the election year of 1916, Erskine's topics were more political and included, among others, addresses on responsible government, causes of war, lack of labor solidarity, anarchism, the hysteria of preparedness and patriotism, and the right of free speech.

Yet, no matter how harshly he criticized special privilege and the prevailing social order, Wood continued to make his living by serving exemplars of the system he tilted against. He explained that he chose to play by the rules that ran society, maintaining all the while his right to advocate radical changes in those rules or in the very structure of society itself. When Emma Goldman chided Eskine for his activities in the progressive wing of the Democratic Party, Wood simply responded, "Emma, I take any wagon going my way."

In 1904, Wood published *A Masque of Love*, a three-part drama that questions matrimony and monogamy; this marked a significant change in Wood's writing and the beginning of his second phase as a writer. At around the same time, he began to celebrate Christmas by sending out Christmas messages, often exquisitely printed, intended, he claimed, not as poetry or literature but as "sarcasm and propaganda." Wood's Christmas pieces most often attack the hypocrisy of Christianity and the commercialization of Christmas. The themes in *A Masque of Love* and the Christmas pieces reflect the views he expressed in prose in *Pacific Monthly* and other publications. Though firmly ensconced in Portland's aristocracy, Wood was growing increasingly discontented with the sociopolitical system. This was the Progressive era and Wood held conspicuously progressive views.

Wood's radical pronouncements did occasionally rankle members of the Portland power structure. In her oral history, recorded in the Bancroft Library, Sara Bard Field remembers that T. B. Wilcox, head of the Portland Flouring Mills and one of the law firm's most influential and wealthy clients, came to Wood and threatened to fire him if he didn't rein in his radicalism, especially his support of labor unions. He was, Wilcox insisted, "going around talking everything that's against the way of life that we all live by and that we believe in." Furious at the suggestion that he could be bought off, Wood refused to muzzle himself and told Wilcox to find another lawyer. It is a measure of Erskine's standing among Portland attorneys that Wilcox backed off and Wood continued to represent Portland Flouring Mills.

Wood's creative writing and social criticism were crowded into an already busy life but clearly it was where his heart lay. He set up a two-room office in the Chamber of Commerce building separate from the law offices of his firm. One room was needed to accommodate the increasingly complex wagon road grant Wood managed for Lazard Freres; the other was a studio where he withdrew at the end of the working day and on Sundays to write or sketch or paint or, as Alfred Powers puts it in *History of Oregon Literature*, to spend "relaxed and happy hours with . . . poets, artists, scholars, philosophers, and social reformers." This was the existence he cared about; here he was nourished and sustained in a way denied him in his profession.

Since his arrival in Portland, Erskine had sought to transfer some of his passion for modern American painting, Impressionism in particular, to the Portland business and professional community. Drawing on his contacts in New York and Connecticut he worked to place paintings by Ryder, Weir, and Hassam in the homes of wealthy Portlanders. He strove to wean the Corbetts and the Ladds and the Ayers from purchases of

European art and get them to patronize the New York circle in which he had such faith. Over many years, Erskine corresponded with J. Alden Weir and those letters, full of negotiations designed to transfer paintings from eastern studios to the western shore, attest to "Ces" Wood's continuing function as arbiter of taste for Portland patricians. In fact, he has been called perhaps the most important art dealer in Portland's history.

Wood (right) and Childe Hassam painting in eastern Oregon in 1908.

In mid-October 1910, Erskine met Sara Bard Field Ehrgott, a woman thirty years younger than he who influenced his writing and changed his life. Married to a Baptist minister, Albert Ehrgott, a man inclined toward the Social Gospel but conservative in matters of doctrine, Sara had gone with him to Burma and then to Cleveland, where she helped elect the reform mayor, Tom Johnson. Again the church called, this time to Oregon. Dismayed, Sara saw the move to Portland as imposing a kind of cultural and social exile. Her friend Clarence Darrow, whom she knew through her older sister, Mary Field, suggested that she get in touch with Charles Erskine Scott Wood who, he assured her, was a force for liberalism in the Pacific Northwest.

As it turned out, when on a speaking engagement in Portland, Darrow invited Sara and Erskine to dinner at a Portland restaurant and saw to it that they sat next to one another. The two found common footing at once. He hungered to discuss literature and reform and so did she. Sara had studied briefly with Professor Thomas R. Lounsberry at Yale and was writing poetry. A friendship developed rapidly. Eager for criticism, Erskine asked the young woman to look over some of his writing that had piled up in a chest in his literary retreat. Here Sara came across a notebook of free verse impresssions of the eastern Oregon high desert. Sara was convinced that the material held great promise. Stimulated and encouraged by her suggestions and enthusiasm, Erskine expanded and shaped the verse fragments into the long poem that he considered his major creative work. The poem appeared first in 1914 under the uninspired title "Civilization." The next year it was published by Baltes Press in Portland as *The Poet in the Desert.*

In order to understand Wood's literary career, the reader must realize that he was reborn as a writer and a man in his relationship with Sara. In her he found someone who affirmed the direction he wished to go. Sara was not only a beautiful woman; her political views, devotion to poetry, and intelligence matched Erskine's. They were soul mates, something both of her children with Ehrgott, Albert and Kay, testified to. Erskine's relationship with Sara begins his most prolific and powerful writing period, the second decade of the twentieth century.

Between 1914 and 1915, Erskine reached a crossroads in his life and career. World War I had begun and Wood became galvanized in opposition to it. He campaigned for Woodrow Wilson, who was against U. S. military involvement, consonant with the strong isolationist mood in the country. In a 1916 speech, printed in a pamphlet "Is This a War for Democracy," Wood called the war, "dirty trade for dirty dollars."

Also in 1914, Max Eastman, an editor of the radical magazine *The Masses,* asked Wood for a contribution, perhaps something humorous. Wood responded with several satirical dialogues that he called collectively "Heavenly Discourse." Here he lampooned prudery and evangelism, but took special aim at the war effort and its abrogation of free speech. Ten discourses appeared before the magazine was barred from the mails in 1917.

Politically, the situation became less comfortable for Wood. His antiwar activities brought his patriotism into question. He came under the investigation of Clarence Reams, Assistant U. S. Attorney General, for writing an antiwar pamphlet, "Ave! Caesar. Imperator. Morituri Te Salutant." In his letter to his superior, the U. S. Attorney General, Reames clears Erskine of any unpatriotic activity but he does suggest Wood to be "not a safe man to advise the President, especially relative to labor conditions." Reames also acknowledges that Wood "has a lot of friends, and a great deal of influence in the community."

During this same period, the rift in the Wood household had become irreparable. Although Nanny Wood was a devoted mother and a valuable asset to her husband in maintaining a gracious social milieu, she found herself linked with a man whose passion for exploration and intensity of experience were foreign to her nature. She simply was unable to share his enthusiasm for art and anarchy. Moreover, for several years her husband's relationship with Sara Ehrgott had involved a good deal more than intellectual companionship. Given his views of marriage as a voluntary union resting on mutual affection and understanding, vividly rendered in *A Masque of Love,* Erskine was prepared to defy convention and seek a life with Sara devoted to creative writing at whatever the price in pain and suffering to all concerned. Since Erskine recognized his financial obligation to his family, such a break would be costly materially as well as emotionally and although his law practice was lucrative enough, his penchant for spending beyond his means kept the attorney in debt. Light on Wood's lack of frugality comes from this excerpt from son Erskine's memoir of his father:

> *It was not only fine books that my father loved, he really loved all things of beauty—fine paintings, sculpture, Oriental rugs, ancient Greek glass, the art of China and Japan. . . . He also liked jewelry, opals and star sapphires, and particularly the pure yellow unalloyed gold rings and jade settings that the old Chinese jewelers used to make in Chinatown in Portland, among whom my father had some friends.*

Wood delighted in the physical world, especially when it gathered into loveliness. He bought real estate not as an investment but for the beauty of the land—and lost money. This sensuous apprehension of the world, of both nature and art, is another pervasive element of Wood's sensibility and of his writing.

Fortuitously, the sale of the wagon road grant that Wood had been negotiating for some years was consummated in 1918. The generous commission—one million dollars paid over several years—permitted Erskine to set up a number of trust funds for his Portland family and freed him to retire from law practice and move to California with Sara, who had gone to Nevada, obtained a divorce, and moved to the Bay area. However, Nanny's Catholicism, combined with her indignation, compelled her to refuse her husband a divorce.

*Erskine and Sara
during their time in
San Francisco*

Erskine and Sara hoped to start a new life together, one
devoted to poetry and their shared vision of a just society, but
Wood found it difficult to extricate himself from the web of
relationships and loyalties that thirty years in Portland had woven.

Wood and Sara spent much of the fall of 1918 in San Francisco.
Sara, who had just learned to drive, took Erskine and her two
children, Kay and Albert, for an outing in Marin County. On a
steep road the car overturned, killing Albert and nearly severing
one of Sara's legs. Wood stayed with Sara a good part of the
spring, nursing her back to health. The accident and the payment
from the wagon road sale shook Erskine loose from Portland. In
the late spring of 1919, they bought a house at 1020 Broadway on
Russian Hill in San Francisco.

In 1918 and 1919, though it was a difficult and traumatic time,
Wood was quite productive, turning out *Maia* and *Sonnets* along
with a revision of *The Poet in the Desert* in 1918 and *Circe, A
Drama with a Prologue* in 1919. *Maia* expresses Erskine's love of
nature and of Sara. *Sonnets*, called "Personal Sonnets" or "Garden
Sonnets," is dedicated to his family. *Circe* makes the power of
human love supreme. The revision of *The Poet in the Desert*

affirms Wood's radicalism and his devotion to poetry, clarifying his vision and shedding much of the blatant propaganda of the 1915 version. It was a significant artistic and psychological feat for Wood to complete during this time four books, each of which deals with a key element in his life. No doubt the increase in his financial fortunes assisted, but his need to present his case in poetry is clearly primary.

The poets' house overlooked San Francisco Bay from Russian Hill. Angled into a corner lot, it featured an enclosed garden and a steep stairway to the front door. Soon after moving in, Sara suffered a breakdown, an aftermath of the loss of her son. She hovered near death for several days. Her recovery was slow. Wood and Sara's daughter, Kay, cared for her together, forging a bond. In fact, Kay grew to prefer "Pops," her name for Erskine, to her real father. The divorce settlement stipulated that Wood not be present when Sara's children came to visit. Once, due to a misunderstanding, Ehrgott found Wood and Sara together when he brought Kay for a visit. "You killed your son," he shouted at Sara over and over as he spirited Kay away. Neither Wood nor Sara wrote much during this time, although both had poems in *Debs and the Poets*, a tribute to Eugene V. Debs, the socialist leader imprisoned for his opposition to World War I.

In 1920, San Francisco hosted the Democratic Convention. Both Erskine and Sara attended as reporters for small, radical publications; among them was Max Eastman's *Liberator*. The failure of the left and a new conservative tone in American politics made the convention depressing but the week was enlivened by visits to their home by William Allen White, the progressive Republican editor of the *Emporia Gazette*, novelist Edna Ferber, and William Marion Reedy, editor of the radical journal *Reedy's Mirror*, one of Wood's venues. "The Flowering Wall," the name they gave their house, became a meeting place for writers, artists, musicians, labor leaders, civil libertarians and others of liberal persuasion. Erskine and Sara befriended a young Ansel Adams. The novelist and lecturer John Cowper Powys came with his brother Llewelyn, who remembers Wood as "Some magnificent old chieftain, victor of a hundred battles. . . . this old, unrelenting, white-maned lion of Oregon." They met the young and beautiful poet Genevieve Taggard, as well as the generous patron of the arts, Albert Bender, who connected them with the Grabhorn brothers who would print several of their books. George Sterling, the Bohemian poet, roused them out of bed at least once. They also formed a friendship with Noel Sullivan, heir to two fortunes and supporter of Langston Hughes, Marian Anderson, and Roland Hayes. The muckraking editor of *The San Francisco Bulletin*, Fremont Older, visited often. The two poets joined the Bay area community of cultural progressives with gusto and were living as they had hoped they might.

Erskine and Sara put their support behind a school for theater arts directed by Maurice Browne and Ellen Van Volkenburg. Browne began the little theater movement in Chicago in 1912, giving rise to hundreds of other little theaters across the country in the next few years. He arrived in San Francisco in 1921 and operated a theatre and offered experimental acting classes. Browne's troupe performed Wood's *Odysseus* and gave space to Blanding Sloan's Puppet Theater which adapted some of *Heavenly Discourse* for production. Sloan's version of Erskine's satire caused something of a sensation. He took liberties with the text, rearranging material and adding questionable scenes, including one of a naked Eve perched provocatively on God's lap while being fondled. The police raided the show and closed it down. Wood would not allow it to reopen, even though a repentant Sloan promised to rewrite the script.

San Francisco's fog, together with constant interruptions of their writing by visitors, led Wood to acquire, as a potential retreat, 34 acres of wooded hillside above Los Gatos, a small town fifty miles south of San Francisco, just west of San Jose at the eastern edge of the Santa Cruz mountains. The two poets spent time at first in a small shack on the property, cooking in a stone fireplace and reading to one another of an evening. Before building on the property, they took Lincoln Steffens's advice to scout out Europe as a possible place to live and in January 1924, Erskine, Sara, and Kay sailed for Italy, docking in Naples. From Sorrento as a base they made excursions to Sicily, saw Greek tragedies at Syracuse, and visited St. Peter's cathedral in Rome, a visit that may well have inspired one of Erskine's most delightful poems, "Billy Craddock in Rome."

After four months in Italy and Sicily, Wood received word that his commissions from the land grant sale were being taxed as annual income, threatening his financial security. The three travelers booked passage home but not before visiting Paris, Vienna, Florence, London, and Normandy. In Paris they met with

Ezra Pound, who liked Erskine's satiric conversations but felt Wood's lampooning of American society was too mild. Also in Paris, the three served as the only witnesses to the marriage of Lincoln Steffens and Ella (he called her Peter) Winter. At the reception they were joined by Louise Bryant, John Reed's widow, and her new husband, William C. Bullitt.

They returned to New York in September 1924 and stayed there for several months, visiting friends and equipping Kay for college at the University of Wisconsin. Wood traveled back and forth between New York and Washington, consulting with lawyers and working on the income tax case. By December of 1924, Sara and Erskine were back in California, having decided to build on their hill in Los Gatos.

House-building got under way in the second week of December 1924. At Erskine's suggestion architect Walter Steilberg abandoned the idea of view as the paramount consideration. Instead, the house would rise from the hollow in harmony with its hill background with the slope or "run-away" in the foreground and protected from the wind. The house resembled a thick staple set into the flank of the hill and enclosing an inner court that was studded with flowers and shrubs up toward and merging with the hill's crest rimmed by live oak and eucalyptus. Thus the house set squarely across the watershed facing the descent that leveled off in a lovely cluster of oaks, forming, with the gentle slope of the grove, a small natural theater. As it worked out, the view of Los Gatos, San Jose, then mostly fruit trees, to the Diablo Range, was partitioned rather than lost, coming in broken vistas through the trees instead of in one staring panorama. A steep and narrow road wound down to the highway where two ten-feet-tall stone felines sculpted by Robert Paine, one half asleep, the other open-eyed, guarded the entrance and passed on the name of the town, Los Gatos, to the hillside dwelling, The Cats.

The finished house of concrete blocks was deceptive, seeming more massive and spacious than it actually was. There was a long living room with a cavernous fireplace, three bedrooms,

Robert Paine's towering stone cats that flank the entrance to The Cats.

27

The Cats, Erskine and Sara's house in Los Gatos

a basement garage and a solarium over the living room roof. Up against the outside of the great chimney, looking out over the court, rose sculptor Ralph Stackpole's figure of Maia, a huge primeval woman with tree-trunk thighs and "breasts like the ever lasting hills." Below Maia, Ray Boynton executed a mosaic of two naked figures holding out their hands to catch manna. Sculptor Beniamino Bufano cast a bas relief of two figures sitting beneath the tree of poetry for the south wall of the courtyard. Bufano also made a fountain for the courtyard, fired with a special blue glaze he brought back from China (a trip Wood financed), at the center of which were a boy and girl, arms intertwined. All in all, this was a house of originality, charm, and power, built to defy fire and storm and earthquake but receptive to the sun.

Shortly after acquiring the hill acres, Colonel Wood had set out what he called a "mountain vineyard," so that The Cats might produce wine as well as writing. Erskine was fascinated by the ancient process of wine making, the fecundity of the earth, the storing and saving for the bare, cold days, the sculpturesque postures of the workers about the press, their arms purpled to the elbows, the rich autumnal tints that hung around them as tapestries. Moreover, the knowledge that more than two hundred gallons of wine drawn from the upper and lower vineyards were bubbling and fermenting in the basement beneath the house in sublime defiance of the Volstead Act delighted the Colonel's anarchist soul.

Assisted by their loyal help, Vincent and Mary Marengo, Erskine and Sara created beautiful grounds with an unusual

28

variety of trees—native oaks, redwood, and madrone, as well as olive trees, cypresses, and a lemon grove. The Cats was their monument to their love and to poetry. On the bluff to the south of the house, two friends erected a tandem bust of Erskine and Sara. On Wood's side, the inscription reads:

I know for everyone
were he but bold
Surely along some
starry path
His soul awaits him.

Sara's side reads:

Had we not clutched
love flying by
Where had you been
Where had I?

In poetry, they declared their love for each other and for the fate that brought them together.

They moved into the house in November of 1925, beginning the happiest time of their lives; they were together in a beautiful place, close to many good friends and able to devote themselves to their writing. Erskine and Sara looked upon The Cats as a refuge from distractions. At first, in fair weather, they worked at stone tables and benches under bay trees; when the California rains came, they withdrew to opposite ends of a long table in the living room. Later on, to gain privacy from a stream of visitors, they built a small house with a kitchen and two writing rooms a few hundred feet above the main house. A dedication, "To Poetry," was hardened in cement on the kitchen wall and the beams of the writing rooms carried quotations. Here the poets set their own pace, able to claim they were not at home when unannounced visitors called at the main house.

Encouraged by writers and friends, Erskine set about revising and bringing up to date his satiric discourse. When he finished in 1926, there were forty conversations, about double the number in existence when *The Masses* was denied use of the mails. Two years later, Jacob Baker, head of New York's Vanguard Press, brought out *Heavenly Discourse* in a fifty-cent edition of three thousand, with a flattering introduction by Floyd Dell and eight line drawings by Art Young, former *Masses* cartoonist and

This portrait of Wood by Hugo Gellert was used as the frontispiece to Heavenly Discourse.

communist. To the surprise of Vanguard and the delight of the author, the first printing was rapidly exhausted. Public demand persisted, requiring a succession of printings and several editions, each of which, after 1928, contained a forty-first discourse dealing with the trial of Sacco and Vanzetti.

After more than a score of printings by Vanguard, *Heavenly Discourse* came out as a Penguin paperback in 1946 and in 1953 there was a Danish translation. The Colonel's confidence from the start that the book would make its own way was thoroughly vindicated.

In 1929, Grabhorn Press of San Francisco printed a collection of Erskine's western verse, *Poems from the Ranges,* that stands as a lyric tribute to the Harney Basin region of eastern Oregon he loved so much. The success of *Heavenly Discourse* prompted Vanguard in 1929 to reprint Erskine's *A Book of Tales* as *A Book of Indian Tales* and a revised edition of *The Poet in the Desert.*

In 1931, Erskine wrote a book of irascibly eloquent, rambling essays against governmental interference with individual liberty called *Too Much Government* that focuses on prohibition, but other favorite targets—censorship, patriotism, prudery, privilege, militarism—also come under attack. Nearing eighty years old, Wood still wrote with grace and fire. This publication was followed by *Earthly Discourse*, a return to satire, published in 1937, but he could not duplicate the success of *Heavenly Discourse* and, appropriately, considering its title, the book never got off the ground. Over these years Erskine was also constantly revising *Sonnets to Sappho* (privately printed), a sequence of fifty-five sonnets attesting to his love for Sara in his later years. He began

Wood dressed in Greek garb reading a 1929 edition of The Poet in the Desert.

but did not complete a historical narrative designed to show his father's role in the acquisition of California. Finally, early in 1940, Wood made a second start on his memoirs, begun in Portland as early as 1913.

Meanwhile, his beloved companion, Sara, was also working at her craft. In the year of *Heavenly Discourse*, Sara's *The Pale Woman* appeared. Five years later, in 1932, her *Barabbas*, a dramatic narrative poem with a religious theme, won the California Book Club's award for the best literary work by a Californian. *Darkling Plain* (1936) was the last of her major works of poetry, but in 1937 she and Erskine printed privately *Selected Poems by Charles Erskine Scott Wood and by Sara Bard Field.*

Because Erskine and Sara were people of broad sympathy and compassion, each with a highly developed social consciousness, The Cats was a kind of clearing house for causes. Both poets spoke in public protest against what they considered the intolerable imprisonment of Tom Mooney, the labor agitator implicated in the 1916 Preparedness Day parade bombing in San Francisco. In 1935, they joined the Provisional American Committee for the Defense of Leon Trotsky, a group supporting the exiled Trotsky's plea for an impartial trial to clear him of the Stalinist charge of treason. At about this time, Wood discovered

that he and Sara were under investigation by the House of
Representatives Special Committee on Un-American Activities,
headed by Martin Dies. Wood wrote a series of letters to Dies,
scolding him for abandoning the fundamental American values of
liberty and individual rights. In 1936, at a Western Writers
Conference in San Francisco, Wood delivered an address that
took the conference by storm and the audience of progressive
writers such as Upton Sinclair, Kenneth Rexroth, and Nathanael
West, concerned with the rise of fascism and interested in
fostering solidarity within their ranks, elected him their president,
seeing him as a symbol of western American independence and
the radical tradition in American thought. It is clear that Erskine
and Sara, despite the protective shell of their hillside house, were
very much of and in the world.

The Cats was not only a distinctive dwelling set in a stunning
backdrop of natural beauty, it was a way of life. Both poets were
committed to writing but beyond that they were dedicated to the
art of living. Out of their devotion to each other and from the
tranquillity and charm of their surroundings, they shaped a
relationship that was as much a thing of their own creation as any
piece of poetry fashioned in their twin studios. Each drew from
the other in a kind of spiritual symbiosis. Sara gave Erskine youth
and graciousness, abiding love, and criticism and advice in his
writing. He gave her something of his vitality and strength
combined with worldly wisdom born out of long and varied
experience upon which she might draw; security, with a chance to
develop her own talent; and a sprawling philosophy of freedom
that she could accept and share. Abundant evidence that some
such relationship existed can be drawn from the couple's double
journal, from explicit statements in letters from friends and
admirers, and from the testimony of those still living who knew
Sara and Erskine and who remember the texture of their life
together. Lincoln Steffens put it this way in a letter written after
returning from a celebration at The Cats of Wood's eightieth
birthday:

> When we drove home from The Cats Monday, I felt that I had
> been in a place of beauty, and I wondered why we didn't go oftener
> to you. The drive there is beautiful, the house, the guests, the spirit
> of it all—the whole and every part are beautiful. Los Gatos is a
> work of art. A play of art. . . . You are, both of you, each one of
> you, beautiful works of art.

Their San Francisco friends made their way to Los Gatos. Noel Sullivan came often, having a house in Carmel and a sister in a convent in Santa Clara. Several times he brought Langston Hughes along. Fremont Older lived nearby in Los Altos Hills, financially secure after his paper's merger with the Hearst chain but unhappy at the accompanying restraints. When Genevieve Taggard visited they would have long discussions on how to use poetry to promote political change. John Steinbeck and his first wife Carol lived near The Cats for several years and would stop over to talk and drink their good, red Princess wine.

Erskine on his 80th birthday.

Through mutual friends, George Sterling and Albert Bender, the Woods became friends with the poet Robinson Jeffers and his wife Una. The reclusive Jeffers did not travel far from Tor House often, but Erskine and Sara would visit them every few months, sometimes picnicking on Carmel Beach. Wood admired Jeffers's poetry and Jeffers had read *The Poet in the Desert*, finding it "noble."

Sara's daughter Kay married James Caldwell, a professor of English at the University of California, in a lavish wedding at The Cats in 1927, and they settled down in Berkeley. Caldwell liked his in-laws immensely and the four of them were often together. In that same year Wood won his income tax case but the stock market crash of 1929 reduced his wealth, though the couple's lifestyle did not change dramatically. Sadness came in the deaths of family and friends. Sara's son Albert, of course, had died in 1918, followed three years later by the death of Maxwell, Wood's favorite son. Nanny died in 1933. Fremont Older died in 1934 and both Lincoln Steffens and Bill Hanley the next year. In 1938, Darrow passed away.

Late in 1937, Wood's phenomenal health failed. He suffered a severe heart attack while staying with his daughter Lisa in San

Rafael. On January 20, 1938, prompted by his weakened condition and by the need to safeguard Sara's inheritance of the estate, the two poets were married by Rabbi Jacob Weinstein of Chicago, in a private ceremony at The Cats.

Wood died on January 22nd, 1944, just one month short of his ninety-second birthday. Sara wrote his son Erskine that "to the last conscious hours nothing but love and humor came from his lips." His body was cremated and his ashes were sown through the live oak grove at The Cats, a wish he expressed in one of his sonnets.

In a long and eventful life, C. E. S. Wood was many things to many people. A hostile view would stress his extravagance, his vanity, his self-conscious, sometimes strident, anarchism. Surely special pleading marred some of his work nor, except for *Heavenly Discourse* and his lyrics, was brevity a hallmark of his style. While admitting his talent and charm, there were those who could not stomach what they considered to be a mixture of hypocrisy, blasphemy, immorality, and self-indulgence. Nonetheless, across the years, Wood's life has an impressive richness and vitality. Touch the man almost anywhere in his several careers and find style, gusto, variety, vision, and Renaissance proportion, characteristics that, as the reader will see, also mark his literary production.

C. E. Scott Wood's first career was short-lived and not of his own choosing. He spent four years as a reluctant West Point cadet, followed by ten years in the infantry as a competent but dissatisfied soldier who had a prominent part in one of the most dramatic and tragic Indian campaigns of North American history. Over that decade the young officer bent his military experience toward his true interests. He turned a brief probe of Alaska and service on the far western frontier into articles published in *Century*, the premier illustrated monthly of the era. By the generous exercise of poetic license he turned Chief Joseph's words of surrender into one of the most famous and quoted speeches in the annals of Indian oratory. As adjutant of West Point, he played host to Mark Twain and delighted the humorist with his hospitality and by secretly commandeering the Academy press to print a limited and elegant edition of the scandalous *"1601."* Taking advantage of detached service, Lt. Wood mingled with east coast avant-garde artists and earned a law degree from

Columbia University that allowed him to resign his commission within less than two years and set up as an attorney in Portland in 1884. Using wit and intelligence, Wood followed his own artistic star even while serving with some distinction in the army.

The second segment of Wood's life was three times as long as his military phase and over those years in the Pacific Northwest, with physical and mental powers at full strength, Wood played an increasingly contradictory and complex role. He saw the region develop from frontier to established society. Living in a center of that society and traveling from it in all directions, Wood could claim to have had a hand in the transition. As a successful attorney, he maintained a varied practice, supported a large family, and managed to hold onto propertied clients while questioning the bases of their security. His work with William S. U'Ren in Progressive reform politics, his association with Harry Lane, his campaign for Woodrow Wilson, and his persistent defense of civil liberties gave him a measure of success on the level of practical political reform, despite views that were regarded as visionary or downright dangerous.

As a poet, satirist, editorialist, and short story writer, C. E. S. Wood left a significant legacy in literature. Through *Pacific Monthly*, widely circulated along the Pacific slope, he commanded a substantial regional audience and his column "Impressions" ruffled the complacency of the literate and essentially conservative reading public of Portland and the West Coast. His contributions to *Liberty* and the *Mirror* involved him in the dialogue of the anarchist and libertarian communities. In the twenties and thirties, Wood enjoyed a good reputation, especially among leftist editors. His work appeared in a number of respectable anthologies and in many of the important literary reviews of the day. He was listed in *Who's Who in American Literature* in the thirties and is listed in the current *Reader's Encyclopedia of the American West*. Wood wrote four books of lasting merit: *A Book of Tales, The Poet in the Desert, Heavenly Discourse,* and *Poems from the Ranges.* Scattered among his other works are a number of fine lyrics, some excellent short stories, and various passages of eloquent and lucid prose. Like Homer, he sometimes nodded. However discursive he could be, though, he was rarely boring, having a bright and teeming mind and a gift for turning a phrase.

As a self-confessed anarchist, Wood tried mightily to disturb Portland's peace. As artist, critic, and man of broad culture, he worked to refine the tastes and sharpen the aesthetic sensibilities of his fellow Northwesterners. Why did generally conservative Portlanders suffer such a man to live and declaim in their midst? Wood was tolerated, perhaps, because his philosophical anarchism was considered too extreme to pose a genuine threat to society, or possibly because they sensed an element of truth to his views. More important, Erskine was a fascinating and polished personality, as at ease in a banker's drawing room or at an Arlington Club banquet as he was on Bill Hanley's eastern Oregon ranch or at an I. W. W. meeting. Prominent Oregonians who detested and decried his radical doctrine liked his company, admired his taste, and trusted his judgment, even when they disagreed with it. Portland patrician Harry Corbett, in a letter to Wood's eldest son, testifies to "Ces" Wood's impact on Portland:

> *I am glad we talked of your father the other day and if we have sense we will do it again on other days and have the memories of him blow the cobwebs out of our brains. He didn't have many cobwebs in his—all was mostly fresh breezes blowing. . . I know that I owe to him most of whatever appreciation I have of fineness and niceties but then, hell, the whole of Portland as it once was, owes much of its culture to him. . . . There are few who can shape the trend of thought of a whole city. Certainly he did that for this town, and just as certainly that same extraordinary influence of his moved into the most unexpected places; from Mrs. Hanley who never knew how beautiful eastern Oregon was till he brought Hassam out and showed it to her, on to quite a few you and I knew on Burnside Street, who reveled in the music of some words he wrote down.*

In California Erskine was able at last to live life on his own terms. The twenty years that he and his good companion Sara spent together at The Cats were a time of vital and original experience. However, that is not to say that their lives were an uninterrupted idyll. There were disappointments. There were money troubles. Each had disruptive bouts of sickness. There was separation from family and there was deep sorrow through the loss of a child for both. Neither could escape the past, but they shared a rare capacity for the enjoyment and enrichment of the present, and misunderstanding and discord seem to have been

*The frontispiece, by Ray Boynton,
from Wood's Poems from the Ranges.
The design is an adaptation of his
mosaic in the courtyard of The Cats,
and Erskine and Sara also used it as
the label for their Princess wine.*

minimal. Their existence was nicely but not evenly proportioned
between solitude and celebration. The solitude was more
important and they gloried in the sense of aloneness on their
private hill. Still, Sara and Erskine also loved good company and
they delighted in planning an evening around the presence of
talented guests—Robinson and Una Jeffers perhaps, or Lincoln
Steffens and Ella Winter, or John Steinbeck, William Rose Benét,
or Mark Van Doren. They gathered to talk, to read aloud and
criticize, and always there was Princess wine from the domestic
cellar. All in all, for Erskine, these must have been truly vintage
years.

If there is a constant factor in Colonel Wood's three careers, it
would have to be rebellion. It is not surprising that a man who,
until his late sixties, felt oppressed by one kind of authority or
another—father, army, legal profession, Gilded Age ethics and
values, Victorian convention—should rebel in the direction of
anarchism, a theory that provides the utmost leeway to the
individual. However, Erskine was not the same kind of rebel after
1918 that he was in the first decade of the century. In the early
period his anarchism sprang largely from having to subdue or
hide artistic, romantic, and literary urges in the face of demanding
responsibilities imposed by family and law practice, both of them
growing. There is a defiant note in this passage from Wood's 1905
journal:

I rebel against the suppression of the individual, the lack of freedom and the falsity—the hypocrisy of the smooth successful life. . . . I am sick of worthy men who force others to their own ideas of worthiness. . . . I would have more hope from a society where men gambled freely if they wanted to, than from a society made to be good by force of law and the thunders of the pulpit. . . . I have more hope that the uplift of the physical and mental man will be resumed when society permits free love than I have from a society which forces the passing glance of young nature to be one dead, eternal gaze. . . . . I deify rebellion. I glory in being a rebel—and a fanatic.

There is a suggestion of Albert Camus' "Dandy," from *The Rebel*, in the Wood of 1905—handsome, vain, and dramatically dressed, reminiscent of Ezra Pound in London at around the same time. Outspoken in his anarchism, Erskine demanded for himself in Portland something of the freedom that John Reed, Floyd Dell, Mabel Dodge and others were seeking and finding in Greenwich Village.

By 1918, Erskine's anarchism is changing in makeup and direction. It is less self-absorbed, more humanitarian. In *The Poet in the Desert,* condemnation of the state and of authority is explicit and severe, but Wood does not renounce all law; rather, he proclaims the law of nature as supreme, as he did in *A Masque of Love.* If people can only learn to understand freedom and adhere to Nature's ordinances—the central one being freedom—then they will evolve their soul as well as their body. However, in *The Poet in the Desert*, Wood marshals his original blend of transcendentalism and anarchism with the goal of gaining social justice for all, a significant development in his thought.

Harry Corbett remembered Charles Erskine Scott Wood as a civilizing influence in Portland. Max Eastman recalled him as an "all-sided lusty man who lived with an Elizabethan gusto." To Lincoln Steffens, he was "that lovely old anarchist." His legacy is one of the spirit—a spirit that impressed those who knew him with his personality and presence; his love of life, learning, and freedom; his aesthetic relish; his range of interests, delight in camaraderie, and joy in the verbal arts, and, in the end, with his wisdom and humanity. C. E. S. Wood was a distinctive human being whose life and writing enhance our understanding of the American character.

First Stage
1877-1901

1t is not certain just when Wood first aspired to be a writer. Perhaps the urge grew in part out of boyhood reading in his father's library, rich in the classics and in Spanish literature, and in part out of the example set by the elder Wood in publishing accounts of his adventures as a naval surgeon in Caribbean waters and the China seas. The first tangible evidence of Erskine's interest in a writing career lies in letters to his father from West Point where the cadet, unhappy with the rigid military academy regimen, threatens to resign and turn to free-lance writing. Dr. Wood expressed stern disapproval of any such notion and the rebellious cadet stayed the course. However, the creative fires smoldered, only to rekindle a year later at Fort Bidwell, a frontier post in northeastern California, Lt. Wood's first station. From there, Erskine sent a manuscript to his older brother Maxwell, at the Navy Department in Washington, D. C., requesting that Max try to place it with *Harper's* or *Scribner's*. Max wrote back that neither editor was interested. That letter is tantalizing in that Max describes the manuscript only as being "too deep for the reading public." Max goes on to suggest that Erskine turn to topics closer to his military experience on the far western fringe. In following his brother's advice, Erskine gave increased attention to the journal he had begun after graduation from West Point, seeking ways to break the monotony of garrison duty.

Lt. Wood, as son of the surgeon general of the Navy, graduate of West Point, and an unusually literate soldier who made no secret of his ambition to write, must have appealed to General O. O. Howard, Commander of the Department of the Columbia, who was a frequent contributor to the newspapers and magazines of the day. At any rate, Howard seems to have taken Lt. Wood under his wing, as was his custom with younger associates throughout his career, and sent Erskine on a number of assignments, usually involving legal problems arising within the judge advocate's sphere, that released him from the more routine duties as a company officer and took him to various posts within the Department including Forts Canby and Stevens in Oregon and Walla Walla in Washington Territory.

Early in the spring of 1877, a promising opportunity opened when C. H. Taylor, an eastern "scientific explorer," with the blessing and support of Professor George Davidson of the United States Coast and Geodetic Survey, applied through channels for a military escort for the purpose of climbing Mt. St. Elias in Alaska Territory. When Lt. Wood learned through General Howard of the projected expedition, he volunteered at once to lead a small party to the far north and by April 6th, 1877, was ready to go. In that year, Alaska—in American hands through purchase from Russia for only a decade—was the nation's newest and rawest frontier. There were small garrisons at Sitka and at Wrangell, but the vast territory was for the most part *terra incognita* for Americans. Aside from the challenge in attempting to scale an 18,000-foot peak, the venture fed Wood's literary ambitions. The expedition failed when Lt. Wood was ordered to rejoin his company, which was preparing to take the field against the Nez Perce and force them onto the reservation at Lapwai, Idaho Territory.

Out of the Alaska adventure and taking his cue from his brother Max, Lt. Wood carved his first publication, "Among the Thlinkits in Alaska," that became the lead article in *Century,* a major east coast magazine. However, even before the *Century* piece, Wood had provided *Harper's Weekly* with a copy of Chief Joseph's surrender speech of October 5, 1877, that *Harper's* carried in November 1877. The speech, in Wood's handwriting, is in the War Department records in the National Archives. That speech, since become so famous, launched the remarkable literary career of Charles Erskine Scott Wood.

During the last two decades of the nineteenth century, Erskine wrote a number of western pieces on such topics as a buffalo hunt, Pacific Northwest Indian chiefs, an Indian horse race, and his account of the pursuit of Chief Joseph. He also wrote a number of anti-imperialist poems and essays that appeared in Benjamin Tucker's *Liberty* and Louis Post's *The Public*. These were hasty, strident, unexceptional attacks on British and American imperialist policies and the verse was jingly and conventional. All in all, this soapboxing was simply not in the same class as Wood's western writing.

In 1898 Erskine wrote a sonnet while going up the Snake River where he had been twenty some years before on his way to join his company as they moved against the Nez Perce in 1877. The sonnet's last lines convey the sympathy Wood felt for the Indians.

This first stage in C. E. S. Wood's writing career culminates with *A Book of Tales* (1901), a collection of myths and legends drawn from his army journals kept during his service on the far Western frontier.

Introduction to "Among the Thlinkits in Alaska"

THIS LEAD ARTICLE IN *Century Magazine* (July 1882) was derived from the army journal Lt. Wood maintained during the expedition escorting C. H. Taylor in an attempt to climb Mt. St. Elias in Alaska Territory in the spring of 1877.

On arrival in Alaska, Taylor and Wood went directly to the trading store and post office at Sitka where Taylor had written to engage a schooner, only to learn that it had been dispatched to Bering's Bay for a load of furs. The next best thing was to procure an Indian war canoe or *yahk*, "as buoyant as a bladder, as graceful as a gull," in Wood's words. Tah-ah-nah-klekh, owner of the canoe, would act as pilot and steersman. An interpreter, two natives, a white prospector, and three enlisted men swelled the party to ten and it left Sitka on April 25, 1877.

Three days later, the party sighted the mouth of the Chilkaht. Proceeding to Chatham Strait, they paddled into Cross Sound and in a sudden turn the sound opened to reveal the Mt. St. Elias alps rising, Wood wrote, "like a shadowy host of snowy domes and pinnacles," chief among them the twin peaks of Fairweather and Crillon. The next stop, Cape Spencer, put the expedition within five days' journey of Yakatat, near Icy Bay. However, at this point, the natives would go no farther. Tah-ah-nah-klekh gestured toward Fairweather and said, "One mountain is as good as another. There is a very big one. Go climb that if you want to."

The party returned to Sitka, and Taylor decided to abandon the enterprise. Erskine, however, obtained a new crew and returned to explore a bay to the southeast of Mt. Fairweather, the first white man to discover Glacier Bay. Discouraged by the vastness and austerity of the land and uneasy about overstaying his leave, Lt. Wood returned to Sitka to find orders to return to Fort Vancouver to rejoin his company, which would soon be in pursuit of the Nez Perce. In addition to recounting the expedition's failure, Wood in the following article describes his brief sojourn among the Thlinkits, telling something of their customs, legends, hospitality, hunting and fishing practices, and the conditions of health among a people little known to *Century* readers.

Note that, through the rendering of "Song of the Salmon Season," Wood manages to include both prose and poetry in this, his first, publication.

AMONG THE THLINKITS IN ALASKA

We set forth in April, 1877, from Portland, Oregon, in the steamer *California,* and steamed northward till we entered the Straits of Fuca. Our purpose was to climb Mount St. Elias, the highest peak in the world above the snowline, to explore the Mount St. Elias alps, and to acquire information about the unknown districts lying nearest the coast, with a view to future explorations. For less is known today of Central Alaska than of Central Africa. From Cape Flattery to Fort Wrangell—nearly a thousand miles—the passage is entirely inland, excepting short runs across the Gulf of Georgia and Queen Charlotte's Sound. The shores are forest-covered mountains, between which the steamer passed as between the lofty banks of a river. One of these channels, Grenville Strait, is forty-five miles long, perfectly straight, and, in some places, only four hundred yards wide. Cliffs and snow-capped mountains wall it in. Avalanches have mowed bare swaths through the fir-trees from the summits to the water's edge, and the mountain lakes, lying a thousand or fifteen hundred feet above the spectator, pour their waters in foaming cataracts into the sea. Twelve hundred miles from the Columbia River bar we touched at Fort Wrangell, a filthy little town at the mouth of the Stickeen, where the miners from the gold-diggings up the Stickeen River spend the winter in squalor and drunkenness. A native village lies, between high tide and the forest, to the east of the town, along a sweep of the rocky beach. Behind the huts may be seen the graves of some Shamáns, or "medicine-men." Their functions, however, are more spiritual than medicinal, for these savages attribute death and disease to the workings of evil spirits. It is the part of the Shamán to exorcise the evil spirits or to call up the good. His remedies are almost exclusively incantations and frenzied pantomime, accompanied with the wild hubbub of his rattles and drum. The Shamáns alone have tombs. All the other dead are burned on funeral pyres. At Wrangell we first saw the tall ancestral columns, which are carved from the trunks of huge trees, and sometimes are eighty and one hundred feet high. Their colossal symbolic carvings represent the totemic genealogy of the cabin-dweller before whose door they stand. They serve the double purpose of frightening away evil spirits and satisfying family pride. A few sick or bankrupt miners were hanging about the American town. One ragamuffin, almost picturesque in tatters and dirt, was seated on the shoe-box steps of the "Miners' Palace Home and Restrent," playing an asthmatic accordion to an audience of half-naked Indians, wearing yellow headkerchiefs and cotton drawers.

After a few hours' stay at Wrangell, we sailed for Sitka by the outside passage around Cape Ommaney and Baranoff Island, as the inside passage is much longer.

As we entered the harbor of Sitka from the sea the general appearance of the place was tropical.* The snowy cone of Edgecumbe first appeared, then the sharp peak of Vostovia—a triangular patch of white against the sky. Everywhere below the snow-line the mountains were green with luxuriant growth. The harbor was protected against the sea by a curved line of reefs, on which grew firs and pines and cedars, with bare trunks and tufts of branches, making them look not unlike palms. The warm, moist atmosphere curtained all the middle distance with a film of blue, and, in the foreground, a fleet of very graceful canoes, filled with naked or half-naked Indians, completed the illusion. A line of surf seemed to bar every approach to the town, but suddenly a narrow channel opened. The ship swung sharply to the right and glided into a long, narrow harbor. The Indian village is built upon the beach, and at evening it was covered by the shadow of the adjoining forest. The green spire on the belfry of the Greek church reached up above everything except the former Russian governor's "castle," a huge log structure perched upon a pinnacle of rock near the sea. The church on the lower ground was surrounded by the rambling, dilapidated houses and hovels of the Russian inhabitants, who then numbered about four hundred, their neighbors being two hundred mixed whites and about twelve hundred Sitka Indians. Sitka was abandoned as a military station shortly after our arrival, since which time several efforts have been made to induce Congress to organize some sort of government there.

When we landed at Sitka we forced our way through a crowd of Indians, Russians, half-breeds, Jews, and soldiers, to whom this monthly arrival is life itself, and went directly to the trading-store and post-office. Mr. C. H. Taylor, of Chicago, who supported the expedition, had written to engage Phillips's fur-trading schooner to take us to Yakutat, where we were to begin our expedition. This schooner was the only craft available for rough work in the ice-drifts, so it was with much anxiety that we asked:

---

* Observations at Sitka during fourteen years give a mean summer temperature, 54.2 Fahr. Mean winter temperature, 31.0; average temperature, 42.80.

"Where is your schooner?"

"Gone to Behring's Bay for a load of furs," was the disappointing answer.

After fruitless efforts to obtain something better, we decided to risk ourselves in one of the large Indian canoes. The Alaskans, having superfluity of time on their hands, devote long periods to the most trifling transactions, and in important bargains, it takes days, and sometimes weeks, to reach an agreement. We found them grasping, shrewd, and unscrupulous.

It was April 16th when we first asked for a large war canoe, or *yahk* (a word which would seem to be related to the yacht of the Germanic tongue), with crew. We negotiated with several of the chiefs, sub-chiefs, and principal men who owned the canoes and slaves to man them. But after wearing ourselves out chaffering with them, we found we could save time by taking the experienced Phillips's advice to "let'm alone." By and by, these aboriginal land-sharks began to offer terms. The winter and spring drizzle set in, and we joined the group of loungers around the trader's stove. We visited "Sitka Jack," an arrant old scoundrel, but one of the wealthiest men of the Sitka tribe. Of course his house stood among the largest, at the fashionable end of the town.

These houses were built of planks, three or four inches thick, each one having been hewed from a log, with an adze formed by lashing a metal blade to the short prong of a forked stick. In constructing the native cabin, the planks are set on edge and so nicely fitted that they need no chinking. The shape of the house is square; a bark roof is laid on, with a central aperture for chimney. The door is a circular opening about two feet in diameter. It is closed with a sheet of bark or a bear-skin or seal-skin. On arriving at Sitka Jack's hut we crawled through the door, and found ourselves in the presence of Jack's wives, children, and slaves, who were lounging on robes and blankets laid on a board flooring which extended along each side of the room. A dirt floor about seven feet square was left in the center, and on this the fire burned and the pot of halibut boiled merrily.

Our arrival was hailed with stolid indifference. The family circle reclined and squatted as usual, and went on with the apparently enjoyable occupation of scooping up handfuls of raw herring-roe, which they munched with great gusto. Sitka Jack was absent on a trading expedition to the Chilkáht kwáhn or tribe. One of his brothers-in-law was chief of this tribe, and being a one-eyed despot of sanguinary principles not only held his tribe under absolute control, but inspired his relatives and connections with wholesome awe. His sister, Mrs. "Sitka Jack," was, therefore, a person of great consequence, and her influence surpassed even the usual wonderful authority of the Alaskan women. Evidently she was the head of the house, and as such she received us haughtily. She weighed at least two hundred pounds. She gave us her terms, pointed coldly at the slaves she would send with us, and told us she was the sister of the terrible Chilkáht chief. As we still hesitated, she threw her weight into the scale, and said she would go with us and protect us. We could not get one of the great canoes holding from sixty to eighty warriors, but finally closed a bargain with Tah-ah-nah-klékh for his canoe, of about four tons burden. He was to act as pilot and steersman. We hired Nah-sach, Klen, and Jack as crew. Jack, our interpreter, was a Sitka Indian who had a smattering of mongrel Russian and English. Myers went with us as prospector and miner.

We had accumulated a cargo that looked fully twice the size of the canoe, which, like all of her kind, was as buoyant as a bladder, as graceful as a gull, and very capacious, so that by skillful stowage we loaded in the entire cargo and left room for ourselves; that is, we could swing our paddles, but we could not change our seats. Jack, or Sam as we had newly named him, was fond of "Hoochinoo." This is a native distilled liquor, colorless and vilely odorous. The stills are large tin oil-cans, and the coils are giant kelp. The Sitkans never set forth on an expedition of unusual importance without first getting beastly drunk. Sam had evidently gauged the importance of this expedition as immense. We loaded him in as cargo, and waited for the last man, Myers, who presently appeared, dragging at the end of a rope a half-grown black dog. Myers took his place, his canine friend was put in the bow, and amid the cheers of idle Sitka we paddled rapidly toward the north. The dog gazed wistfully at the retreating crowd, then suddenly sprang into the water and swam ashore.

For a time we were in mortal terror, lest we should capsize the shell by our awkwardness; an anxiety on our part that was epitomized, at our first landing, in Myers's fervent exclamation:

"Thank Heaven, I kin shift my foot!"

One drowsy evening we saw the peak of Edgecumbe for the last time. The great truncated cone caught the hues of the sunset, and we could note the gloom gathering deeper and deeper in the hollow of the crater. Our Indians were stolidly smoking the tobacco we had given them, and were resting after the labors of the day with bovine contentment. Tah-ah-nah-klékh related to us the Thlinkit legend of Edgecumbe:

A long time ago the earth sank beneath the water, and the water rose and covered the highest places so that no man could live. It rained so hard that it was as if the sea fell from the sky. All was black, and it became so dark that no man knew another. Then a few people ran here and there and made a raft of cedar logs, but nothing could stand against the white waves, and the raft was broken in two.

On one part floated the ancestors of the Thlinkits, on the other the parents of all other nations. The waters tore them apart, and they never saw each other again. Now their children are all different and do not understand each other. In the black tempest Chethl was torn from his sister Ah-gish-áhn-akhon ['woman-who-supports-the-earth']. Chethl [symbolized in the osprey] called aloud to her, "You will never see me again, but you will hear my voice forever!" Then he became an enormous bird, and flew to south-west till no eye could follow him. Ah-gish-áhn-akhon climbed above the waters and reached the summit of Edgecumbe. The mountain opened and received her into the bosom of the earth. That hole [the crater] is where she went down. Ever since that time she has held the earth above the water. The earth is shaped like the back of a turtle and rests on a pillar; Ah-gish-áhn-akhon holds the pillar. Evil spirits that wish to destroy mankind seek to overthrow her or drive her away. The terrible battles are long and fierce in the lower darkness. Often the pillar rocks and sways in the struggle, and the earth trembles and seems like to fall, but Ah-gish-áhn-akhon is good and strong, so the earth is safe. Chethl lives in the bird Kunna-káht-eth. His nest is in the top of the mountain, in the hole through which his sister disappeared.

He carries whales in his claws to this eyrie, and there devours them. He swoops from his hiding-place and rides on the edge of the coming storm. The roaring of the tempest is his voice calling to his sister. He claps his wings in the peals of thunder, and its rumbling is the rustling of his pinions. The lightning is the flashing of his eyes. *

---

* Bishop Veniaminoff, Wrangell, and Dall have given versions of this legend.

We passed a succession of evergreen islands with steep, rocky shores, and in the distance we could see the jagged alps of the main-land. The trees were principally fir, hemlock, and cedar. The evergreen underbrush was so dense and so matted with ferns and moss as to be almost impenetrable. The accumulation of moss was frequently ten or fifteen feet deep. Peat-bogs and coal-fields were common features of the islands, but the coal was found to be sulphurous and bituminous. Clams were abundant and good. The smallest, when opened, were about the size of an orange. The largest shells were used as soup-plates by the natives. The waters of the archipelago at all seasons are alive with halibut. They are caught with a peculiar hook, fastened to a thick line made of twisted cedar-root fiber. Our bill of fare in Alaska included clams, mussels, herring, herring-roe, codfish, salmon, porpoise, seal, ducks, geese, and halibut—eternally halibut. Venison and wild goat and bear's flesh were to be had only occasionally, and the craving for good warm-blooded meats was incessant with us whites. Another intense craving was for sweets. We devoured our supply of sugar, and when it was exhausted we consumed much seal-oil, and chewed the sweet inner bark of a species of cedar, of which bark the Indians dry great quantities for the winter.

On the 27th we sighted the mouth of the Chilkáht. Professor Davidson of the Coast Survey has been up this river a little beyond the upper village. The two villages are governed by the Chilkáht chief before alluded to as "Sitka Jack's" brother-in-law. He is a despot and does not encourage explorations of his river, though recently he has become so envious of the gold mines on the Stickeen, that it is said he will help gold prospectors to ascend his river. This one-eyed chief is very savage and vindictive, but as he holds a monopoly of the fur trade up and down his river he is very wealthy and influential, and can be of great assistance to any expedition.* He owns many slaves, mostly captives from the tribes of the interior or from hostile coast tribes. So little distinction is made between the bond and the free that at first a stranger finds it difficult to detect the slaves. They sit around the fire and eat from the same dish with their owners, who joke with them, and place them on footing of perfect social equality. But the slaves hew the wood and carry the water and paddle the canoe. They cannot marry without the consent of their

---

* A good plan of exploration would be by two parties cooperating: one to go up the Yukon, the other up the Chilkáht, to meet at a depot of supply previously located on the upper Yukon.

master, and they are unpleasantly liable to be offered as sacrifices on their master's grave.

From Chatham Strait we paddled against head winds into Cross Sound. In a sudden turn the whole vast sound opened to us, and the Mount St. Elias alps appeared like a shadowy host of snowy domes and pinnacles. Chief among them were the twin peaks Fairweather and Crillon. About this time we met a canoe-load of Hoonáhs, who had come ninety miles to dig their spring potatoes. On a sunny slope, sheltered by surrounding forests and sentinel peaks, these people had long ago planted some potatoes procured from the Russians at Sitka, and every year they come come to dig last year's crop, and sow the ground for the following spring. The tubers were about the size of large marbles. In the gardens of Sitka are grown excellent potatoes, beets, turnips, radishes, lettuce, cabbage, and such hardy vegetables. The soil is not suitable for cereals, neither is the season long enough.

Near Cape Spencer we camped on a little island, where Tsa-tate, a young man of the Hoonáh kwáhn, had his summer hut. Three families lived here with Tsa-tate; and, though he was much younger than the other men of the family, he was the head of his clan. Tsa-tate's cabin was like all the other wooden huts we had seen. The cross poles and rafters were hung with fish and snow-shoes and nets. The sides were covered with traps, bows, spears, paddles, and skins of bear, sable, and silver-fox. The women sat around the fire, weaving baskets of different shapes and colors from the fiber of a long, fine root, which they soaked in water and split into threads. One old woman was chewing the seams of a pair of seal-skin boots so as to soften them, and another was pounding some tobacco leaves into snuff. A man with a fiery red head was carving a pipe in which to smoke the tobacco we had given him, and a sick baby, tenderly watched by its mother, lay in a corner, with its mouth and nostrils stuffed full of some chewed-up weed. As darkness came on and the halibut fishermen returned from the sea, we all gathered about the central fire in Tsa-tate's hut, and Mrs Tsa-tate lighted the pitch-wood candles, and with down and resin dressed an ugly gash in the sole of her husband's foot. The children slept or poked the fire with an immunity from scolding that would have cheered the heart of every civilized five-year-old. A young girl sat demurely in a corner. Until they are of marriageable age, and entitled to wear the silver ornament through the lower lip, the maidens are carefully watched by the elder women of the family. An old woman stirred and skimmed the boiling pot of porpoise flesh. Tsa-tate, reclining comfortably on a divan of bear skins, answered our questions and repeated tribal legends. He pointed to his son, a boy about five years old, who, he said, would be his successor, as head of the clan. It was difficult to ascertain the exact law of succession among the Thlinkits, but the chiefship seems to follow the direct line, though, as in all other savage nations, this is scarcely a rule, for the lineal heir may be set aside in favor of a more acceptable man.

In the inheritance of personal property, the collateral is preferred to the lineal relationship. The wives, or more properly the widows, being personal property, pass to the collateral next of kin of their husband's totem, for the marriage of two people of the same totem is considered a kind of incest. The widow, in any event, takes with her such possessions as have always been peculiarly her own. She also takes her own infant children; naturally, then, she would take to her new husband the children's inheritance, which may account for the habit of regarding the male collaterally next of kin as proper heir. If there be no male survivor competent to receive the widow, or if he purchases freedom with goods, she then passes into the open matrimonial market, with her pecuniary attractions.

Sometimes the heir rebels and refuses to accept his former sister-in-law, cousin, aunt, or whatever she may be. Then her totemic or family relatives wage war on the insulter and such of his totem as he can rally around him, the object being either to enforce her right or extort a proper recompense. Among the Asónques, further to the north and west, I saw a young fellow of about eighteen years of age who had just fallen heir to his uncle's widow. As I looked upon her mummy-like proportions I thought that here was reasonable cause for war. Sometimes a husband already liberally provided for will come into misfortune in the shape of one or more widows. The only escape is by purchasing freedom.

In fact, there seems to be no hurt to a Thlinkit's honor that money or goods will not heal. The scorning of a widow, the betrayal of a maiden, and murder, all demand blood or pecuniary compensation. If in a feud all negotiations fail, and Kanúkh (symbolized in the wolf), the God of War, be unpropitious, and send private war, then the principal antagonists, with their totemic adherents, don their helmets and coats of paint, and stand facing each other in two lines, each line holding to a rope with the left hand, and wielding heavy knives with the right. They advance, and hack and hew, with more yells than bloodshed, until one side or the other cries the Thlinkit for *peccavi*. In this duel, any warrior violates the code who lets go the rope with the left hand, unless he be wounded, or torn from it; when he has let go, he is then out of the fight and must retire.

If the strife be inter-tribal, or public war, the plan of combat is surprise and sudden capture. The villages, from necessity as well as from choice, are placed always at the edge of high tide. The forces of the aggressive tribe embark in a fleet of war canoes, and by a swift and stealthy voyage strike the village from the sea and endeavor to take it by storm. If they are resisted they generally retire at once. The Chilkáht kwáhn came down suddenly upon the main village of the Sitka kwáhn while I was near by, but succeeded in getting possession of only half the houses, so the opposing forces divided the village between them and kept up a lively but rather harmless combat for three days, at the end of which the invaders were bought off with some loads of furs. A member of the Sitka kwáhn had murdered his Chilkáht squaw in a fit of passion, and this was the cause of the conflict. The goods paid over as recompense went principally to the relatives of the murdered woman. In these tribal conflicts the captured are enslaved, the dead are scalped, and all property taken is held as booty. Hostages and participants in rope duels do not take food from the right hand for several days, because, figuratively (and literally), it is unclean. A head powdered with down is a sign of truce.

We were now within five days' journey of Yakutat, which is near Icy Bay, at which place one of the Mount St. Elias glaciers ends in the sea. Threats and bribes were alike useless. Pay or no pay, our crew would not put to sea. Tah-ah-nah-klékh pointed to the mountain, and said:

"One mountain is as good as another. There is a very big one. Go climb that if you want to."

Thus perished our hope of climbing Mount St. Elias. We turned our course directly to the main-land, about thirty miles away, and landed a little below Cape Spencer. A sea-wind filled the coast-waters with icebergs, and we had great difficulty in picking our way through them. I noticed that, when journeying through the floating ice in good weather, our Indians would carefully avoid striking pieces of ice, lest they should offend the Ice Spirit. But when the Ice Spirit beset us with peril, they did not hesitate to retaliate by banging his subjects. After picking our way through the ice for three days, we came upon a small temporary camp of Hoonáhs, who were seal-hunting. We found little camps of a family or two scattered along both shores. One of the largest glaciers from Fairweather comes into the bay, and thus keeps its waters filled with the largest icebergs, even in the summer season, for which reason the bay is a favorite place for seal-hunting. The seal is the natives' meat, drink (the oil is like melted butter), and clothing.

I went seal-hunting to learn the art, which requires care and patience. The hunter, whether on an ice floe or in a canoe, never moves when the seal is aroused. When the animal is asleep, or has dived, the hunter darts forward. The spear has a barbed detachable head, fastened to the shaft by a plaited line made from sinew. The line has attached to it a marking buoy, which is merely an inflated seal's bladder. The young seals are the victims of the Thlinkit boys, who kill them with bow and arrow. These seal-hunters used a little moss and seal-oil and some driftwood for fuel.

In the morning we arose late, and found that our friends of the night before had silently stolen away, taking with them much of our firewood.

Mr. Taylor decided to return home, and we accompanied him to Sitka. There I reëngaged Sam and Myers, and, obtaining a new crew, returned at once to a bay about twenty miles south-east of Mount Fairweather. My purpose was to explore the bay, cross the coast range, and strike the upper waters of Chilkáht. On the shores of the bay we found hospitality with a band of Hoonáhs. Leaving the crew with our large canoe under the charge of Myers at this place, I took a smaller one and went with Cocheen, the chief of the band, north-westerly up the bay. After about forty miles' travel we came to a small village of Asónques. They received us with great hospitality, and as our canoe had been too small to carry any shelter, the head man gave me a bed in his own cabin. He had a great many wives, who busied themselves making me comfortable. The buckskin re-enforcement of my riding trowsers excited childish wonder. I drew pictures of horses and men separate, and then of men mounted on horses. Their astonishment over the wonderful animal was greater than their delight at comprehending the utility of the trowsers.

The Alaskan women are childish and pleasant, yet quick-witted and capable of heartless vindictiveness. Their authority in all matters is unquestioned. No bargain is made, no expedition set on foot, without first consulting the women. Their veto is never disregarded. I bought a silver-fox skin from Tsa-tate, but his wife made him return the articles of trade and recover the skin. In the same way I was perpetually being annoyed by having to undo bargains because "his wife said *clekh*," that is, "no." I hired a fellow to take me about thirty miles in his canoe, when my own crew was tired. He agreed. I paid him the tobacco, and we were about to start when his wife came to the beach and stopped him. He quietly unloaded the canoe and handed me back the tobacco.

The whole people are curious in the matter of trade. I was never sure that I had done with a bargain, for they claimed and exercised the right to undo a contract at any time, provided they could return the consideration received. This is their code among themselves. For example: I met at the mouth of the Chilkáht a native trader who had been to Fort Simpson, about six hundred miles away, and failing to get as much as he gave in the interior of Alaska for the skins, was now returning to the interior to find the first vender and revoke the whole transaction.

Among themselves their currency is a species of wampum, worth about twenty dollars a string, beaver-skins worth about a dollar a skin, and sable or marten worth about two dollars a skin. From the whites they get blankets worth four dollars apiece, and silver dollars; gold they will not touch (except around Sitka and Wrangell), but they accept copper and silver.

They are a laughing, good-natured people, ordinarily very quiet. Even their large meetings are subdued and orderly. They are undemonstrative. The mothers do not fondle nor play with their children much, but a stranger can win their hearts by kindness to their little ones. They consider corporeal punishment a disgrace, and I did not see a child struck during the time I was among them. A rebuke, a sharp tone, or exclusion from the cabin seemed to be the only punishments. Even the dogs are curiously exempt from punishment and abuse, and a more wolfish, starved, mangy lot of curs it would be hard to find. Good bear-dogs they will not sell at any price. With all their gentleness of voice and manner, and their absolute respect for the rights of the smallest and youngest of the family, their love and affection seemed of the coolest sort. Etiquette required only about forty days of ostensible mourning. The loss of children seemed to cause the greatest grief. They have a curious habit of blacking the face with a mixture of seal-oil and lamp-black, or burnt pitch, but I believe this custom, whatever its origin, is now merely a kind of toilet, to be used according to the whim of the individual.

From this Asónque village I went, with a party of mountain goat-hunters, up into the Mount St. Elias alps back of Mount Fairweather —that is, to the north-east of that mountain. For this trip our party made elaborate preparations. We donned belted shirts made of squirrel skins, fur head-dresses (generally conical), seal-skin booties fitting very closely and laced half-way to the knee. We carried spears for alpenstocks, bows and arrows, raw-hide ropes, and one or two old Hudson Bay rifles. The climbing was very laborious work. The mountains, where not covered with ice or snow, were either of a crumbling schistose character or ice-worn limestone, and sometimes granite. The sides were terribly rugged; some of the face walls were about eight hundred feet sheer, with a foot slope of shell rock or *débris* of two hundred or three hundred feet more. Ptarmigan were seen on the lower levels where the ground was bare, but I saw nothing on which they could feed. The goats kept well up toward the summit, amid the snow-fields, and fed on the grass which sprouted along the edges of melting drifts. They were the wariest, keenest animals I ever hunted. The animal is like a large white goat, with long, coarse hair and a heavy coat of silky underfleece. The horns, out of which the natives carve spoons, are short, sharp, and black.

After crossing this coast range the country seemed much the same— rugged, bleak, and impassable. The Indians with me, so far as I could understand them, said it was an exceedingly rough country all the way over, and that the Chilkáht River had its rise among just such alps as those around us, only it was warmer in the Chilkáht mountains, and there was more grass and plenty of wild goats, sheep, and bears. We found a bear that, so far as I know, is peculiar to this country. It is a beautiful bluish under color, with the tips of the long hairs silvery white. The traders call it "St. Elias's silver bear." The skins are not common.

Being unable to go further overland I returned to the Asónque camp. There we fitted ice guards to a small canoe, and with ice-hooks pulled our way through, and carried our canoe over the floes and among the icebergs to the extreme limit of so-called open water in that direction. The ice-guards were merely wooded false sides hung to a false prow. From this point, also, I found the interior impenetrable, and went to a temporary camp of seal and goat hunters, who were camped on a ledge of rocks above the crunching and grinding icebergs. The head man of this camp was a young fellow of about thirty who was both Shamán ("medicine-man") and hereditary chief. He was the most thoughtful and entertaining Thlinkit I had met. He told me that within his own lifetime this place where we now were had been solid ice. He would listen with breathless attention whenever I spoke, and then reply in low, musical intonations, almost like chanting. His narration of the traditions of his people was pathetic in its solemn earnestness. He said:

You are the only white man that has ever been here, but I have heard of your people. Before I was born—a long time ago—a ship came to the mouth of this bay, and gave the Thlinkits iron to make knives like this one. Before that they had made knives from copper or from stone, like this.

Then he would pause, fix his eyes on me, and hold up his knife. When he saw I had absorbed his words, he would give a graceful wave of the hand and continue:

Then the Thlinkits had many furs—foxes, and bear, and sable,—all the people were warm, all were happy, and lived as Yéhl had set them to live [or after Yéhl's example, I don't know which]. There was plenty to eat, and plenty to wear. Now, sometimes we are hungry and wear ragged robes.

Here he paused again, picked up the corner of his squirrel robe and raised it with a sweeping forward gesture, which he maintained till his words had produced their full effect, when the sing-song intonation would begin again.

Coon-nah-nah-thklé, for that was his name, showed me his sorcerer's kit. There was an immense drum of stretched seal-skin or goat-skin, made to accompany him in his incantations, and to terrify the wicked spirits preying upon the life of the sick person. The drum had formerly belonged to a celebrated Shamán, and his spirit was either in the drum itself or had passed into the possessor of the drum, I could not determine which. I found it to be a common belief that anything that had belonged to a dead wizard possessed some inherent virtue. For this reason it was almost impossible to secure Shamán instruments. These Shamáns claim to be able to see the "life" or soul leaving the body or being dragged from it by spirits, and it is their business to seize the soul with the mouth and breathe or force it back into the body. The dress they wear depends upon what malign spirits they determine are at work. I only saw one Shamán exorcising, and I do not believe he would have continued had he known I was observing him. He kneaded, pounded, yelled, chanted, frothed, swayed to and fro, played tunes all up and down the suffering patient, blew in his mouth and nostrils, and literally worried the life out of him. In general practice the Shamán continues this performance till the wretched patient declares he is better or well. If he cures, the Shamán gets large pay. If he kills, he restores the goods he has previously received on account. If any one who is not a regular Shamán does anything for a patient who dies, the self-constituted doctor is held responsible, and must pay forfeit in life or goods. If the patient is obdurate and will not declare that the spirits have left him, the Shamán makes that statement for him.

The hair is generally worn long by the Alaskan women; always short by the men, except the Shamáns, who never cut or comb the hair, nor are the matted locks benefited any by the habit of powdering and greasing for occasions of ceremony. The hair is kept tied up, except when the Shamán is exercising his peculiar functions. Then it is shaken out in long, snaky ropes, which dance over the shoulders. Some take these ropes of hair and stick them all over with flat scales of pitch, increasing thereby the Medusa-like appearance of the head.

I made for myself a fair reputation for sorcery while in the Coon-nah-nah-thklé's camp by a judicious use of my repeating-rifle and revolver. The chief and I shot at a mark, and I am afraid he was the better shot. He gave me a little amulet (whale totem), which he said would bring me good luck if I would hang it on my rifle. Then he took the weapon and passed his hands over it, and blew on it, which he said would prevent its ever hurting him.

The spirits of the Thlinkit mythology are classified as Ki-yékh, spirits of the air; Tah-ki-yékh, spirits of the earth; Te-ki-yékh, spirits of the water; and Yékh, subordinate or minor spirits. The spirits of those killed in war become Ki-yékh, and the aurora is the flashing of their lights when they are dancing their war dances. Hence, an auroral display is a sign of war. The chief deity of the Thlinkits, the Bramah, the Creator, is Yehl. One would suppose that he would be the deity of the Tinneh, or interior Indians. Yet among the Thlinkits the raven is held peculiarly sacred for his sake, and the early writers (Veniaminoff and Wrangell) declare the raven to be a foul and ill-omened bird among the Tinneh. Yehl is symbolized in the raven for the reason that one of his chief exploits, the bringing of fresh water to the Thlinkits, was done under the guise of a raven. The sum of the Thlinkit philosophy is, "Live as Yehl lived." Their great totem is Yehl's totem or the raven totem, the raven being the symbol. Another scarcely inferior totem is the Kanúkh (wolf), the wolf being the symbol. The third (and as far as I know, the last) totem is Tset'kh (the whale). Who Tset'kh was before he was a whale and what he did I could not learn.

Their totemic system is the most curious one that ever came to my notice. The totemic relationship is stronger than that of blood. The child follows the totem of the mother, and in family quarrels the opponents must array themselves with their totems; hence, half-brothers are often called on to fight each other. I used to be surprised at having my vagabonds tell me perfect strangers were their "brothers" or "sisters," until I found it meant brother or sister in the totem. The Kanúkh (wolf) totem is the warrior caste. Men of this caste are the soldiers of the whole people, and are led in war only by chiefs of their own caste. Kanúkh is either the older brother of Yehl or an older deity—I don't know which. He is now the god of war and patron saint of the "wolves," but the myths tell of a celebrated encounter between him and Yehl. It is difficult to arrive at the religion of the Thlinkits from the stories of these deities. In my short visit I certainly could not, and Veniaminoff, who lived among them, has left little information on the subject.

A very wise old raven was pointed out to me as the embodied spirit of a defunct Shamán. Suicides are very frequent, because the tired person wishes to enter upon a happier existence; this and the superstition as to the aurora points to a belief in a spirit life. Then again all bodies are cremated (except Shamáns), and whatever may have been the origin of the pyre, the reason given now is that the spirit may not be cold on the journey to the Spirit Land. A Thlinkit, in answer to my questionings, replied:

"Doctors won't burn."

"But why don't you try?" I persisted.

"Because we know they will not burn."

I once saw a body ready for the funeral pyre. It was lying behind the cabin in a crouching attitude, with a native blanket from the wool of mountain goats thrown over it, and its robes and possessions near by. A hole had been cut through the rear wall of the cabin, for if the corpse had been carried through the entrance, it would have left the dread mystery of death upon the threshold, and the living could not enter. The Shamán attends to the burning. One day a little boy of the Sitká Kwáhn was pointed out to me as a Shamán. He wore the untouched long hair. I asked how they knew so soon that he was to be a Shamán.

"Oh," they answered, "he was alive a long time ago as a Shamán." At the proper time, this boy must take his degree in the college of Shamánism by fasting in solitude in the wilderness. No one must approach him, and his food must be the roots of the earth. When he has become sufficiently spiritualized, the Great Shamán will send to him the otter, to impart the secrets of his order. The novice will meet the animal. They will salute three times. He will fall upon the otter and tear out its tongue and take off its skin. Then in a frenzy he will rush back to his tribe and madly bite whatever comes in his way. These bites are often dangerous, but are sought for as wounds of honor. This frenzy fit among the Haidáhs is called becoming "Taamish." If the otter is not forthcoming in due time there are various artifices to compel his presence, such as getting the tooth or finger of a dead Shamán and holding it in the mouth. After the Nawloks, or evil spirits, have thus wrestled with him, the Shamán ever after has his own attendant retinue of Nawloks and Yekhs, or even of higher spirits, whom he summons to his aid. In supernatural matters, therefore, his word is law.

At Coon-nah-nah-thklé's, I found the people using stone-axes, knives, and other implements, some of which I brought away with me. They were made of hypo-chlorite and slate, tempered in oil. The children there were greatly frightened at me, and would not let me approach them. On my return I encountered another Shamàn, and purchased from him a finely carved medicine rattle. But a skinny hag snatched it from my hand, just as I had concluded the bargain, and compelled the "Doctor" to return me my tobacco. She said the rattle had been the favorite one of her dead husband, a Shamàn, who had left her and his rattles to this nephew, the "Doctor," who certainly did not seem too happy over it. By judicious coaxing and tobacco I succeeded in pacifying her, and renewed my trade with the nephew. The rattle is carved with crane's, owl's, and raven's heads, and has queer long-tongued demons turning back somersaults over it.

From Cocheen's I turned southward and homeward. I had applied for a year's leave with the purpose of exploring the interior of Alaska, and now was anxious to return to Sitka for the reply. In Chatham Strait, near Cross Sound, the old head chief of the Hoonáhs, came and begged me to go to his island to doctor his boy who was very sick. I went but was loath to do any doctoring; for the Thlinkit custom of killing the doctor in case his patient dies, is discouraging to a beginner. The boy was feverish and had a complication of troubles, so I gave him hot-water baths followed with a seidlitz powder. The effervescing of the powder put me at once at the head of the Shamáns. During my stay I built up an extensive practice. I made for the chief some camphorated soap liniment. Eye troubles are common among the Thlinkits, and are due to the glitter of snow and ice and the irritation caused by the smoke in the huts. One feeble old man to whom I had ministered was surely dying, and I was anxious to be off before that event. I visited all my patients preparatory to departing. I gave to some dried onions stewed in sugar, to others cod-liver oil, and diluted alcohol to the feeble old man to keep him up until I could get away. From the father of the sick boy, then nearly well, I took a fee of some finely carved spoons made from horns of the mountain goat.

At this camp I found traces of a custom which prevails to some extent in Central Africa and is said to obtain throughout the interior of Alaska. When a stranger of rank visits a chief, the latter presents his guest with a wife from among the women of his household. In morals the Alaskans are much inferior to most Indian tribes of the plains. Avarice is their ruling passion. They are the most knavish and cunning of traders. Theft, if successful, brings no disgrace. The detected thief is laughed at and ridiculed. I saw old Cocheen look with fond admiration on Kastase-Kúch, his son, when the latter drew from under his robe some articles he had purloined from the village where we had lodged for the night. Their gratitude seemed small and they have no expression for "I thank you." Flaws in gifts were always carefully examined and critically pointed out to the giver. An Alaskan who shot at some decoy ducks near Sitka, went to the owner of the decoys and demanded the return of his wasted ammunition. Two Alaskans were driven to sea in a canoe. A schooner picked them up, but would not or could not take their canoe as it was still blowing a gale. The rescued demanded payment for the lost craft. Another fellow came to the doctor of the post at Sitka and begged for medicine for his brother and then asked the doctor to pay him for carrying it to the brother. I lent Tah-ah-nah-klékh a goat-skin robe of mine and at the end of our voyage asked him to clean it. He did so and demanded full payment. We did not lose much by theft, because our crew knew very well the value would be deducted from their wages.

Thlinkit virtues are hospitality, good-nature, peaceableness, filial obedience, and, after their own code, a respect for solemn contracts or engagements. Even when very angry they only sulk. They are demonstrative only in the expression of surprise. My host, the old

Hoonáh chief, was disinterested kindness itself. At his bountiful board I had a seat between his youngest and prettiest wives. They prepared seal-flipper for me with a celery-like dressing of some plant. We lived in ease and luxury and a little necessary grease and dirt. When the fire was stirred, and the spears and paddles were put away for the evening, my host smoked his pipe and told tales of the land of Tinneh, where all the best furs were and where the mountains were bleak and merciless. His youngest son, a sturdy little fellow of five, shared the pipe with his father, and they passed it from one to the other with amusing solemnity.

I told of a wonderland where the *yahks* were as large as islands and moved against the wind without the help of hands; of great horned animals giving milk; of other great animals on which men rode; of thousands of great stone houses; of the vast multitude of white people. The Thlinkits received my stories, as they do every statement, with courteous deference. When I rose to go to my own camp the chief selected the handsomest bear-skin from a pile of them, and bade his youngest wife present it to me. When next he came to my camp I gave him, among other things, a fine woollen blanket. He folded it about him and said he would not use it as a hunting blanket. When he went away he would leave it at home and when he died it should not go with his other effects to his wives and children, but he would be burned in it and it would go with him to the Unknown.

A niece of the Chilkáht chief, one of the comeliest of her race, who had married a hideously ugly, but very rich old Hoonáh, the second man in the village, mended my clothes and my sealskin boots and sang sad songs or chants for my entertainment that were quite wonderful, I thought, for their flowing measure and rhythm. This is one which I learned to understand the best, called "The Song of the Salmon Fishing":

> Why is the young man sorrowful?
> Oh why is the young man sad?
> Ah-ka. His maiden has left him.
> The long suns have come,
> The ice now is melting;
> Now comes the salmon
> He leaps in the river,
> In the moon's gentle twilight
> He throws up a bow—
> A bow of bright silver.
> Lusty and strong he darts through the water,

He sports with his mate;
He springs from the water.
All the dark season
He has lain hidden.
Now he comes rushing,
And ripples the river.
Purple and gold, and red and bright silver
Shine on his sides and flash in his sporting,
How he thrashes the net!
How he wrenches the spear!
But the red of his sides
Is stained with a redder;
The maid of the young man leans o'er the salmon
White laugh her teeth,
Clear rings her laughter;
Which passes canoes all busy and happy,
Which outstrips the noise of the many mixed voices
And pierces the heart of her sorrowful lover.
She has forgot him,
She joys with another.
All for another she chases the salmon,
Ah-ka. Your sweetheart has left you.
So do they jeer him,
Ah-ka—your sweetheart is here at the fishing!
Ah-ka—how like you this gay salmon season?

The crabs I saw at this village were wonderful for their size. Two crabs were brought to me, the largest of which measured a little more than six feet on a line joining the extremities of its outstretched mandibles. The body was eighteen inches long. When broken in pieces one crab filled a camp kettle, and four men made a hearty meal off it, and it was all very good. The boy archers of the village who brought me the crabs held their bows horizontally, and strained the bow against the front of the thumb and back of the little fingers, the arrow passing between the fore and middle fingers, a mode of archery peculiar to the Alaskans. Many of the men and boys of the village were making boxes and firkins, and shaping bows, and paddles. They used dried dog-fish skin for sand-paper.

In this village were many little bee-hive huts, temporarily constructed of mats or bark, which were due to one of the most universal superstitions, and especially cruel, as influencing these people. These huts were the temporary shelter to which women were driven at certain times when they most needed comfort and attention, that is, at the periods of childbirth, etc.

When a maiden reaches a marriageable age her lover demands his bride from her parents, and if they answer favorably he sends the purchase-money or goods, and on the appointed day seats himself outside her hut with his back to the door. If they are willing to accept him he is invited in. The maiden sits modestly in a corner. The relatives form a circle round the fire and sing and dance. The wedding gifts are displayed and critically examined. They are laid upon the floor, and the girl walks over them to her lover. According to the Russian priest, Veniaminoff and Wrangell, the marriage ceremony is not complete until bride and groom have fasted four days, and lived away from each other for a month. They then live together as man and wife. I had no opportunity of confirming the accuracy of these statements.

A man frequently takes the name of his son, but before doing so, he gives a festival and announces his intention. He does not give up his former name or names, but assumes a new one as the father of his son; or he takes the name of a dead ancestor, but first gives a festival in honor of that departed progenitor. They call such a ceremony "elevating" (or reverencing) the dead. Another festival is of a political character. It is to gain popularity and influence. To this end the ambitious person will save for years till he has an accumulation of this world's goods. Then he makes a feast of unlimited eating and drinking, and all this store of wealth is distributed to the guests present. Festivals also celebrate the arrival of distinguished guests.

In the gray dawn, as we were about to push from shore, the old chief came to us accompanied by two of his wives. My blanket was wrapped round him. He said I had a good heart. I was a young chief now, but some day I would be a great one. Among the Thlinkits, he said, when a friend was leaving on a long journey, they watched him out of sight, for he might never return. I was his friend. I was going away to my own land. He would never see me again. Therefore he had come to watch me out of sight. He then motioned to his elder wife, who handed me a beautiful sable skin, and he continued: "Wherever you go among Thlinkits, show them this and tell them I gave it to you."

The breeze was freshening. I wrapped my capote about me and stepped aboard. We paddled rapidly out to sea, and it was not long before the three figures were lost to view. We were about three hundred and fifty miles from Sitka. In three days we reached Koutzenóo, a large village opposite the entrance to Peril Strait, where most of the native distilled liquor is made. Here we witnessed a drunken revel of indescribable abandon, during which naked and half-naked men and women dragged themselves about the place.

With a comparatively mild climate throughout the Archipelago, with most valuable ship-building timber covering the islands, with a cedar that now sells at one hundred and fifty dollars a thousand feet in Sitka, with splendid harbors, with inexhaustible fisheries, with an abundance of coal, and the probability that veins of copper, lead, silver, and gold await the prospector, with the possibility of raising sufficient garden vegetables, and with wild cranberry swamps on nearly every island; with all these advantages it is surprising that an industrious, amphibious, ship-building, fishing colony from New England, or other States, has not established itself in Alaska. One drawback is that Congress has not yet organized a territorial government, but when this region shall have been opened up to individual enterprise and settlement, it will then be discovered that Alaska is a valuable possession. There is lacking neither the wealth nor the will to contradict this, but to those who are really interested I will say what the opposition does not say:—Go and see! The round trip from New York will cost you about six hundred dollars, which does not include hotel expenses.

IN THE SUMMER OF 1879, C.E.S. Wood, now a first lieutenant and married, was back on frontier duty in the Pacific Northwest. From the notes he took during an Indian-white council held where the Wenatchee River enters the Columbia in what was then Washington Territory, he wrote this account of an Indian horse-race for *Century*. The piece testifies to Wood's skill as observer and reporter.

AN INDIAN HORSE-RACE

In the summer of 1879 we—that is, the American people—were trying to settle the Methows, Chelans, Weenatchees, and half a dozen other tribes upon the reservation Secretary Schurz had marked out for them. Although there was to be no compulsion used, still homes were to be broken up; many of the interested parties had been hostile only the summer before, and concessions were to be made on both sides. Indian negotiations are ponderous. They cannot be hurried. I was the adjutant-general of the expedition, that is to say, the scribe or reporter, and I expected to have none of the responsibility and all of the fun. The first general meeting was at the mouth of the Weenatchee, in the heart of the ruggedest Alps of America. The great Columbia tore through the mountain pass in a grand sweep, tossing and foaming. This bend of the river inclosed a level plain some mile or so broad, and just opposite the blue Weenatchee came from the mountain glens to join the Columbia. This plan was the council-ground. We arrived first and went into camp. The pack-mules luxuriated in good rolls in the sand, the canvas village arose, and very soon bacon and coffee led us to supper by the nose. Next morning our friends began to arrive. The news of our presence flew in that way so mysterious even to those who know the Indian's tireless night-and-day riding and system of signaling. Hour after hour the Indians arrived, singly, by families, bands, and almost by tribes, trooping in with herds and loaded pack-animals, men, women, and children—for they brought their homes with them.

The tepees of buffalo-skin were put up, the smoke of many camp-fires arose, and the hill-sides became dotted with grazing ponies. All the life was barbaric. The smoky smell and flavor of everything belonging to these people were not more characteristic than each one of a thousand other things. The picturesque troop just coming in, the shy women in buckskin shirts and leggins (riding astride), their saddles hung with bags, strange utensils, and sometimes the papoose swinging in his swaddling cradle at the pommel; wild-eyed, elfin-haired, little bronze children, perched naked on top of some bales of household goods; the untamed, half-naked boys on their bare-back horses, and galloping along in premature dignity; the motley horde of patient pack-horses loaded out of sight under mats, robes, tepees, poles, pots, bows, spears, guns, and a thousand barbaric things of shape and color defying description. Last, or perhaps first, in the train came the grave, anxious-looking men in fur mantles or loose buckskin shirts, or with yellowish copper-colored, naked bodies, and only the breech-clout and fringed leggins, their hair loose or braided, and their faces painted black, red, yellow, white, whatever color pleased best their idea of an imposing toilet. Each had his gun, perhaps slung in a gayly fringed case, but more generally carried in the hand across the saddle. Then the saddles, most of them of native manufacture, curious, often profusely decorated. The ponies with tails and manes sometimes clipped, sometimes gay with interwoven feathers, and sometimes ears, tail, and mane all cut close to the body in very wantonness of the grotesque.

Then the camp with its wild groupings, its color, its gorgeous setting in the evergreen and snow-clad hills; the eternal snow-peaks high in air against the blue sky; the irregular streets of dusky tepees; the lounging men, the playing children, the sneaking dogs, the working women! It is the thrilling life of the wilderness. What a pity it should all be passing away and no great artist think it worthy of his brush!

There were on this ground the best horses of the whole North-west, belonging to rival tribes that had been renowned for horses from the time of Lewis and Clark. There were races almost every hour, but the one I choose to describe came off on the last day of the council, after morning adjournment, so that the elders of the tribe could be present.

The course was a straight stretch of about a mile along the half grass-grown plain between the camps and the foot of the mountain. The starting-point was marked on the ground; the finishing-point was determined by a horse-hair lariat stretched along the ground and held by two Indians, one from each of the competing tribes.

The finishing-point was nearest the camps, and here the horses took their stand, stark-naked, save the fine buffalo-hair lariats knotted around their lower jaws. They were little beauties, clean cut as barbs, one a white and the other a gray; the skin fine, the sinews clean and silky, nostrils immense, heads small, bony, necks graceful, slim. I say little, for they were undersized, as compared with our thoroughbreds, though larger than the average Indian horse. Their tremendously deep chests led one to believe the assertion of a twenty-miles' galloping race which the gray had won. By each stood its rider, a young Indian boy, slim and sinewy as his horse, and as naked, save the most meager breech-clout. These horses were each the pick of the tribe to which he belonged, and as a matter of course all the members of these tribes adhered to their own especial steed.

Crowds began to flock to the stand. The racers were examined again and again; hands were passed over their bodies a thousand times, it seemed to me. I believe there are no better horsemen in the world than our horse-Indians. These examinations were made to see that all was sound and fair, and also by individual bettors to aid their judgments. The crowd naturally ranged themselves into two parts, each on the side of its favorite horse.

Presently the owner of the white horse stepped out and threw to the ground a new saddle and a bundle of beaver and other pelts. Some one from the opposing side threw in a separate place a bundle of blankets. This was their wager, one against the other; each would remember it, for now all the bets would be piled indiscriminately in two opposing heaps, guarded by appointed watchers. As each threw down his stake, he must watch who matched it, and with what. If he accepted, well; if not, he refused the bet, and either some other took it up or the stake was increased to satisfy the first bettor. The women and young boys were fringing the outer edge of the assemblage, many of them guarding the household treasures, which were in readiness for their husbands or fathers to stake.

It did not take long for the Indian excitement to grow, and soon the bets were showering down and the pile "swelling visibly" with such rapidity that it was marvelous how account could be kept. Blankets, furs, saddles, knives, traps, tobacco, beads, whips, and a hundred other things were staked.

Ponies were led apart in two groups, some wealthy Indians betting six and ten ponies at a time. The excitement grew to a fever. The men even tore the robes and belts from their persons and threw them as wagers. They whispered to boys, who hurried to camp and came up with new things.

Squaws appeared with armfuls of buffalo, wolf, bear, and fox robes, beaded garments, brass pots, etc. Their lords snatched these and bet with seeming recklessness. They took ear-rings from their ears and blankets from the backs of their wives (after having stripped themselves almost naked). The women seemed to enjoy this contribution they made to the wealth and pluck of their husbands. The more ardent bet the last pony they owned in the world, leaving themselves afoot, and some risked their rifles on the race. Their rifles are the last things parted with, but under the all-conquering gambling passion these too will be sacrificed and the bow and arrow resorted to till another weapon is procured.

The excitement, the surging crowds, the calling, the hurrying to and fro, the reckless shower of bets forming at last two piles five or six feet high and twenty in diameter—all were in strange contrast to the little jockeys who stood by their horses, apparently all unconcerned, while the betting was going on. Those in charge had fastened around each horse's body a thick horse-hair lariat doubled; this was knotted tightly but hung loosely, leaving a space of several inches between it and the horse's belly. When all the bets were laid, the riders vaulted to their places, and bending their knees, thrust them between the lariat and the horses' sides, thus drawing the lariat very tight and binding themselves like centaurs to their slippery steeds; and yet by simply straightening their legs they could throw off the band and be released.

The racers now walked with long, supple strides down the course to the starting-point, accompanied by the starters, friends, admirers, jealous watchers, etc., some on foot and some on horseback. The whole mile of track soon became a lane hedged by groups and lines of Indians. The intentness, the care, and the suspense were catching. I began to feel a thrilling excitement and an impatience to know which of the beauties would win and which tribe be beggared.

The eagerness to watch the start made them crowd up the track at one end of the line, in spite of the shrill cries of the Indian watchers to clear the track. But the track would be cleared soon enough.

A faint cry at the other end of the line, a whirl of the horses, a tumult down there, a waving of whips, a wild yelling growing nearer, louder, and here they come—flying. Side by side, the naked riders plying the lash with every terrific bound; the Indians bordering the track packed to a dense mass, surging to and fro, yelling and throwing up their whips; the mounted ones running their horses at full speed after the flyers, but being rapidly left. Here they come! heads out, eyes strained, nostrils stretched, forehoofs seemingly always in the air, the whip-thongs falling with a quickening vigor. A hoarse, wild shouting, a deafening burst of yells, a *swish* in the air, an apparition before the eyes, a bound over the finish line, and the race is over, the white just half a length ahead, and there they go down toward the river, the boys pulling them in for dear life.

Ere they were led back the bets had been claimed, each person taking his stakes and those things which had been pledged against them. Other races were made. The piles of wagers grew again, and again dissolved. Bets were all that was needed to prolong the sport, for if the stock of swift horses—their regular "race-horses"—should by chance be exhausted, slower ones were speedily matched. In these intertribal contests the tribe never deserts its own horses, so that if their antagonists have superior animals, the losers will be stripped to beggary. A transfer of property takes place, and the paupers with happy carelessness hobble off with a few sore pack-animals to carry their diminished possessions.

The Indians are shrewd jockeys, but their own races are as a rule fair and honest trials of speed. The decision of the umpires is never demurred to unless palpably unjust, and on these rare occasions the settlement is either by a quarrel or more usually by a renewal of the race. And while an Indian is willing to gamble on anything, even a tortoise race, his true delight, the very exultation of his soul, is in a long race between horses of wonderful speed. There is nearly always with each band some one favorite steed of supposed all-surpassing powers, and it is the races between these pets of the tribe that inspire the chief interest. The great spring gatherings are among the most picturesque features of Indian peaceful life. The bands and tribes meet near some vast plain or meadow bordered by the forest or the mountains and watered by pleasant streams. Here the women dig the edible roots and weave mats and baskets. The children hunt in the edge of the woods with mimic bows and arrows or fish for trout in the swarming brooks; while each band bring forth their favorite and trust their fortunes to its speed.

The victor over all for the year gains a wide reputation, and is coveted by some three or more thousand Indians. They cherish their race-horses, but apparently from selfish motives, for in the races they are utterly merciless; the most gallant efforts of a defeated brute seem to inspire neither admiration nor gratitude.

Our assembly was not one of these gala meetings, but with savage thoughtlessness our tawny friends turned from the breathless debating of vital affairs of state to the hilarious excitement of horse-racing. The chiefs, it is true, stood aloof, with a dignity partly natural and partly affected, to impress the white dignitaries; or they mingled in the crowd in a stately way, keeping their keen interest tempered with the gravity begotten by their responsibilities.

After dusk the Indian lads would take possession of the deserted track and run their ponies in break-neck scrub-races.

Introduction to "Chief Joseph, the Nez-Percé"

When Lt. Wood was recalled from Sitka, he could not know, of course, that he was about to enter one of the most dramatic and tragic episodes in the history of Indian-white relations on the North American continent. From the time of Lewis and Clark, the Nez Perce had been friends with the whites. They were a proud and talented people, breeders of the famous Appaloosa horse. They were semi-nomadic, ranging over the vast Columbia plateau, though each band had its homeland. In 1855, at a great council at Walla Walla, Washington Territory, 3,600 Nez Perce were given a reservation of 5,000 square miles, but a subsequent treaty in 1863 whittled the area down, eliminating the Wallowa and Imnaha valleys that Old Joseph and his son, Young Joseph, called home. The treaty also shattered Nez Perce unity. About two-thirds of the Nez Perce, nominally Christian, most of whose land lay within the new boundaries, went on the reservation. Old Joseph refused to sign, shredded a copy of the treaty, and destroyed his once-treasured New Testament. Thirty-seven other chiefs refused to sign, and became known as non-treaty Nez Perce. For more than ten years the United States government tried to get these bands on the reservation. Finally, in the summer of 1877, they agreed to go to Lapwai. They were given 30 days to make the move and the troops remained in the vicinity to see that the Indians complied. Some Nez Perce killed two whites, enacting untimely revenge for Nez Perce killed earlier, and the war was on.

The first serious encounter was on June 17th, in White Bird Canyon, Idaho Territory, where cavalry and volunteers under Lieutenant David Perry were badly mauled by the Nez Perce. On June 26th, Lt. Wood joined General Howard's command and was made the General's aide-de-camp, a position he held throughout the campaign. The Nez Perce war was essentially a running fight, marked by several pitched battles, of some 1,500 miles, most of them over extremely rugged terrain, lasting from mid-June until the Indians surrendered in the Bear Paw Mountains, Montana Territory, on October 5th, 1877, only about fifty miles from the Canadian border. For the most part, the Nez Perce, led by Joseph, his younger brother Ollokot, Toohoolhoolzote, Looking Glass, Lean Elk, and White Bird, outmaneuvered and outfought the U. S. army, hoping at first to join the Crow on the buffalo plains and then turning toward Canada and the encampment of Sitting Bull's Sioux.

At one time Joseph was thought to be a military genius. Actually, credit for the masterful strategy and tactics of the Indians must be shared among the aforementioned chiefs; Joseph was most impressive as spokesman for his people. What one historian has called the "flight of the Nez Perce" has gained renown in the annals of Indian-white warfare, in large measure through the continued and widespread publication of Chief Joseph's "Surrender Speech" taken down by Wood. However it is not clear how much, if any, of the speech came from Joseph's lips at the time he gave his rifle over to Colonel Nelson Miles. The speech is included in this account of the pursuit of Joseph, one of only three eye-witness descriptions of the complete campaign.

Chief Joseph, the Nez-Percé

Chief Joseph, or "Young Joseph," as it became the habit to call him during his father's life-time, fought for that which the white man calls patriotism when it has been crowned with success. He and the survivors of his band are now exiles in the Indian Territory. He has appealed to the authorities at Washington, claiming that by the terms of his surrender, as he understood them, they were to be allowed to return to Idaho, and to settle on the Nez-Percé Reservation. This reservation lies at the bottom of the trouble with Joseph's people. They prided themselves on having received Lewis and Clarke, Bonneville, Fremont, and other white men, with the hand of friendship, and on never having falsified their early promises. Up to the time of Joseph's outbreak, though Nez-Percés had been killed by white men, only one white man had fallen by the hand of a *Chu-lé-pa-lu*, the slayer being *Sa-poon-mas*, of Big Thunder's band.

Joseph's father joined the other independent chiefs of the tribe in a formal treaty concluded in the Walla-Walla Valley on June 11, 1855, but which was not ratified until 1859. By this treaty, the Indians gave up all claim to the country excepting certain specified tracts. Old Joseph and *Appush-wa-hite* (Looking-glass) entered into the contract with great reluctance, and only on the express stipulation that the Wallowa and Imnaha Valleys should be guaranteed them as their especial district. Soon the white man wanted these valleys, and in 1863, a supplementary treaty was made (ratified 1867), taking those valleys away from Old Joseph. But he would have nothing to do with this second treaty, he and his band becoming known as the non-treaty Nez-Percés. He said: "I have kept my faith; let the whites keep theirs." A majority of the other chiefs, however, agreed to the new allotment, for their particular interests were not injured; and the commissioners for the United States claimed that Joseph was bound by a majority of his peers. False as was the whole theory of treating with the Indians, the inevitable evil results could have been softened only by good faith on both sides. The faith pledged to Joseph in 1855, when the country was a wilderness, could not now be kept in its spirit, and through that loop-hole the commissioners sought escape. But no matter how consistent their action may have seemed to them, to the Indians it was false and absurd. With them, as with all warlike, nomadic peoples, the decision of a majority is not regarded as binding the minority; this principle is unknown. In their institutions, the autonomy of the individual is so complete that a chief approaches absolutism only in proportion to his personal strength of character, and the strongest never dreams of such an attempt at power, but acts upon the will of his people expressed in council; and if there be but one man who dissents, his right to depart from the action of the others is unquestioned.* So Old Joseph would not leave his valleys, and there he died and was buried, and *In-mut-tu-ya-lat-nut* (Thunder Rolling in the

---

* The character of the tribal Germans as presented by Caesar and Tacitus is in many respects in interesting parallelism with that of the native North Americans.

Mountains), or "Young Joseph," took his place. On the same principle, "Young Joseph," since his confinement in the Indian Territory, points out that to his mind the essential thing about a contract, namely, "the agreement of the minds," was wanting in this supplementary treaty. His parable in effect is as follows: "A man comes to me, and says, 'Joseph, I like your horses, and I want to buy them.' I say I do not want to sell them. Then he goes to my neighbor and says, 'Joseph has some good horses, but he will not sell them,' and my neighbor says, 'Pay me and you may have them.' And he does so, and then comes to me, and says, 'Joseph, I have bought your horses.'"

He first came into notice as chief during the Modoc troubles of 1873. His band became very restless and defiant. A commission was ordered, and on its recommendation the Wallowa was set aside for Joseph's exclusive use by an executive order of June, 1873. But this valley was so beautiful and fertile that two years later the order was revoked. Joseph, however, resisted intrusions into his territory; and in 1876 one of his Indians was killed by a white man, in a quarrel over some stock. This led General Howard, the commander of the military department, to ask for another commission, to "settle the whole matter, before war is even thought of." This commission recommended that if the principle of decision by majorities should be held to apply, Joseph ought to be required to go upon the reservation. Thereupon, at the request of the Interior Department, General Howard was directed to occupy the Wallowa Valley with troops, and, if necessary, to drive Joseph upon the reservation. Indian runners were sent out to inform the "non-treaties" of the decision against them. They refused to hearken to such messages, and prepared to defend themselves.

Joseph would not believe that his case had been truthfully presented, and yet not determined in his favor. He hastened to the agent at Umatilla, and declared that the interpreter at Lapwai could not have spoken the truth to the mixed commission. He begged for another interview. Two councils were held, one at Umatilla, and one at Walla-Walla, in neither of which Joseph appeared, but sent his brother Ollicut (killed in the last fight) to represent him. A general council was called to meet at Lapwai. Joseph and all the non-treaty bands were to be present. For several days the motley hordes poured in from the mountains. There were men, women, and children, with troops of horses, and all the picturesque paraphernalia of the camp.

They came singing the monotonous chants of the wilderness, with gaudy blankets flaunting in the wind or girded at the loins. The horses were daubed with color and plumed with eagle feathers. As they galloped and curveted, the fantastic head-dresses, crests, and flowing locks of their riders, the red leggings or bare brown legs, arms, and breasts, the eagle-feather and bear-claw trimmings, made a highly colored and animated picture.

On May 3d, the first day of the council, Joseph spoke of the importance of the subjects to be discussed, and asked for delay till all could be present, and for plenty of time for deliberation. He was told that White Bird would be waited for if he wished it. Here an old *tooat* (priest) stood up and said to the interpreter: "For the sake of the children and the children's children of both whites and Indians, tell the truth!" The orders of the Government were interpreted to the Indians, and they were told that the department commander and the Indian agent were there to hear all they had to say, no matter how long it might take; but that the Indians must comprehend at the outset that the views of the Government would be enforced.

On the second day White Bird was present, and the debate became so hot and so hostile that Joseph suddenly asked for an adjournment. The next day the council opened more calmly, but finally *Too-hul-hul-suit*, whose anger had forced Joseph to seek the adjournment the day before, said plainly: "The others may do as they like. *I* will *not* go on the reservation." For this he was arrested and confined. Thereafter Joseph and White Bird managed the council smoothly. They either agreed or seemed to agree to everything, and promised to be on the reservation by June 14. At their request *Too-hul-hul-suit* was released. On June 14, 1877, the non-treaty bands began their horrible murders of men, women, and children. The small band which began the work swept over the Camas Prairie and Salmon River country, falling upon the unsuspicious dwellers in their lonely cabins, firing the houses, and throwing the living into the flames. Soon after his capture, while he was a prisoner in a little tent on the bank of the Missouri, Joseph said to the writer: "I intended to go on the reservation. I knew nothing of these murders. Had I been at home, they would not have happened; but I was away on the other side of the Salmon River, killing some beef for my wife, who was sick, and I was called back by messengers telling me what the young men had done. Then I knew I must lead them in fight, for the whites would not believe my story." Nevertheless, the story may be true. About a year after this talk with Joseph, an Indian in Idaho told me that after the last council with General Howard, at Lapwai, the allied bands of non-treaties met in a rocky cañon near the Salmon River, and argued peace and war for ten days; that Joseph urged peace, and the others war, even taunting him with cowardice; that on the last day two young men whose fathers had been killed by the whites took three companions and committed the first murders.

News of the outrages was received at Fort Lapwai, the nearest military post, not far from Lewiston, June 15, and by eight o'clock in the evening the garrison, consisting of two companies of cavalry, was on the march. By dawn of the next day, they entered White Bird Cañon, a basaltic-walled, rough-ridged defile leading from the table-land of Camas Prairie to the Salmon River, six miles distant. Into this cañon the troops marched, accompanied by some citizen volunteers. The Nez-Percé record had been one of such unbroken peacefulness toward white men that no one knew what sort of antagonists they would prove. Our advance was met four miles from the entrance to the cañon by nearly the entire hostile force—some three hundred warriors. Leaving their women and children and noncombatants—in all about seven hundred souls—in the camp behind them, they advanced, throwing out a line of mounted skirmishers which deployed and maneuvered in fine order. They came on yelling, under cover of a herd of horses driven ahead of them, and by military skill and savage adroitness combined, they soon turned our flank and poured in a deadly fire. The citizen volunteers, who had been given the key position to hold, broke and fled, panic-stricken.

This demoralized the soldiers, and the sad affair was only saved from being a rout and total massacre by the coolness of the few who preserved military order and thereby escaped alive. The Nez-Percés returned to their camp completely victorious, and probably suffered very slight loss. During the heat of this fight Joseph's wife gave birth to a daughter. At his surrender this was the only child left to him, his other daughter, a girl about ten years of age, having been cut off from camp, and lost during the *mêlée* of the final engagement.

After this fight or "massacre" at White Bird Creek, the Indians had the country to themselves. The whites fled to Idaho City, and hurriedly constructed a stockade; and the hostiles gathered into the mountain glens most of the horses of the region, and pillaged the settlements and slaughtered the cattle. General Howard concentrated all the troops of his department as quickly as possible, and, putting himself at their head, moved on the hostiles. These abandoned their lair in the White Bird Cañon, and crossed the Salmon River into the heart of the Craig Mountains just as the troops reached the river-bank. Now began a doubling chase in this rugged country. Joseph, with his great herds of horses and ranch cattle, which he killed as he needed them, chose the nearly inaccessible paths; and the incessant rain, the slippery or rocky steeps, all combined to foil the breathless efforts of his pursuers. Returning to the Camas Prairie in a wide sweep through the mountains, Joseph penned up two companies of cavalry in a stockade, and cut off and killed Lt. Rains and ten men who had been sent out to reconnnoiter.

Encouraged by this continued success, which he hoped would draw malcontents to him from the neighboring reservation, Joseph went into camp on the North Fork of the Clearwater, and here, by redoubled exertions, the troops overtook him on the morning of July 11. It was a test case—all the hostiles under Joseph against all the soldiers under General Howard. The Indians, naturally a brave tribe, now flushed by success and rendered desperate by their lot, seemed not unwilling to try the issue. Leaving their picturesque camp and cone-like tepees protected by the broad mountain stream, they crossed over to meet us, and, swarming out of the river-bottom, occupied the rocks and fir-crowned heights of the ravines transverse to the main valley, leaving the troops only the alternative to deploy as skirmishers, and throw themselves flat on the sunburnt grass of the open. Joseph promptly took the initiative, and tried the favorite and hitherto successful tactics of working around our flanks and getting in the rear; but in this he was checked each time, and our line finally developed into a crescent with the baggage and hospital at the rear and center. Nothing could be bolder or more aggressive than the conduct of these Indians. Twice this day they massed under shelter, and, leaving their war-horses in the timber, charged our line so savagely that they were only repelled by as fierce a counter-charge, the two lines advancing rapidly till they almost met; and when the Indians turned they did so only to regain cover. Their fire was deadly, the proportion of wounded to killed being but two to one. A large number of the casualties occurred in the short time before each man had protected himself by earth thrown up by his trowel bayonet. At one point of the line, one man, raising his head too high, was shot through the brain; another soldier, lying on his back and trying to get the last few drops of warm water from his canteen, was robbed of the water by a bullet taking off the canteen's neck while it was at his lips. An officer, holding up his arm, was shot through the wrist; another, jumping to his feet for an instant, fell with a bullet through the breast. So all day long under the hot July sun, without water and without food, our men crawled about in the parched grass, shooting and being shot. The wounded were carried back to an awning where the surgeons were at work; the dead were left where they fell. All day long the Indians fought hard for the mastery. Among the rocks and scrubby pines their brown naked bodies were seen flying from shelter to shelter. Their yells were incessant as they cheered each other on or signaled a successful shot.

Joseph, White Bird, and *Too-hul-hul-suit*, all seemed to be in command but—and as one of Joseph's band told the writer—Joseph was after this fight called "the war-chief." He was everywhere along the line; running from point to point, he directed the flanking movements and the charges. It was his long fierce calls which sometimes we heard loudly in front of us, and sometimes faintly resounding from the distant rocks. As darkness covered us, the rifles grew silent, till only an occasional shot indicated each side's watchfulness.

The packers and non-combatants had been set cooking, and during the evening a sort of pancake and plenty of ammunition were distributed to each man. A spring in a ravine was secured, but one man sent to fill canteens never returned, and it was found that the enemy were in possession of it. Next day, however, the spring was retaken. All through the night, from the vast Indian camp in the river-bottom, rose the wail of the death-song and the dull drumming of the *tooats*. The dirge of the widows drifted to us through the summer night—now plaintive and faint, now suddenly bursting into shrieks, as if their very heart-strings had snapped. But mingling with these unpleasant sounds came the rapid movement of the scalp-chant, *hum, hum, hum,* hurrying to the climax of fierce war-whoops.

With the dawn the stray popping of rifles grew more and more rapid, till as the sun shot up into the sky both sides were hard at work again. Joseph, unlike his men, did not strip off his clothes for battle, as is the Indian custom, but wore his shirt, breech-clout, and moccasins; and though (as I was told by one of his men) he was wholly reckless of himself in directing the various fights, he did not receive a wound.

On this second day, the Indians being more determined, if possible, than on the day before, and our side having received reinforcements, General Howard, at two o'clock in the afternoon, ordered a charge upon their position. Colonel Marcus Miller led the attack, which was desperately resisted. Some of the Indians made no effort to retreat, and were killed in their rifle-pits. But this ended the fight. They fled across the river, hastily gathered the women and children who had not been sent off the night before, and throwing on pack-animals such effects as they could secure in their haste, they were soon seen speckling the distant hills, as they streamed away to Kamiah ferry and the Lo Lo trail.

Much of their camp was taken standing, the packs and robes lying about, and the meat cooking at the fire. Evidently, the enemy had not anticipated defeat. We followed them to Kamiah ferry, which they destroyed, and disputed the river, while they robbed their kinsmen, the Kamiah Indians, and collected their herds in a mountain glade. At this place Joseph sent in a flag of truce; some of the wounded and some young braves came in, but he did not. The writer was told long afterward, by an Indian of that region, that Joseph wished to surrender rather than leave the country or bring further misery on his people, but that, in council, he was overruled by the older chiefs, *Ap-push-wa-hite* (Looking-glass), White Bird, and *Too-hul-hul-suit*; and Joseph would not desert the common cause. According to this informant, Joseph's last appeal was to call a council in the dale, and passionately condemn the proposed retreat from Idaho. "What are we fighting for?" he asked. "Is it for our lives? No. It is for this land where the bones of our fathers are buried. I do not want to take my women among strangers. I do not want to die in a strange land. Some of you tried to say, once, that I was afraid of the whites. Stay here with me now, and you shall have plenty of fighting. We will put our women behind us in these mountains, and die on our own land fighting for them. I would rather do that than run I know not where."

But, the retreat being decided on, he led this caravan, two thousand horses and more, women, children, old men, and old women, the wounded, palsied, and blind, by a seemingly impassable trail, interlaced with fallen trees, through the ruggedest mountains, to the Bitter Root Valley, where (a fact unprecedented in Indian warfare) he made a treaty of forbearance with the inhabitants, passing by settlements containing banks and stores, and near farms rich with stock, but taking nothing and hurting no one. So he pushed on; he crossed the Rocky Mountains twice, the Yellowstone and Missouri Rivers, and was within one day's march of Canada when he was taken. Not knowing that General Gibbon had been summoned by telegraph to intercept him, Joseph, after leaving

Bitter Root Valley, encamped to rest awhile on the banks of Big Hole Creek, in the valley of the Big Hole, situated in Montana.

After making a reconnaissance and finding (with slight loss) that the Indians had a rear guard holding the narrow Lo Lo trail, we hurried to reach the Bitter Root Valley by the Mullan road; but Joseph made a demonstration in the shape of a raid on Kamiah, and such were the reports and the popular feeling that General Howard abandoned the Mullan road and returned to push in on the Lo Lo trail. For ten days we toiled along this pathway. The marching hour was sunrise, the camping hour sunset. Often the hillsides were so steep that we could not sleep comfortably without digging out a bed. Each cavalryman had been required to start with ten pounds of grain for his horse, but several times horses and patient pack-mules were tied up at night without a mouthful of any kind of fodder. Meanwhile, General Gibbon had hurried down from Fort Shaw, and, finding that he was three days too late to head off Joseph, pressed on his trail over the Rockies toward the Big Hole. On August 6 we were still locked in the mountains, but we were encamped in a beautiful glen, where, for the first time, there was good grazing. Hot springs gave delightful baths, and a cold brook furnished trout for supper. Everyone, down to the most stoical mule in the packtrain, felt cheered. Soon a courier from General Gibbon arrived in hot haste, informing us of his intentions and whereabouts. A sergeant was sent with similar information to General Gibbon; and before daylight next morning we were harder at work than ever, trying to overtake Gibbon before he should strike the Indians. For three days we pushed on with no word from our courier. Then (August 10) General Howard, with an aide-de-camp and twenty Indian scouts and twenty cavalrymen, commanded by Lieutenant Bacon, made a forced march ahead of his command to join Gibbon. The latter had discovered Joseph's camp in the bottom-land of the head-waters of the Big Hole. This bottom-land was covered with thickets of willow bushes, and was full of treacherous bogs. Jutting into it from the western side were the timber-covered knolls and promontories of the Rocky Mountain foot-hills, while away to the east rolled the open Big Hole prairie. At dawn General Gibbon made his attack; and though he had less than one-third the force of the enemy, so complete was the surprise that with almost any other Indians there would have been a rout. The soldiers poured into the camp, firing into the teepees, and, in the gray light, shooting indiscriminately everything that moved. Naked warriors with only their rifles and cartridge-belts ran into the willows and to the prairie knolls overlooking the camp, and instantly from these positions of vantage opened a telling fire. Women and children, roused from sleep, ran away screaming with terror, or, surrounded by enemies, begged by signs for mercy. (It is needless to say that no women or children were intentionally killed.) Some few women armed themselves in desperation, but most of them fled or hid under the overhanging banks of the creek or in the bushes.

The yells of the soldiers, the wild war-whoops of the Indians, the screams of the terrified women and children, the rattle of rifle shots, shouts of command, the cursing of the maddened soldiers already firing the nearest teepees, contributed to the horrors of the battle, which was made more terrible by the presence of mothers and babies in the blue rifle smoke that made the dawn more dim. Joseph soon had his men strongly posted on the commanding positions, and their destructive fire stopped further firing of the camp, and drove the soldiers to one of the timbered knolls. General Gibbon's horse was killed, and he himself was shot through the thigh; but he kept command, and, sitting propped against a tree, directed the construction of some rifle-pits and log fortifications.

Stung by the attack, but more (as Joseph later explained) by the loss of their women and children, the Indians tooks the offensive most savagely. They fired the long grass and timber, but a fortunate change of the wind saved the wooded knoll. They wormed through the grass to within forty or fifty feet of the rifle-pits. They climbed to the tree-tops. One of them was so securely perched behind a dead log that he killed four men in one rifle-pit before he himself was picked off, and then his naked yellow body fell so close to the fortification that his friends did not venture to recover it. This night, after burying the dead, Joseph sent his women and impedimenta under escort by way of the Lemhi country, where they again made a treaty of forbearance with the settlers. All the next day the fight continued, but about midnight the last of the warriors withdrew and hastened after the main body.

General Howard with his small party bivouacked this same night about twelve miles from Gibbon's position, being unable to proceed because of the darkness. At twilight he had captured some citizen stragglers from Gibbon's wagon camp, who told a dismal tale of utter annihilation. General Howard was too experienced in deserters' stories to credit all this, but nevertheless he caused camp fires to be built as if his whole command was at hand, and with the earliest dawn was sweeping along at a gallop to give the aid of his forty rifles to Gibbon. Some naked and mutilated bodies of our people were passed, a howitzer wheel was found by the trail, and the wagon camp was found silent and deserted; so it was with forebodings that we rode on, to be cheered, however, as we turned the point of a hill and came suddenly upon Gibbon's camp, and were received with hearty hurrahs. The commander himself was dressing his wound, and directing the soldiers in the care of their comrades; for no medical officer was with this command, and about one-half of them were killed or wounded.

Joseph had turned north-eastward toward the National Park of the Yellowstone, and his rear-guard had crossed the Corinne stage-road a few hours before General Howard's command reached the same point. This was a great disappointment, as we had every reason to believe that this time we would intercept him. The next night we encamped in a prairie dotted with clumps of cottonwood trees and called Camas Meadows. That night, just before dawn, our sleeping camp was startled into half-bewildered consciousness by a rattling fire of rifles, accompanied with the *zee-zip* of bullets through the air and through tent canvas, and by unearthly war-whoops. It was a back hit from Joseph. Our men, still half stupid with sleep, groped about for shoes and cartridge-belts and swore at the mislaid articles; but each one knew his drill, and as fast as he equipped himself he crawled away from the dangerous white tents, formed on the line, and began replying to the enemy. The mule-herd, successfully stampeded, was flying in a terror momentarily increased by the naked Indians yelling demoniacally at its heels, while Indians in front were shaking the bells stolen from the necks of the lead-animals. These Indians had crawled in among the herd during the night, and cut the hobbles and taken off the bells. Our cavalry were at the picket line trying to saddle, and at the same time to control, their frightened horses, while the Indians who had remained behind were doing their best to stampede and add to the disappearing mule-herd. Our own Indian scouts, naked and lithe and silent, glided through the bushes and from rock to rock. The dawn showed the mule-herd far away over the prairie, disappearing toward the hills. The cavalry was already in hot pursuit, and overtook and recaptured the herd, but only for a moment; for Joseph had so calculated his plans that at this point our troops ran into an ambush of the whole Indian force, and could not pay any attention to the herd, the most of which Joseph finally secured. The foot troops then moved to the support of the cavalry, and the engagement became general, and was only ended at about two o'clock in the afternoon by the withdrawal of the Indians. We then returned to our camp, and made a reduction and rearrangement of baggage to suit the crippled pack-train. Joseph said after his surrender that about forty of his youngest men had made all the noise and firing of the first attack. The herd being stampeded, all joined in at the rear, and hurried to where he was waiting to receive them and cover their retreat. He said that that night he was camped about twenty miles from us, and had been watching us all day, and at sunset or a little later had started the stampeding party on their dangerous expedition. He said further that he was tired of always finding General Howard close behind him, and wanted to "set him afoot," but that he was very much disappointed in finding the cavalry horses picketed that night, for he would rather have had the horses than the mules, and expected to get them both; for said he, "You didn't picket your horses other nights, so I didn't expect it this time."

The loss of pack-animals, and the destitution and sickness among the men, compelled a halt of three days, during which time Joseph reached the Lower Geyser Basin of the National Park, and captured some tourists. His young men first came upon them and shot the men. A Mr. Oldham was shot through both cheeks, but we found him wandering through the woods. Mr. Taft also escaped. A Mr. Cowan was shot from his horse, and again shot through the head while his wife held him in her arms. He was left by the roadside supposed to be dead, but the wife and her sister were not harmed, and after being held in Joseph's camp for some time were released. White Bird took them out of camp, showed them their ponies, and said, "Go. That is the way. Do not stop to water your horses. Hurry! Hurry!" Both he and Joseph feared they would be waylaid by the young warriors. Mr. Cowan was found by us in a dying condition, but strange to say recovered; and he and his wife were eventually restored to each other. A miner named Snively also escaped to us from the hostile camp. He said he was well treated, and that Joseph used him as guide, for he was wandering in these mysterious regions without any exact knowledge of the country. The time he thus lost enabled us to take a shorter line and press closely on him. General Sturgis and the Seventh Cavalry, fresh in the field, were ahead of Joseph; and again we confidently expected to hold him in the mountains, from which there was but one pass in the direction Joseph was going, and another toward the Stinking Water. But every attempt to communicate with Sturgis was, as we afterward found, unsuccessful. The bodies were found of every courier sent out, of every miner or white man caught in the mountains; for at this juncture the Indians spared nobody. Joseph made a feint toward the Stinking Water pass, and having got General Sturgis moving in that direction, he slipped out under cover of the hills, by way of Clarke's Fork, and crossed the Yellowstone toward the Musselshell basin. He had led his whole people much over a thousand miles, through the ruggedest wilderness of the continent, and now he again paused to rest at Rocky Cañon. But Sturgis, reënforced by General Howard's freshest cavalry, overtook him here, and again he started the caravan of women, children, and old men, under escort, while he and the warriors held their position and protected the retreat. Thus he made a running fight of two days, extending one hundred and fifty miles to the lakes near the Musselshell. Here he distanced all pursuit, and was never again overtaken until he had crossed the Missouri, nearly completing a retreat of almost two thousand miles, and was within thirty or forty miles of the British line, and not much farther from the vast hostile camp of Sitting Bull. During this march every vicissitude of climate had been felt: the cold, drenching rains of early spring, and the heat of summer, the autumn extremes of temperature, when the midday in the mountains was very hot, and at night water froze an inch thick in the buckets. The men who pursued Joseph through his entire course were mostly foot troops. They were necessarily reduced to the most meager supplies, and found the country ahead of them swept clean by the hostile tribe.

On September 12, General Howard sent word to General Miles that Joseph had foiled all attempts to stop him, and earnestly requested him to make every effort to intercept the Indians. This dispatch was received by General Miles September 17, and the next day he began the march which resulted in Joseph's capture. Joseph, who did not know of any other available troops in the field, and was watching only Generals Howard and Sturgis, was encamped along Eagle Creek. The country around was all bare, rolling, grass prairie, at this time covered with a light fall of snow. The camp lay in the sheltering hollows—the lowest, and therefore for fighting purposes the worst situation. A blinding snow-storm shielded General Miles's approach on the morning of September 30, until he was almost upon them. Instantly, on discovering the advance, the Indians seized the crests of the knolls surrounding their camp, and the cavalry charge was successfully repulsed. Every officer or noncommissioned officer who wore a badge of rank was killed or wounded, save one. Joseph and his elder daughter were on the other side of the creek, among the horse-herd, when the first charge was made. Calling to the girl to follow, he dashed across and joined his men, taking command; but his daughter and many others were cut off by the cavalry charge, which captured and drove off the herd. These people fled to the distant hills; some were murdered by the Sioux; some probably perished from the severe weather; but Joseph's daughter was restored to him some six months afterward. The troops held most of the higher crests commanding the camp. The Indians with wonderful labor and ingenuity literally honeycombed a portion of the site of their camp, and other more advantageous transverse gulches, with subterranean dwelling-places, communicating galleries, etc. Their dead horses were utilized as fortifications and as food. Here they held their own, refusing all offers of surrender, and saying in effect: If you want us, come and take us. Joseph visited General Miles under flag of truce, but at that time would not surrender. His people held Lieutenant Jerome as a hostage till Joseph was returned to them. Had he not lost the herd that moved his motley horde, it is more than probable that Joseph would have made another of his successful fights in retreat. On October 4 General Howard, with two aides, two friendly Nez-Percés (both of whom had daughters in the hostile camp), and an interpreter, arrived in Miles's camp while the firing was still going on. The two old Nez-Percés, "George" and "Captain John," rode into Joseph's camp next day. They told him General Howard was there, with promises of good treatment; that his whole command was only two or three days behind him. With tears in their eyes they begged Joseph to surrender. Joseph asked if he would be allowed to return to Idaho. He was told that he would, unless higher authority ordered otherwise.

Then old "Captain John" brought this reply (and his lips quivered and his eyes filled with tears as he delivered the words of his chief):

Tell General Howard I know his heart. What he told me before—I have it in my heart. I am tired of fighting. Our chiefs are killed. Looking-glass is dead. Too-hul-hul-suit is dead. The old men are all dead. It is the young men, now, who say 'yes' or 'no' [that is, vote in council]. He who led on the young men [Joseph's brother, Ollicut] is dead. It is cold, and we have no blankets. The little children are freezing to death. My people—some of them—have run away to the hills, and have no blankets, no food. No one knows where they are—

*perhaps freezing to death. I want to have time to look for my
children, and to see how many of them I can find; may be I shall
find them among the dead. Hear me, my chiefs: my heart is sick and
sad. From where the sun now stands, I will fight no more forever!*

It was nearly sunset when Joseph came to deliver himself up. He
rode from his camp in the little hollow. His hands were clasped over the
pommel of his saddle, and his rifle lay across his knees; his head was
bowed down. Pressing around him walked five of his warriors; their
faces were upturned and earnest as they murmured to him; but he
looked neither to the right nor the left, yet seemed to listen intently. So
the little group came slowly up the hill to where General Howard, with
an aide-de-camp, and General Miles waited to receive the surrender. As
he neared them, Joseph sat erect in the saddle, then gracefully and
with dignity he swung himself down from his horse, and with an
impulsive gesture threw his arm to its full length, and offered his rifle
to General Howard. The latter motioned him toward General Miles,
who received the token of submission.

Those present shook hands with Joseph, whose worn and anxious
face lighted with a sad smile as silently he took each offered hand.
Then, turning away, he walked to the tent provided for him.

His scalp-lock was tied with otter fur. The rest of his hair hung in a
thick plait on each side of his head. He wore buckskin leggings and a
gray woolen shawl, through which were the marks of four or five bullets
received in this last conflict. His forehead and wrist were also scratched
by bullets. White Bird, the only other surviving chief, would not
surrender, but with his immediate family passed between the lines that
night and went to British Columbia. As has already been explained,
Joseph could not have controlled this, even if he had known of it. In
surrendering he could really act only for those willing to follow him.

On the second day after the surrender the prisoners were disposed
of according to the terms of the following letter, the final result being
that they were taken to Fort Leavenworth, where many died of malarious
fever, and the others removed to the Indian Territory, where they now
are:

*Head-quarters, Department of the Columbia. In the Field. Battle-
field of Eagle Creek, near Bearpaw Mountain, Montana. October 7,
1877.*

Colonel Nelson A. Miles, Fifth Infantry, Commanding District of the Yellowstone.

Colonel: On account of the cost of transportation of the Nez-Percé prisoners to the Pacific coast, I deem it best to retain them all at some place within your district, where they can be kept under military control until next spring. Then, unless you receive instructions from higher authority, you are hereby directed to have them sent, under proper guard, to my department, where I will take charge of them and carry out the instructions I have already received.

> *O.O. Howard,*
> *Brigadier-General, commanding Department.*

Joseph at this time must have been about thirty-seven or thirty-eight years old. He is tall, straight, and handsome, with a mouth and chin not unlike that of Napoleon I. He was, in council, at first probably not so influential as White Bird and the group of chiefs that sustained him, but from first to last he was preëminently their "war-chief." Such was the testimony of his followers after his surrender, and such seems to be the evidence of the campaign itself.

INTRODUCTION TO "MAN'S BATTLE WITH THE TITANS IS BEGUN"

AS THE POSTSCRIPT INDICATES, Wood wrote this sonnet upon his return to the country he had passed through to join Howard's troops and begin the Nez Perce campaign. Written around the century's turn, it reflects a great change in the Northwest and in Wood's own circumstances, as well as a sense of nostalgia for more vital times.

The poem appeared in 1918 in *Sonnets* and is the first of a number of occasional works—works written for or in response to a particular occasion, often a wedding or funeral, a coronation or military victory—featured in this anthology. Occasional poetry had its heyday in the sixteenth and seventeenth centuries, when royalty commissioned poems and masques for birthdays and other state occasions.

This is a form of which Wood was quite fond. He turned it to his own purposes, writing poems for birthdays (his own and those of people close to him) and at Christmas. He also delighted in writing long inscriptions, sometimes poems, in the books he often gave as gifts.

Sonnets is a book of occasional verse, carrying the dedication, "Throughout aye many years begot of introspective sense and love for kith and kin." The book contains many sonnets dated and dedicated to specific people. One sonnet has this epigraph, "To my son, Berwick, on his way to Cornell, 1906." Another has this postscript, "On learning of an accident to Maxwell in the Black Forest, Germany, 1903." The poem below has the postscript, *"Going up the Snake Rivwer twenty odd years after making the same journey to the Nez Perce War (1877)."*

MAN'S BATTLE WITH THE TITANS IS BEGUN

Man's battle with the Titans is begun,
  And on the narrow strip beneath the heights
  Orchards cluster, flecked with sunny lights,
An oasis from the parched desert won.
So heavy hang the peaches in the sun
  That limbs are propped, and children, happy wights,
  Plunder unchecked with shrill cries of delight
As in the fragrant shade they laughing run.
When first I saw where now these shout and play
  An Indian camp nestled in solitude,
  I, young moustached, with shoulder-strap and sword,
And through these hills despairingly at bay
  The brown men stood, with wives and naked brood.
  The orchards bloom, but gone the tawny horde.

With the turn of the century, the frontier phase of C. E. S. Wood's writing culminated with the publication of a unique little book. Erskine's second son, Maxwell, and his chum, Lewis A. McArthur, operated a hand press in the attic of the McArthur home on Glisan Street. McArthur would go on to be a director of the Oregon Historical Society, secretary of the Oregon Geographic Board, and author of *Oregon Geographic Names*. The two fourteen-year-olds had been putting out intermittently a little newspaper called *The Bee*. Seeking a more substantial publication, Maxwell asked his father to write a small book for printing on the Attic Press. Wood obliged by collecting nineteen tales told him by far western frontier figures, most of them Indians, between 1875 and 1878, when Wood was exploring Alaska or serving as aide-de-camp to General O. O. Howard in the Nez Perce and Bannock campaigns.

Wood tells the tales with appropriate directness and simplicity but with little intent to achieve ethnological authenticity. Jarold Ramsey writes in *Coyote Was Going There* (1979) that, "[Wood's] transcriptions of *Indian Tales* are by no means scholarly . . . but neither are they merely fanciful or sentimentalized." "To make quantity," Wood wrote a twentieth imaginative legend of his own, "The Tale of Shshauni and Susshupkin," "born of the longing of the heart."

Erskine had in mind a book in the spirit and style of the famous printer and designer William Morris. He sent to New York for special type and to Holland for quality paper. The boys printed an edition of 105, part of them bound in morocco and part in vellum tied with green ribbon; the tops were gilt edged but the other edges were left in the deckle. The books went to a select group of subscribers. Vanguard Press of New York published a reprint in 1929 under the title *A Book of Indian Tales*. Copies of the Attic Press edition are collectors' items and very expensive.

HOW YEHL ESCAPED FROM THE FIRE DEMON
AND BROUGHT FIRE TO THE THLINKITS

While we were slipping down Peril Strait through an endless summer day, the afterglow remaining until the sun rose again, I resting prone upon the bales in the canoe, Tah-ah-nah-klekh, his terrapin eyes ever upon the sea and sky, told me this tale.

The Thlinkits had no fire. They were cold and unhappy. All the fire was in the great Smoking Mountain to the north, guarded by the fierce Fire Demon. If any tried to steal some, he threw them into the midst of his world-big furnace and piled huge logs upon them, so that smoke and flame flew out of the top of the mountain and the earth shook with the fury of the Demon and trembled at the groans of his victims. Yehl was sorry for the Thlinkits; therefore he shot hundreds of the little bird Kun and from the skins of their breasts he made himself a cloak, sewing into it such magic that when he drew this cloak about him he became invisible, or could change himself into any beast he wished. He slew the terrible crane Kutzghahtushl, whose bill cleaves the clouds and makes the lightning; and, casing himself in its skin, he could fly swift as light. Then he changed himself into the raven, a very large bird of purest white. He flew northward to the fire mountain and alighted before the great cavern that led into it, to the fires of the Smoke Mountain's Demon. Devils of the earth, the air and the water guarded this cave, and whomsoever approached they tore in pieces or delivered to their master. None could kill them, for they were devils immortal. Some slept while others watched, and the only entrance to the fire was always guarded. But Yehl, throwing over him his invisible cloak, passed safely through them and on into the blackness, as it seemed forever, till it began to grow warmer and warmer and lighter and lighter. Then suddenly he came into the vast chamber where the fires leaped and roared forever, lighting the rocks with a glare unendurable. On a huge rock, the shadows black at his back, sat the mighty Demon. Yehl took his proper form and spoke to him. Who are you? said the sorcerer. Before the land came out of the sea, I was, said Yehl. Then the fire devil drew himself up as high as the mountain and said: Before ever the world was or the liver came up from below, I was. When Yehl heard this, his heart trembled and became small; but presently he asked the

Demon to tell him his adventures. After he had finished, Yehl commenced to tell of his own adventures; and on this matter he talked for many days, never pausing until from weariness of listening the mighty devil fell asleep. When he snored so that the earth trembled, Yehl took a firebrand and started to escape. At once the devil awoke. He flew at Yehl with fury; but Yehl quickly changed again into a raven, and, taking the firebrand in his beak, flew into the smoke and up through the chimney of the mountain. But the throat of this flue narrowed so that Yehl could not get through with his firebrand; and the devil, seeing this, threw on log after log and piled the great fires higher than ever, so that the mountain quivered and the smoke rolled up black as pitch-smoke. At last Yehl escaped, but shriveled in size and changed from white to black; and the ravens have been so ever since. When the Fire Demon knew that Yehl had escaped, he changed himself into an eagle and flew in pursuit of him. The flight of these two was like that of an arrow, or a falling star. The air cracked: smaller grew the firebrand, and nearer came the terrible Demon. At last Yehl was overcome: he could do no more. The fire was burning his claws, so he dropped it. Down after it swooped the great Devil bird, and Yehl made his escape. But the Demon was too late; the fire fell among the pebbles on the shingle beach of an island and, breaking into thousands of sparks, flew into the stones. The Demon returned to his cavern, and for three days shook the whole earth in his anger. But ever since that time, even to this day, fire can be knocked out of the stones.

Introduction to "The Love of Red Bear and Feather Cloud"

Sarah Winnemucca, a Northern Paiute of southeastern Oregon and northwestern Nevada, told Lt. Wood one of the most interesting of the tales he collected. He met her during the Bannock War of 1878-1879, the last major Indian-white conflict in the Pacific Northwest.

The Northern Paiutes and the Bannocks sprang from Shoshonean stock. Denied the natural abundance that Pacific Northwest coast peoples enjoyed, these hunting, fishing, and gathering folk often had to be migratory. Thus, for them the reservation system was inappropriate. According to General George Crook, who was critical of governmental policy, the Paiutes and Bannocks had two painful alternatives, "the warpath or starvation."

Coming on the heels of the Nez Perce campaign, the Bannock-Paiute outbreak was something of an anticlimax. It also lacked the shape and dimensions of a war. Rather, it was a series of skirmishes and encounters, sometimes deliberate, sometimes accidental. Matters were further complicated because some of the Paiutes, Chiefs Winnemucca and Egan in particular, were against war but tended to be intimidated by the more aggressive Bannocks.

Sarah Winnemucca rode into Sheep Ranch on June 15, 1878, seeking the army's help in protecting her father Chief Winnemucca and his people from the Bannocks. General Howard, recognizing her value as interpreter, guide, and go-between, agreed, and she served with his command for the three months' campaign. Wood made friends with Sarah Winnemucca, as he had with Chief Joseph, and learned from her stories and customs of her people including their protocol of courtship. At the end of hostilities she and her people were sent to Yakima, far from their homes in southeastern Oregon. Sarah Winnemucca took to the public platform espousing Indian rights, wrote her life story, and, when she died of tuberculosis at the age of 47, was probably the best-known Indian woman in the nation.

The Love of Red Bear and Feather Cloud

When Buffalo Horn and Ehegant went on the warpath in 1878, there came on a panting and foaming horse to our camp at Sheep Ranch, Sarah, daughter of Chief Winnemucca, called in her own tongue, The Pretty Shell Flower, who told us her father and his band were held by the hostiles. After their escape she rode with us till the end of the campaign; and riding under the blazing sun over the dusty sage plains of the Malheur, she told me this tale.

A long time ago, before Fremont or any white man came to this country, my people, the Piutes, held all the land from the Columbia to below the Humboldt; all Nevada, California and Southern Oregon. There was plenty of food and furs and they were happy. But our enemies conquered, so that at last the Piutes just had a little desert land in the Humboldt Valley. The chief of the Piute nation was my father's ancestor, but this is so long ago I cannot tell you how long. The daughter of this chief was a beautiful maiden. Her name was Feather Cloud, because of the small white cloud seen at her birth. She was smooth-armed, her eyes were very bright, but she always looked modestly down when in camp or among the men or the elders. She could sew with the deer sinew and tan buckskin, and kept her father's moccasins always soft and dry. No one could make such fine baskets of the hazel and the willow twigs, or of the rye grass and the maiden-hair fern stems. She could make mats from the inner bark of trees and of the tules. She was very neat and clean and her hair was glossy as the blackbird's back. Her father had many ponies, but he was offered many more for the pretty Feather Cloud. No, said he, she shall make her bed where she chooses. She was eighteen years old.

In the tribe, but living in another band, was a young man named Red Bear. He was tall, straight and braver than an eagle. He held his head up and looked every one in the face as an eagle does. He was not afraid of any one. He had no father, no mother, no squaw. His tribe had brought him up till he could hunt for himself, and he did not seem to care to get horses or robes or any riches. What he killed more than he needed he gave with the hides to the old people, and sometimes he asked an old woman to make him a new robe or pair of leggings. So everybody liked Red Bear and every one was afraid of him.

Red Bear had seen Feather Cloud for the first time at the Wreath Feast to celebrate her coming to womanhood. The feast was in the spring-time, as it always is. The day was warm; the birds played through the branches and sang in the tree-tops. The pine squirrels and the gophers ran about chirping; everything was glad to live. That morning Feather Cloud with all her companions, young girls of sixteen or eighteen, had gone into the forest to gather flowers and make wreaths. They found the most flowers on the edge of the woods, in the open places where the sun was, and here they sat them down and made wreaths of violets, purple and yellow; anemones, yellow lilies, and purple iris, lupin, and larkspur, the wild currant so pink, and strawberry blossoms. When the time had run and the shadow had reached the mark, the wreaths were counted; and as Feather Cloud had the most, she was crowned queen. She was clothed with flower wreaths. The others were ornamented also with wreaths. No one today could dispute her will; what she ordered was law. Every one laughed and was very happy. She decreed foot-races, and the maidens ran like frightened fawns, and wreaths were given as prizes. She decreed dances, and they took hold of hands and danced in circle, sometimes very slowly. She ordered many games and moved about like a queen.

Red Bear had been hunting that day. He had killed a black bear coming out of a large hollow tree. The hide was on his arm as he came through the woods. Suddenly he was near to the maidens as they were dancing. Feather Cloud was in the center; her teeth and her eyes and her feet were all laughing, she was so happy and excited. Red Bear looked on her and loved her. She was very beautiful to him, the most beautiful in all the earth. But he said nothing, for men are not allowed at the wreath games. He stood still like a pine tree, but when the dance was done he walked forward and laid the bearskin at her feet and walked away. She said nothing and he said nothing. Only he looked into her eyes as boldly as a hawk and she looked into his and was ashamed.

In the evening the great camp fires were lighted and the meat and the nuts were roasted, and the tribe sat around to see Feather Cloud and the maidens dance and celebrate the end of the feast. None but the relatives of Feather Cloud could take part. But Red Bear stood in the ring of onlookers and watched Feather Cloud. The more he watched, the more his heart seemed to go out to her hands and feet and the more hungry he became to take her for his wife; and he said to himself, I have found the one I wanted. So all evening, while Feather Cloud and her companions chanted and danced and celebrated the end of the feast, Red Bear sat in the shadows of the fire and let love eat into his heart. The next night, after the custom of his people, Red Bear went to the no-o-pee of Feather Cloud's father and sat at her feet like a statue. He did not speak, nor she nor any one; for no one at such a time must speak inside the no-o-pee. Feather Cloud was awake; for all day she had wondered if Red Bear would come to her no-o-pee as he now was. After he had sat a long time, she arose and moved to the other side of the tent and lay down again, and Red Bear moved and sat at her feet as before. Then after a time he went away. It would have been wrong to have offered him any hospitality.

The old chief, the father of Feather Cloud, did not like that he should come wooing his daughter; and outside the no-o-pee, in the day-time when he could talk, he said to Red Bear: Red Bear, the beaver seeks a mate in its own village, the wolf in its own band; you are not of my band, and Wounded Elk is to be my son. He has horses and a skin no-o-pee; he has relatives who will give rich presents and who will fight for him. You have nothing and are alone. Then Red Bear said: Skins for a no-o-pee are easily killed, and beaver and mink for her to wear, instead of a robe of rabbit skins. Bears are in the mountains. They will be glad to lend their skins for us to sleep on. Do you not know I kill more than two others, or even three? Horses can be taken from the enemy. But all these things are nothing. What you need is a strong heart which will fight your battles, drive away your enemies, widen your hunting ground, make your name feared. You cannot get this with presents. Wounded Elk is a dandy; he is very lazy. I will drive him away as you drive a dog from the fire. You must not drive him away, you must go away yourself. If I go, I shall come back for Feather Cloud and to be chief, said Red Bear.

That night Red Bear sat at the feet of Feather Cloud in the no-o-pee, as before, and the next day he spoke to her and said: By the law, I cannot speak to you in the no-o-pee, but now I can tell you that you are dearer to me than my own hand. Your father is not pleased that I have nothing. Does he think you would ever go hungry? Does he think you would not be warm in the furs of the otter and sable? You are my eyes and like my very blood. You shall dry my moccasins and keep the fire burning and make soft buckskin and bring children to my tent. And does he think you shall not always have meat and skins? You shall put the sinew on my bow-back and make my war-bonnet. Does he think you shall be given to our enemies? These things your father wants are easy to get. Will you wait for me? Then Feather Cloud put her eyes on the ground and said in a whisper, I will wait.

That night again Red Bear sat at her feet, without speaking as is the law. Then he was gone. More than a moon passed, and Red Bear was not heard of. No one knew whither he had gone. Then came Wounded Elk, who had been far to the north, to the Great River. And he came to the no-o-pee after all had lain down for the night, and sat at the feet of Feather Cloud. But she slept or pretended to sleep, and the old chief, who was watching, waked her up. She did not move from the place, and presently she slept again, or pretended to sleep. Thus it went on until the thin edge of the moon had cut through the sky three times and three times had slid back again behind the sky. And the heart of Feather Cloud was very heavy, for she knew naught of Red Bear and her breast was empty for him. Then her father began to upbraid her, saying: See how patient is Wounded Elk. He needs you for his no-o-pee. He is young and strong. He has many horses. He will be good to you. If you are sick he will take care of you. You are waiting for Red Bear, who has forgotten you. This must stop; you must take Wounded Elk. Then Feather Cloud would look at the ground and say, I do not love Wounded Elk. Tell me what it is that I do not do right for you, that you turn me away from your fire. And her father would say, You shall not marry him if you do not love him; I shall not force you. And so three more moons crept out of the sky and back into it again. Then came Wounded Elk with his father and his relatives; and they brought many fine horses and robes and offered them all for Feather Cloud. Then her father said: Now I will give you to Wounded Elk whether you like it or not. But Feather Cloud sat down in the dust and put dust on her head and cried; and again she asked: What have I done that you like horses better than me; and her father answered: Very well; you need not go to him if you do not love him. But now listen; this is the Feast of the Autumn; you may keep it with the maidens. If Red Bear returns before the Midwinter Festival and wants you, you may go to him. But if he does not return, you shall belong to Wounded Elk. This comforted her a little, and she told every one that went away from the tribe to tell Red Bear to hurry back. But after they traced Red Bear as far north as the Bannacks, or to the Blackfoot country, they lost him. No one knew where he was.

Feather Cloud's heart was too heavy for the Autumn Festival; but she also gathered the nuts and the seeds, pine nuts, hazel nuts, sweet acorns, grass seeds—and the roots, wild anise roots and camas and many others. For five days they gathered; then the women brought all these to the great fires, bearing them on their heads in the close-woven stiff baskets like buckets, the maidens walking behind the older women and all chanting the song of thankfulness to the Earth as they walked. Then around the fires they ground up the seeds in the stone mortars. Also they roasted the nuts and roots in the fire. They cooked all that had been gathered in the five days, and they sang songs and danced and made a great feast to celebrate the Autumn Season and to thank the Earth. They cooked no meat of any kind, because meat they had all the year round.

When the winter had well begun and all the no-o-pees were hidden among the willows in the little valleys, the camp was attacked one morning by the Snakes, enemies from the North. They were beaten off, but a few were killed on each side and many were wounded. Feather Cloud's father got an arrow in his side, but not too deep. He pulled it out and stopped the hole with fresh pitch from the pine and with owl feathers. There was a young Snake taken prisoner, and they were getting ready to torture him, but he commenced laughing and calling the Piutes women and liars. He said they had been coaxed to come on this expedition by Wounded Elk, who wanted his chief killed; then he would be chief and would marry the daughter. While he was telling this tale and jeering at such a people, Wounded Elk rushed forward to where the prisoner was bound, and brained him with a war club. The old men and women were angry that he should have done just what the captive wanted and released him from their torture. Wounded Elk was sorry, and gave dried venison for a feast. But Feather Cloud believed what the captive had said.

The Midwinter Festival is for three days, to celebrate the sun's getting stronger and climbing higher into the sky. For in winter the sun is sick. The night before the first day of the feast, Feather Cloud did not sleep at all, for she had given up all hope of seeing Red Bear, and snow lay on the ground too deep for good traveling. When the day came, all began to gather in the great medicine lodge. The fires were built higher and the drumming of the drums and the whistling of the flutes began. So they kept up the dancing and the chanting all day. When one was tired another would take his place. The young men would dance and tell what they had done. The day and the night ended, and the old chief said to Feather Cloud, Tomorrow you must have Wounded Elk. He called the Snakes to kill you, said she. That is a lie told by a captive to madden him, said her father quietly. Tomorrow you shall marry him. I am old.

Feather Cloud wept all night. Her eyes were like fire. She ran into the woods and hid. That day they did not find her, but the next day they found her and brought her to her father, who said: Why do you do this? Is marriage like death? You can leave him if you do not like him. I shall give you to him. That is all I can do.

So Feather Cloud made herself clean and put on her feather trimmed white tunic, and braided her hair very smooth, and sat very sorrowful in the medicine lodge with her eyes cast down. In the evening the fires were built very high. It was the last hours of the feast. The pipes were sending out blue smoke and the fluters were whistling and the drummers drumming. Wounded Elk stepped into the circle, and slowly twisting and stepping, began to chant. He was telling of his life and what he had done. He told how a wounded elk had nearly killed him, but he had stabbed it. He told how he had brained the captive. These were the most honorable things he had to tell.

When he had finished, a young man with only his loin cloth on and a great war-bonnet of eagle feathers which hid his face, stepped into the circle and began to dance. He was beautiful as a cougar. When he began to recite, then the heart of Feather Cloud gave a jump. I am a Piute, he said, and I have the heart of a man. I do not talk of killing elk. What is that? That is to get food; a boy does that. I have gone across the mountains to where the land runs to meet the sky, and there is the end of the world. I found a party of Crows on the warpath. They were coming here. I crept among them at night like a snake and stabbed seven of them. This is the way they died. I was not afraid, I laughed at them. I followed them again for a week. I made no fire, I ate raw meat and I was cold, but I am not a baby. Then I crept among them again and killed five. It is hard to kill five men in the dark. You must strike just right and hold your hand on their mouths. Again I got away and hid in the rocks. They were now afraid. They considered together and determined to turn back. Each man had two horses for travel and three war-horses. To steal these horses from a war party one must be brave as a grizzly and sly as a coyote. I slipped among them and cut their lariats. I tied them together, and, going back, I stabbed one of our enemies; but my hand slipped a little and he made much noise. Then I jumped on the back of one of the horses and gave our war cry and drove them off. They followed a little, but were afraid. They did not know how many there were. I laughed at them and was not afraid. I had twenty horses, and for three days and nights I only stopped a little. Then I found buffalo in a large valley, and I rode to the head of the herd and killed the best cows as they ran, until I had more meat and robes than I wanted. Then I hid my horses and went among the Blackfeet and traded for some fine blankets, made from the wild goat's hair. Then I loaded my herd with jerked buffalo and robes and blankets and some fine bows and many things and came among the Snakes. No one knew me to be a Piute. No Piute has ever done what I have done. There among the Snakes I heard the messages from Wounded Elk. He asked them to come slay his own blood, to kill his own chief. I say it is true. I say I have stayed behind the rocks three days keeping off the Crows who wanted my blood. I say I have fought hand to hand with Spotted Hawk, a Crow chief, and fell upon him so tired I could hardly kill him; but I have not killed a captive. That is for the women. I say Wounded Elk is a Snake, a liar, a coward; he is worse than the dirt beneath my feet. Then the stranger, who had been dancing and singing faster and louder, stopped in front of Wounded Elk and threw his war-bonnet far from him; and there was Red Bear, his eyes shining like a snake's. Wounded Elk leaped to his feet as if a snake had bitten him and looked for a way to escape. Then quickly he grabbed a hatchet pipe from an old man squatting near, but before he could use it Red Bear had grasped him by the waist and hurled him clear over into the fire, leaping upon him instantly like a wild cat and fastening his fingers on his throat. No one interfered, and presently the body of Wounded Elk was carried out.

Then Red Bear went to where Feather Cloud sat with her head hanging down, and said, I have horses and robes and a skin no-o-pee, more than another could give, though he had many relatives, and from your relatives I ask nothing. Then spoke the old chief and said I will give you my war-bow and you shall be my son. A bowl was put in the hands of Feather Cloud, filled with roasted acorns. She offered this, standing, to Red Bear; but instead of taking it from her he took her by the wrist and drew her to him. Then he took the bowl from her and handed her some of the acorns to eat, then he ate some and thus they were married. He became the great war chief of the Piutes and drove back their enemies till again they wandered over what is now California, Nevada, and part of Oregon. Feather Cloud was happy, for she had waited for him a long time, and a marriage feast was made and the old people gave much advice to them how they should live and at the end they went to live in their own no-o-pee.

IN THE SUMMER OF 1875, in Warner Valley in southeastern Oregon, Lt. Wood met Debe, a young Klamath Indian on his way home to kill a medicine man and recover five ponies that had been given the medicine man under promise that he would cure Debe's brother of measles; the brother had died. Erskine, exercising his not inconsiderable powers of persuasion, talked Debe into delaying long enough to kill antelope and swan to his brother's ghost and for the Klamath to spin a tale or two.

How the Coyote Stole Fire for the Klamaths

Toward evening, when the sky was red on the edge of the mountains and while we were roasting antelope ribs on the coals, Debe told me this tale.

In the beginning the Klamaths had no fire. The only fire in the world was guarded by two very bad-hearted old devil-women, not the same as those who barred out the salmon; two different ones. They lived in their great lodges, which are now the white-topped twin mountain. The fire was inside the mountain. Again the Coyote came to the Man and said: Why do you not get some fire for yourself and your children? The Man said, I cannot; the devil-women have it. Then the Coyote said: I will get it for you, because you were good to me; wait, I shall be back. The Coyote went to all the animals and told them they must do as he said, and help steal fire from the witches. Then he put them in a long line, from the Fire Mountain to the home of the Klamaths, each one about as far from the next as he could make a good run. The swiftest and strongest he placed nearest the devil-women's lodges. The eagle was first, just a little way off; then, a long way down the mountain, was the cougar; then the bear; then the elk and deer; then, across the open prairie, the antelope, the swiftest animal; then the rabbit, with his long bushy white tail; and all the animals down to the squirrel, and last of all the frog. The frog was not then so small as he is now: he was a large animal and could give great leaps; but he was the slowest. He was put at the edge of the river, where the Klamaths lived. The Coyote, when he had got all the animals ready, came for the Man, and together they went to the fire lodges of the old women. When they were there, the Coyote made the Man wound him a little bit in the skin of one leg, not much; and the Man cut himself, too, and smeared plenty of blood over the Coyote. Then the Coyote went limping on three legs to the lodge, and crept in, whining and crying. What is the matter, Italapas? said the devil-women, cracking their great teeth together as cranes clash their bills, only louder. The Man has tried to kill me, said the Coyote, and showed his wounds; but I have bitten him so he will die. Smell; some of this blood is his. Then the old women sniffed the blood and gnashed their teeth more than ever, and laughed so the mountain shook, and down in the mountain you could hear the rumble of their laughter. Lie down by the sacred fire, said they to the Coyote. He lay down and commenced to lick his leg. After a time he pretended to fall asleep, and stretched himself out before the fire and snored. Presently the devil-women dropped their chins on their breasts and dozed. Then, like the dart of a salmon, the Coyote seized a brand and fled. The hags followed after him, screaming and gnashing their teeth. They were nearly on him, when he handed the brand to the eagle. Away flew the great bird, his wings hitting the air like a tempest in the pines. But the old women followed fast and never grew tired. The eagle was glad to give the fire to the cougar; so it went down the line, the devil-women just missing it each time, and shrieking with anger as they pursued each new fire-bearer. They were so close to the rabbit that, just as he gave it to the bat, one old woman seized his tail and pulled it off: that is why rabbits are stump-tailed. The bat took the fire; he could not fly very fast, but always, just as the old women thought they had him, he would dodge. They could not touch him, for he dodged this way and that, and brought the fire safe to the squirrel. When the fire got to the squirrel, it was much smaller than it had been, but it had been fanned into a blaze, and in carrying it he scorched his back; so that his tail was drawn clear over his back, and the brown is on his fur to this day. At last it came to the frog; but he, knowing he could not outrun the old women, swallowed the fire and jumped into the river. Then, with yells of rage, the devil-women gave up the chase and went back to their lodges. Their fire went out, and there they stand today, cold and white. When they had gone, the frog came up and spit the fire out into a log; which is why it can be got by twirling one stick of wood very fast on another. The fire had burned the frog inside so badly that he shrank to the little fellow he is now, and his eyes nearly popped out of his head with pain.

How the Spirit Coyote Passed from Earth

The weight of brotherly duty pressed so upon Debe that he would delay no longer; but the night before he left to kill the medicine man and get back the five ponies, the crystal sky sparkling above us, he told me this tale.

In those days the Coyote was a spirit Coyote; he was a friend of the Man: they were cousins and talked together. The Coyote loved the night: all night long he would sit and watch the stars. There was one large star, more beautiful than the moon or the sun. He was in love with the star, and would talk to her, night after night, and all night long. But the star would not answer him: she walked across the sky, looking at him, but saying nothing. The Coyote grew more and more crazy for the star. He noticed that always, as she walked through the sky, she passed very close to a certain mountain peak, so close it would be easy to touch her. The Coyote traveled as fast as he could, a long, long way; till, very tired, he stood on this mountain, at the place the star always touched. He would not sleep for fear of missing her, so he sat and waited. In the evening he saw her coming: she was very beautiful. He could see now that she and the other stars were dancing; they moved through the sky dancing. The Coyote waited; his heart was nearly bursting through his skin, but he kept very quiet. The star danced nearer and nearer; at last she was on the mountain. He reached up as high as he could, but he could not quite touch her; then he begged her to reach her hand down to him. She did so, and took his paws into her hand. Slowly she danced with him, up from the mountain; far up into the sky, over the earth. The Coyote got very dizzy; his heart was afraid. They went higher into the sky, among all the stars. It was bitter cold and silent. None of the stars spoke. The Coyote looked down, and fear made his heart very cold. He begged the star to take him back to the earth. When they were at the very top of the sky, the star let go of the Coyote. He was one whole moon falling; and when he struck the earth, he knocked a great hole in it. His blood turned to water and made a lake. This is Crater Lake, in Klamath County. When the Coyotes talk to the stars at night, they are scolding the star that killed their father.

Seconò Stage
(1899~1911)

The period of the second stage in C. E. S. Wood's literary development also saw both the emergence of the United States as a world power and the rise of the Progressive movement on the local, state, and national level, led by the likes of Robert LaFollette of Wisconsin, Theodore Roosevelt of New York, Hiram Johnson of California, and William S. U'Ren of Oregon. Erskine was more progressive than most of his contemporaries but he was too much an individual to be confined to a party or a label. William Deverell, a historian of the American West, links Wood with a loose community of radical intellectuals in the West who distrusted and challenged the prevailing power structure; people like Lincoln Steffens, Portland physician Marie Equi, or newspaperman Fremont Older. Deverell calls them, and others like them, a "radical elite."

Despite his radical opinions, Wood was a pillar of Portland society during these early years of the twentieth century. His law practice was thriving, and he and his gracious wife were prominent members of Portland's upper crust. He was a director of the Portland Public Library Association, a charter member of the exclusive Arlington Club, a trustee of the Portland Art Museum, and an effective broker for the work of his eastern artist friends, J. Alden Weir, Olin Warner, Albert Pinkham Ryder, and Childe Hassam.

Because of his growing interest in writing and the literary life, Erskine managed to find time for a writing apprenticeship that took a number of forms. In 1904, he wrote a dramatic piece, *A Masque of Love*, that examines love in several guises. He also wrote a good deal of occasional verse. Wood's tradition of writing Christmas pieces began in 1906, and in 1918 he published privately a collection of over seventy occasional pieces that he called "*Sonnets*."

Meanwhile, a mounting radicalism was the spur to much of Erskine's creative work and he was publishing in two of the most

C.E.S. Wood's Oregon State Bar photograph, 1903

liberal periodicals in the country. Between 1900 and 1908, he wrote poetry and articles, both sharply critical of imperialism on the part of Britain and the United States, for Louis Post's *Public* (which later moved from Chicago to New York to become the *New Republic*). In the more radical *Liberty,* edited by Benjamin Tucker, an avowed anarchist, Erskine wrote "The Law, Marriage, and Freedom," along with several short stories, some of them exotic fanciful tales, others dealing with poverty and economic injustice, but in all of them the theme was the tyranny of authority. However, the bulk of Wood's writing was reserved for *Pacific Monthly,* Portland's premier literary and cultural magazine in the Progressive era. During its thirteen years of publication, Wood was by far the heaviest contributor, using the magazine as a vehicle for honing his writing skills, participating in the literary life, and pulling away from the practice of the law.

INTRODUCTION TO *Pacific Monthly*

WILLIAM BITTLE WELLS LAUNCHED *Pacific Monthly* in Portland in the fall of 1898, hoping that it would become the far western counterpart of New England's prestigious *Atlantic Monthly*, although he did not neglect the business and promotional dimensions that characterized other literary and cultural magazines such as *Overland Monthly* in San Francisco and *Out West* in Los Angeles. Meanwhile, Lischen Miller—whose husband, George Melvin Miller, was the brother of Joaquin Miller, Oregon and California pioneer poet—with the advice and support of C. E. S. Wood, founded *Drift*, a magazine designed to encourage literary talent in the Pacific Northwest. After only two numbers, *Drift* merged with *Pacific Monthly*, Lischen Miller serving as assistant editor and bringing with her Wood's continuing interest in the enterprise.

Under Wells's direction, *Pacific Monthly* grew in size and circulation so that, by summer of 1904, it was averaging 30,000 copies a month. Still, the magazine needed capital if it was to remain afloat. Wood persuaded his banker friend Charles Ladd to provide financial support. As Ladd increased his investment, ultimately to the tune of about $300,000, he took over the monthly's management to the extent that, feeling undermined and betrayed, Wells sold his interest in the magazine to Ladd and, at the end of 1906, his name was dropped from the masthead.

C. E. S. Wood's early offerings to *Pacific Monthly*, beginning in 1899, were for the most part provocative social and political comment with a dash of art criticism. Late in 1903, Wood agreed to write for *Pacific Monthly* for a year, and the January number of the magazine for the first time carried "Impressions," several pages of Wood's opinions, a column that became a regular feature. Here Erskine held forth on a broad spectrum of topics: imperialism, single tax, birth control, socialism, anarchism, divorce, art, books, and Progressive legislation such as the initiative and referendum, direct primary, and direct election of senators. He was vehemently against war, censorship of any kind, prohibition, land monopoly, and big business. He defended Emma Goldman and Margaret Sanger. He derided John D. Rockefeller and Andrew Carnegie. He was pro-labor and he believed women should have the vote. He hated and distrusted constituted authority and for a dozen unbridled years, through "Impressions," he served as Portland's stormy petrel, striving to ruffle that city's placidity. It is to editor Wells's credit that, although his own views were conservative and conventional, he let the Colonel go his own way.

Wood, however, did not go unscathed. An irate Portlander wrote the Pacific Monthly Publishing Company in 1908:

> *When I inadvertently subscribed for your beautifully gotten up magazine, I was not aware that your paper was a full-fledged organ of socialism, anarchy, and destruction. You modestly brand the American people as ignoramuses and their government as a farce. . . . I cannot as a patriotic American citizen, lend even the slightest moral support towards a magazine containing such unpatriotic and ignominious ideas; a magazine which defends such despicable parasites as Emma Goldman.*
>
> *Do not send any more copies, as I do not care to have the paper in my home.*

By this time, Lute Pease was editor of *Pacific Monthly*, having been appointed by Charles Ladd in 1908. Pease, a former *Oregonian* reporter and cartoonist and a veteran of the Klondike stampede, was not one to suffer fools gladly. In reply, after expressing regret at losing a subscriber, Pease signed off with: "Here's to you across acres of exploding bombs, and the ruins of property, law, and morality."

More serious was the opposition of B. S. Josselyn, vice-president of Pacific Monthly Company and president of Portland Railway, Light & Power. He had no use for Wood's socialist-anarchist views and believed they curtailed the magazine's circulation, discouraged advertisers, and alienated the business community. He wished to substitute a series of articles on Christian Science. Pease, who admired Colonel Wood and found in him a kindred spirit, did not agree. He pointed out that "Impressions" was not an expression of the monthly's policy and moreover was readable, stimulated discussion—unfavorable as well as favorable, with the latter predominant—and saved the magazine from "the charge of being innocuous, colorless, or uninteresting."

Aware that *Pacific Monthly*'s mission was in part promotional, Wood waxed lyrical over western Oregon's weather: "I have no apologies for our rain. It is liquid silver and it silvers the whole landscape. Through it the hills fade to delicate shadows, earth and sky are one, and all silver. Come up in the Wintertime and see us you crepe-skinned mummies from the lower regions, and get an Oregon complexion."

In addition to his controversial "Impressions," Erskine contributed poetry, short stories, essays, and book reviews to *Pacific Monthly.* After 1908, the monthly received a steady stream from Wood's pen, often under assumed names. Wood resorted to noms de plume in part to permit his work to be judged on its own merit and in part to disguise the heavy reliance of the magazine on a single writer during the last four years of publication. For example, Erskine submitted a short story in 1908 through a "little gnome of a man," whom Pease suspected was not capable of writing the story. The manuscript bore the exotic signature Felix Benguiat. Pease soon penetrated the deception and drew on Wood for thirteen other stories, all of them published under pseudonyms such as Francis du Bosque and Orrin Seaman. He signed his western ballads as William Maxwell (his father's given names), his political satires as Jared Mallet, and, for some reason, he signed one poem as Gustave Korter.

From 1904 to 1911, the years of Wood's closest connection with *Pacific Monthly,* he appeared in its pages 136 times. C. E. S. Wood was more versatile and more ubiquitous than any other contributor. Except for Jack London's *Martin Eden,* serialized in *Pacific Monthly* between 1908 and 1909—the magazine's greatest publishing coup—Erskine's work was on a par with that of other contributors such as John Reed, Ella Higginson, George Sterling, David Starr Jordan, Joaquin Miller, Mary Austin, John Muir, and William Rose Benét.

As for *Pacific Monthly* itself, the combination of Lute Pease as editor and Fred Lockley as business manager during the last four years of its life brought it to the peak of its performance with a circulation approaching 100,000. But Ladd's withdrawal of support, along with the unprecedented payment of $7,000 to Jack London for *Martin Eden,* saddled the monthly with a deficit. Early in 1912, *Pacific Monthly* sold out to *Sunset* magazine for $20,000, although to this day the name *Pacific Monthly* appears on *Sunset*'s masthead.

Introduction to "Anarchy and Anarchists"

EARLY IN THE TWENTIETH CENTURY Colonel Wood was known in Portland as "the philosophical anarchist," a designation he readily acknowledged. On many occasions—in conversation, from the public platform, in correspondence, and in print—he sought to make his particular brand of anarchism clear. His *Pacific Monthly* column was a natural and convenient venue for this purpose. Often, as in the selection from "Impressions" of February 1904, reprinted here, he tied his theme to a current incident. This column was based on the story of English labor leader and anarchist, John Turner, who was first detained at Ellis Island, pending deportation under an alien law enacted shortly after the assassination of President William McKinley, and then arrested while addressing a trades union meeting in New York City. As it turned out, according to the *New York Times,* Turner was not deported and he left for England under his own steam while predicting class warfare and the ultimate triumph of United States workers in the industrial struggle.

In all instances, Erskine argued that his anarchism was nonviolent, insisting that the fundamental doctrine of anarchism holds that in all matters there shall be the greatest amount of individual liberty compatible with equality of liberty. In 1912, a writer in *Sunset* put a favorable, even a conservative, spin on Wood's anarchism when he wrote that Wood "would like to see larger experiments in freedom, because freedom gives the widest scope to self-interest, and self-interest is the primal governing force."

Perhaps one of the many aphorisms scattered through "Impressions" will serve to give Wood a last word on this topic: "There are many shades of opinion among anarchists, for it is a school of free thought."

ANARCHY AND ANARCHISTS

Secretary Cortelyou is attempting that for which Charles I. and Louis XVI. lost their heads.

John Turner, while peaceably addressing (on the subject of Trade Unions) a peaceable meeting at New York, was tapped upon the shoulder by United States deputy marshals, led from the stage, and, without trial or hearing, was imprisoned without bail until he could be forcibly deported from this country. As "Liberty" very truthfully remarks, this could not be done even in Germany. The warrant for this un-American act is found in a law passed by an hysterical congress after President McKinley's assassination. The evil aimed at by the law is murder. The law should be interpreted as meaning one who advocates the use of force against those in authority. Indeed, the law so reads. The real meaning of the word "anarchist" is one who believes that the ideal form of society is that in which self-interest, guided by intelligence, is the basis of action rather than a law made by a few, or a majority, and enforced upon all. For example, the anarchist would disbelieve in an enforced tax in order that the children of some might have collegiate educations in high schools and state universities. Jefferson, in his ideals, was an anarchist. He said that government was best which governed least and Thoreau carried this to its logical conclusion by saying the ideal government was one which did not govern by force at all, and he wrote his essay on the duty of civil disobedience, showing that there are laws which, as a duty, we should resist and disobey. Herbert Spencer was an anarchist or individualist. Tolstoi, preaching peace and liberty, could not come here under this law, but emissaries of the Czar could freely advocate among us an autocratic despotism.

One who advocates a change in or abolishment of the present form of government, is by an ignorant assumption thought to be an enemy to peace and order. In the same way those who formerly thought there might be a better form of government than the absolute despotism of kings were thought to be not only enemies to peaceable society, but to God himself.

Mr. Edward M. Shepherd said in his letter written to the Turner mass-meeting in New York, "Is it credible that in our day and in our land, there should be found men in places of great power, who do not see that nothing is so conservative, nothing so safe, as an absolute liberty to think and to speak and to write, so long as there is no urgency or invitation to vice or to violence?"

Just as kings used to lop off the heads which spoke against kingship, so this foolish and useless law seeks to put our particular form of government beyond all criticism or discussion.

Our constitution says treason shall consist in acts of levying war against the United States. But this fool law makes it a crime for any one to talk against organized government, meaning, of course, as *now* organized, for no man advocates chaos. Nor will society ever submit to chaos. But there may be order and organization without a majority ruling a peaceable minority by force. Whether we believe in the anarchistic ideal or not, the doctrine of free speech, for which so much blood has been shed, means that any man shall have a right to voice any peaceable doctrine. Riot and bloodshed may yet come to this country in an effort to adjust the economic laws which still separate the monopoly favored few from the poor many; but the man who advocates peaceably a peaceable doctrine is responsible to no greater and no less degree than Voltaire and Rousseau are responsible for the blood of the French Revolution; Milton and Hampden responsible for the bloody overthrow of the Stuarts; and Adams and Franklin responsible for the blood of the Revolution.

If this law meant by anarchists those who advocate the murder of rulers, it did not mean John Turner, for like all true anarchists, force is absolutely absent from his arsenal. Like every real anarchist, he must sternly reprobate the use of force against others, in order to be consistent in his creed that force must not be used against him. Label a man anarchist, and under this law, though his whole life is peace, and his whole doctrine is peace, and his every act has been and is peace, he may be hurried to an Atlantic Liner—a new sort of Bastille.

Mr. Turner was, in fact, discussing trades unions. Some people do not believe in trades unions; some people do not believe in Christian Science; and some do not believe in Christianity; but if there is any topic under heaven which can not be freely and peacefully discussed because some set of men who happen to be in power do not believe in it then free speech is at an end and progress has stepped backward.

Again quoting from Mr. Shepherd, "Has not America, has not civilization come to everything now dear to them, to everything on which their civilization and happiness depend, through the triumph of beliefs which were once odious and once treated as criminal and for which men were deported and even burnt and crucified?"

Among the presidents of the Turner mass-meeting were Felix Adler, Carl Schurz, Charles Sprague Smith, Ernest Crosby, John De Witt Warner, and a great number of other earnest men who realize, though the masses do not, that eternal vigilance is the price of liberty. During this meeting Turner remained in his prison at Ellis Island, where he now is. He is chief organizer of the Retail Clerks Union of Great Britain, and a member of the London Trades Council. He has delivered these same speeches all over England and says: "I came here to discuss economic questions and social problems, and I was very much surprised when the Immigration officers stepped up to me while I was speaking at the Murray Hill Lyceum. They searched me and then brought me here." The *Evening Post* says, "The first attempt at enforcing the anti-anarchist act passed after the assassination of President McKinley is not only ridiculous but alarming to all who hold to American ideals of personal liberty. Last night Secretary Cortelyou's United States marshals broke into a meeting and arrested John Turner as an avowed anarchist."

To show how little the world changes and how men clothed with a brief authority quickly assume the role of tyrant, I quote from what Commissioner Williams said: "We'll ship him back to England on the first British steamer that leaves this port; if the *Teutonic* sails first, Mr. Turner will be deported on the *Teutonic*; we have been laying for him to appear here for the past three months." So these precious Bastille commissioners of Secretary Cortelyou were "laying" for a peaceable trade unionist for three months. It would seem, therefore, that this anarchist is obnoxious not because of any anarchistic theory, because he never uttered any, but because he is an advocate of organized labor, and we may take it that his deportation is at the secret behest of those who are opposed to organized labor. If organized labor is not dull witted, it will take alarm at this attack on free speech and free institutions; it will insist that so called "representatives" in congress must really represent the people; and it will turn to philosophical anarchy itself as a relief from oppression by government by so-called majority.

Tyranny depends upon power, not upon the form of government; it exists in a republic where the power is secured by a majority, as well as in a kingdom, where it is "God-given." A meeting which was to be held in Paterson, New Jersey, and which was to be addressed by Bolton Hall, a son of the distinguished Presbyterian clergyman, the late Rev. John Hall, and himself an eminent lawyer, was, by order of the mayor and interference of the police, not permitted to proceed. Mr. Hall stated to the authorities that the meeting had no connection with the Turner arrest except to protest against it as an invasion of the right of free speech, but the mayor and the police would not even permit the meeting to be held. Mr. Hall and others assured the authorities that they would warrant the entire peaceableness of the meeting and the true American character of its doctrine, and he pointed out the constitutional right of the people to peaceably assemble and discuss their grievances. The mayor snapped his fingers at the constitution and replied, "If you people had your way, *we* would not be running things," and the meeting was not held. In the days of our colonial forefathers, the meeting would have been held, or there would have been blood shed.

The fact is, as those in authority grow more strenuous and militant, and expend the people's millions on battleships and world powerfulness, the people themselves grow more and more timid and less capable of self-help. The coming generations of this country seem likely to have little knowledge of what true liberty is and what their inalienable rights are. Every one ought to know that the constitution guarantees the right of the people to peaceably assemble and discuss their grievances; that this right was secured not only by the blood of the Revolution, but by oceans of blood before it; that every assemblage of citizens is just as capable of interpreting that clause of the constitution as is the Supreme Court of the United States; and that every assemblage of citizens has the same authority to enforce this constitutional right as would any body of police or soldiery. It is one of the fundamentals which comes back to the people themselves for interpretation and enforcement, and I, for one, shall not hesitate to maintain here and elsewhere that I am sorry that the mayor and police of the City of Paterson were not led out into their own square and shot, if such an extreme step were necessary on the part of the citizens to preserve their inestimable, constitutional, and elemental right. Every state in the Union has a law under which any speaker who incites to murder and riot may be arrested and punished, so that this law is absolutely unnecessary to protect any portion of the community against any incendiary utterances, but it does give the federal authorities and the central government one more excuse to invade the liberties of the people.

The *New York Daily News* says of this precious law:

The law under which the immigration officials are holding John Turner a prisoner without bail . . . is as stupid a piece of legislation as congress has achieved for several years. Its unconstitutionality is obvious. The Supreme Court may, perhaps, say otherwise, but any law abridging freedom of thought and speech is in violation of the spirit of the constitution and no amount of legal sophistry can make it other than what it is. This fool law essays to pry into the mind of a foreigner arriving at a port of the United States and to judge him by what he believes or disbelieves. . . . It could be invoked to keep Herbert Spencer from setting foot on American soil.

But the Supreme Court of the United States will, in my opinion, declare this law unconstitutional on some of the following grounds: *First*—That there is a spirit in our constitution beyond the mere words, and that spirit is indicated by the past history of England as well as America, from which our constitution was evolved. That the clauses of the constitution which secure to the people free speech, a free press, the right to peaceably assemble and discuss grievances, the right to bear arms, and which make treason to consist of some overt act, all indicate that the government itself, both in its acts and in its form, is not sacred from discussion, and that the citizens themselves have an inherent right to invite any man, from any part of the world, to join or aid them in their discussion.

Second—That the whole history of this country from the time of the colonies has been that of an asylum for those persecuted for opinion's sake, and that no immigrant has ever been barred from this land because of his political theories: on the contrary, many driven from their own country by the despotisms of Europe have been welcomed here. That the power given to congress to regulate immigration is a delegated power and must be strictly construed, and judging by the intent of the document, and by our history, the discretion of congress is limited to matters of race, economics, and health, and it can not under the guise of regulating immigration, bar any man from these shores because of his religious or political opinion.

Third—That the statute is a restrictive and a penal statute and should be strictly construed, and must be interpreted by the evil sought to be remedied and it does not apply to peaceable men discussing theories of government or of a voluntary social association.

Fourth—That its attempted application is an invasion of the right of the states to a republican form of government and to local self-government, especially in criminal or quasi-criminal matters.

The material portions of this useless and senseless law, which ought to brand every man who voted for it as unfit to represent a free people, are appended in a footnote.*

They talk of deporting anarchists. If they mean philosophical and peaceable anarchists, Warren, a descendant of Warren of Bunker Hill, was the great American anarchist. If they mean by anarchist those diseased and unsettled minds, which brood upon the tyrannies of government until a death stroke at the visible head of government is the consummation of their brooding, we ourselves have bred the only assassins who have struck at our presidents. Have we got to learn all over again what the world is supposed to have learned hundreds of years ago, that the greatest safety lies in liberty and the greatest danger in tyrannous repression? You can not imprison ideas. You can not kill them. There is one thing certain, that the progress of humanity has been toward liberty, and there is another thing certain, that humanity will still continue to progress toward liberty, and those who would gain for the world more liberty are true prophets, and those who would take away anything of the liberty which has been so dearly gained are walking backward into a pit.

---

*Sec. 2. That the following classes of aliens shall be excluded from admission to the United States: Anarchists or persons who believe in or advocate the overthrow by force or violence of the Government of the United States or of all government or of all forms of law or the assassination of public officials.

Sec. 38. That no person who disbelieves in or who is opposed to all organized government or who is a member of or affiliated with any organization entertaining and teaching such disbelief in or is in opposition to all organized government or who advocates or teaches the duty, necessity, or propriety of the unlawful assaulting or killing of any officer or officers either of specific individuals or of officers generally of the government of the United States or of any other organized government because of his or their official character, shall be permitted to enter the United States or any territory or place subject to the jurisdiction thereof. This section shall be enforced by the Secretary of the Treasury under such rules and regulations as he shall prescribe.That any person who knowingly aids or assists any such person to enter the United States or any territory or place subject to the jurisdiction thereof or who connives or conspires with any person or persons to allow, procure, or permit any such person to enter therein, except pursuant to such rules and reguations made by the Secretary of the Treasury, shall be fined not more than $5,000 or imprisoned for not less than one nor more than five years, or both. (Enacted March 3, 1903.)

WOOD'S VIEWS ON DIVORCE are consistent with his broad philosophy of human freedom and are ahead of his times. He frankly acknowledges the important role of sex in marriage and he deplores laws that make adultery the sole justification for divorce; thus, in his words, "guilt receives from the law the freedom denied to innocence."

By the time of these "Impressions" in August and October 1904, Erskine and Nanny are no longer conjugal lovers and Erskine has taken a mistress.

DIVORCE

I t is appropriate to the blossom and nesting time of the year that thoughts of love and mating should stir the breast, and, if love and mating, why not divorce? They are the blossoms. It is the fruit.

Anti-Divorce Congresses are bursting into bloom all over the land— the Mothers' Anti-Divorce Congress in Chicago; the Anti-Divorce League in New York; and the anti-divorce sentiment in the Methodist convention at Los Angeles.

Now, as you can not stop the slow glacial flow by hitting it with an axe, nor hasten it by giving it a kick, so the divorce question will evolve its own solution regardless of the "antis" or of me.

To have no divorces presupposes infallibility of judgment in every boy and girl, man or woman. It presupposes the same likes, dislikes and affinities, character and development at forty as at twenty.

Are human beings infallible in judgment? No! Hence divorce. Is the man or woman of forty the same as at twenty? No! Hence divorce.

Is the love of twenty the same as the love of forty? No! Hence divorce.

There are but few regular divorces among our brothers and sisters of the lower animals, because their marriage is merely mating for perpetuation of species. When you come to think of it in cold blood, human marriage has that for its foundation stone, too.

It has other elements, also, but I suppose no marriage ever took place which was not really a sexual mating. Men do not marry men and women do not marry women. It is a great universal law, and not to be blushed at or stammered over except by those minds who find themselves "purer" than the universal God.

The birds and beasts find their escape from the divorce courts in the fact that they were never legally married. But the boy or girl of seventeen and nineteen or eighteen or twenty, impelled by this same all-compelling goad, who mate with as little discretion as the robins—they are to be kept together in hell, in bands of legal steel, because it seems to some one that God has belied himself and decreed to be lifelong what He has made in most cases impossible of being lifelong.

It is significant that God, as generally understood, is man-created, in that His edicts are always those of the hierarchy in power, and as the hierarchy itself develops so God's edicts change.

Moses decreed free divorce. He said, "Write any one of your wives a bill of divorcement and let her go." If Moses were the mouthpiece of God, this was the law of Omniscience; but Christ said it was only because of the hardness of heart of those old polygamists, and as God could not change their hearts, he did the best he could.

Christ said there must be no divorce except for adultery. Again, if this be the word of God that is the end of the discussion, and yet divorce is growing and ought to grow until people's own sense of happiness or duty is the sole controlling force.

Many a drunkard, gambler or tyrant of uncontrolled temper makes home more a hell and marriage more a failure than the adulterer. If divorce at all then the logic of it is divorce in every case where the true foundations for marriage have failed. There is a deal of solemn talk by parrots about the home and children. No home and no child is bettered by forcing people together who would be apart. Instead of decreasing, divorce will increase, for it means greater freedom. The only law which ought to keep people together is their wish to be together or their own free sense of duty and fitness.

DIVORCE AGAIN

So many communications have been received by this magazine and myself, concerning the article on divorce in the August number, that some further discussion has been requested by the editors. All of the comments were in a kindly tone, but most of them disagreed with me, and some expressed regret that I was an advocate of such views.

I have felt for a long time that it matters little what comes to any man of praise or blame. Any one man's career is soon over, and the only questions the future will ask are, "Was he honest?" "Did he aid the truth?" Only time can tell whether a man has aided the truth; but as discussion is fatal to error and favorable to truth, I believe any agitation— -even hostile agitation—of a question of morals is better than stagnation. All men should unite in saying, "Let the truth prevail."

In the first place, I have to suggest here, as I have had occasion to do in other discussions, that, merely because a man advocates freedom, he is not to be understood as desiring to abolish, even if he could, all decency, all loyalty, all unselfishness. The men who opposed human slavery in this country, by the same curious perversion of ideas, were supposed to be opposed to all law and order and rights of civilized society. The word "freedom" to the slaveholders of the South meant "License," "Anarchy" and such other false-logic, bugaboo words.

Now, in every state of society—and whether divorce be free or not— fidelity, loyalty, steadfastness, tenderness, unselfishness, have been and will be more valued than fickleness, disloyalty and selfishness. No one can, even if he would, ever make the worthy unworthy, or the base of higher value than the noble.

The question is, Shall men and women regulate their own marriage relations by their own sense of right, decency, loyalty and fitness, or shall the law undertake to judge for them and keep together those who would be asunder? If the law must keep cat and dog chained together for the good of the state, then Plato's "Republic" offers the only logical plan—which is that the law must determine beforehand who may marry, and see to it that cat and dog are not chained together. It is recognized that the marrying is solely the affair of the mating couple—even the breaking of the engagement is solely the affair of one party (except the action for damages for the breach of contract). But as soon as the couple is wed, then, whether they have children or not, or whether they possess

115

property or not, the state says they must stay together, even though both be tugging at their chains.

It is not enough that they wish to separate. One must commit adultery, or be a drunkard, or commit some other brutality. When one does this, then the other, in spite of children, in spite of property rights, may have a divorce, and all this nonsense about public policy requiring people to live together who wish to be apart falls to the ground.

The fact is, this vacant theory which is chattered by parrots about the state having a vital interest in the home and family is borrowed from the canon law. The church, of course, did have an interest in keeping up the home, because marriage was a sacrament of the church, and must not be trifled with, and, of course, the state—that is, human society—has an interest in its units or families being decent and prosperous. But I ask sound argument and sound logic and sound morals to prove to me that the state or any one else has any interest in perpetuating a family hell upon earth or in keeping together a couple either one of which intensely abhors the union. The result of the forced union is neglect of children, demoralization of the home atmosphere, and often adultery.

The state has no greater interest in a family than the family itself, and has no greater interest in children than have the parents; and when the useless interference of the law is removed, society will find that the real bond is either love or that sense of duty and high morals which is the only true law, or lastly, a fear of the opinion of society. Instead of morals being worse with free divorce, they will be better, and conduct now excused or extenuated will no longer be tolerated.

The logical conclusion is that what begins with the parties alone, and the foundation of which is the will of the parties, should end with the parties alone, and when that foundation has fallen.

The needless injury done by the law may be illustrated by a very common case. When the man or woman has been guilty of such an offense that the law permits a divorce, and the couple themselves recognize that there must be a divorce, and are willing for the sake of their children to separate quietly, they can not do so, but the law actually compels them to come into court and blazon abroad the mistakes and unhappiness which belong peculiarly and privately to themselves. The brutality of the law is illustrated by another case, not uncommon. When one of the married pair goes to the other and frankly and honestly admits that time and circumstance have produced a change, that he or she loves another, the law does not permit them to separate quietly; it does not permit them to separate at all; but if the one who has changed commits adultery, then guilt receives from the law the freedom denied to innocence. Such a chain upon human freedom can only be productive of deception and immorality.

There was in some of the communications a certain shocked sense that marriage should be called mating, sexual mating. Undoubtedly marriage is of two elements: sexual affinity, or love, and congeniality, or friendship. With youth, the mere blind instinct called love is apt to sway, and hence so many matrimonial mistakes. Unless calm friendship, esteem, fellowship exists, the marriage can not be life-long happiness. But to deny the great part which sex plays in marriage is to be blind to nature. We may refine it as much as we please, and the falsely modest may ignore it as much as they please, yet sex, and sexual love, will continue to make marriages until the end, as it has made mating from the beginning.

I do not mean that the mere sexual mating is before the eyes of young couples, but I mean the force is there, just as the force of gravity controls us, though we are unconscious of it.

In conclusion, as marriage is a mating, freely made by the parties alone, founded upon a desire to live together, neither society, state, children, nor anybody else is benefited by compelling people to live together who have ceased to desire it. If one repels a marriage association so earnestly that his or her moral nature and sense of right fail to make the union tolerable, it is better he or she should be bid to depart in peace. When one hates, where both should love, it is better to let them adjust their mistake as freely as they were permitted to make it. When this day arrives—as it will—then the woman (usually the injured party) or her relatives will, before the marriage, be sure that she is not to be the toy of the year, and by contract will secure her and her children's property rights. In short, freedom and self-help will hereafter, as always, make for truer happiness and truer justice.

With the utmost respect for those who believe marriage to be God-ordained, and all its phases fixed by divine decree, I recognize that with these no discussion of this question is possible; for, as the Godhead is omniscient, there can be no question of its edicts. But the history of religions—Christian, Buddhist, and Mohammedan—and the practical departure today of the law from religion in this respect, show that the divine edicts will not be accepted by society as unchangeable. Therefore a general discussion is, I think, pertinent and useful.

DURING THE REGION'S FRONTIER ERA of journalism in the third quarter of the nineteenth century, Oregon newspaper editors indulged in a particularly vituperative brand of journalism that became known as the "Oregon Style." The practice lingered as Colonel E. Hofer, editor of the *Salem Journal* demonstrates in this attack on C. E. S. Wood early in 1905. Erskine had no trouble defending himself as the following excerpt from "Impressions" suggests. Ironically, twenty years later in *Overland Monthly*, Colonel Hofer praises Wood extravagantly, opining that he would make a most appropriate national poet.

ARGUMENT

"More Fame for C. E. S. Wood."—Salem Journal

"That undeveloped jumble of intellectual confusions labeled C. E. S. Wood of Portland, has been lecturing to the Woman's Club of that city. What have the women of that town been doing to deserve such punishment? Besides, he discussed national banks and the tariff. That is the limit, and we look for arrivals at one of the state institutions."

The above was taken from the editorial page of the *Oregonian* (reproduced from the *Salem Journal*). The fact that it refers to me is wholly immaterial. I reprint it to show the intolerance which those armed with a printing press show to difference of opinion. This courteous and dignified utterance does not attempt either a statement of views or a discussion, and is only worthy of notice as illustrating the essential blackguardism which exists in this particular case, and the cowardly bullying which often characterizes those who feel secure in spilling ink upon the passerby. I understand it was written by one Colonel Hofer, editor of the *Salem Journal*. He evidently believes that the pen is mightier than the sword, and a great deal safer. I do not intend to intimate that there are in the journalistic profession many of so coarse a fiber. From such a kernel we must expect chaff.

Wood was a consistent supporter of women's rights and a friend of Abigail Scott Duniway, the leading suffragist in the Pacific Northwest during the Progressive era. However, under the topic "Woman Suffrage," in his "Impressions" of August 1905, he argues that suffragists will not win the vote until they swell their ranks and strengthen their demands. The means, he insists, must be voluntary cooperation.

Woman Suffrage

Friday, June 30, I had the honor to address the National Woman's Suffrage Association, and among other things said in substance that missionary work of this righteous cause should be done among women, and especially to promote the economic freedom of woman; that woman suffrage would not come till women themselves demanded it, and women would not demand it while they were in a state of mental and physical servitude to husbands, brothers, fathers; that economic independence would make for mental independence and self-assertion.

The Rev. Anna Shaw, a most eloquent and able woman, commenting on this, said that it was useless to wait until all women wanted the suffrage, because all women never would, just as men do not now want it; and cited, as example, that the Democratic party gave the suffrage to the laboring man, though all laboring men did not ask it, and the Republican party gave it to Negroes, though they did not ask it. But it seems to me that history shows that no government has ever cared for abstract justice. No government has ever instituted a just reform until it became practically expedient to do so—through forcible demand or hope of gain.

Now, the Democratic party gave the suffrage to the laboring men because it knew this would add to the voting strength of the Democratic party—and in this it was correct. The Republican party gave the negroes the suffrage because it knew the negro vote would be Republican, and would give the Republican party hope to control the South, though "justice" was the platform cry in each case, yet abstract justice did not enter into either case.

The cause of woman suffrage depends, at present, wholly on inherent abstract justice. No party has anything to gain from it so neither party will voluntarily hand it to them. If women will become interested, and will, as a body—not, of course, every woman—but if the general mass will make either party feel that practically the solid woman vote will, because of inherent circumstances, go to that party—women will get the suffrage at once. If the great body of women will become so interested as to know their rights and demand them in no uncertain terms, making both parties feel that they will not submit longer to this injustice, but that every home in the land will feel their decided revolt, each party will hasten to be the first to earn the woman gratitude by advocating the woman vote. An aroused popular opinion is all controlling everywhere.

Women are the mothers and instructors of men, and if the general opinion among women was earnestly for the right to vote there would in two or three generations be a body of men voters taught to believe in the justice of woman suffrage.

The existing political powers will not offer the voting franchise to women till they see some selfish gain in it. Women must, and only women can, make them see that gain—the hope of new recruits or the fear of moral revolt.

The women of the land offer neither that hope nor that fear. They are indifferent. Portland is a city of more than a hundred thousand inhabitants and not once was the church, in which the National Association met, filled. Women of national and worldwide reputation were there; eloquent women were there; but apparently there were not five hundred women in Portland who took any interest in this interesting subject and this interesting convention.

Notwithstanding the greater freedom of women today, women, as a whole, are still dependents, still under masculine domination, still idlers or drudges. They do not, as a whole, care anything about the suffrage question; so I remain obstinate in my belief that the work of these leaders in a just and righteous cause should be among the women.

All things come to a vast and united body of the people which knows what it wants and insistently demands it. Women must, as a class, demand the suffrage; women as a class must be economically and mentally free. These, in my belief, are the prerequisites.

Introduction to "Direct Primary"

OREGON PLAYED SUCH A prominent part in the national period of political reform known as the Progressive Era (1890-1912) that the battery of legislative measures advanced by this movement—such as the initiative, the referendum, the recall, and the direct primary—were known collectively as the Oregon System. The architect of that system in Oregon was an itinerant blacksmith and journalist named William S. U'Ren. U'Ren was an ardent disciple of Henry George, economist and reformer, who argued that taxes should be confined to the economic rent derived from land; what George called the "unearned increment" or "single tax." As population grew and the amenities of living increased, property values rose. Such gains George sought to return to society since the increment had come about through no action of the property owner. In a capitalist society, the single tax was considered to be confiscatory. U'Ren saw the way to achieving the single tax through the initiative and referendum (I and R) amendment to the state constitution.

For a time "Ces" Wood also was a single taxer. He also favored direct legislation and he worked to help U'Ren draft and pass the I and R amendment. Following this success, the first initiative action passed by the people in 1902 was the direct primary law. Prior to this, United States senators had been elected by each state's legislatures. Wood strongly approved of the clause in the law, labeled Statement Number One, that pledged legislators to elect the U.S. senator chosen by the people. It read: "I will always vote for that candidate for the United States Senator in Congress who has received the highest number of the peoples' vote for that position in the general election next preceding the election of the Senator in Congress without regard of my individual preference."

In Wood's "Impressions" for April 1906 he explained why he considered Statement Number One an important political reform. However, he believed that a Republican legislature would never send a Democratic senator to Congress. He was wrong. In 1909, Governor George E. Chamberlain, a Democrat, was confirmed by a Republican legislature as a U.S. senator. Thanks to the success of Statement Number One, Oregon found a way to the direct election of U. S. senators nine years before the passage, in 1913, of the 17th amendment.

THE DIRECT PRIMARY

THE INITIATIVE AND REFERENDUM

If these laws are failures then popular self government is a failure and Alexander Hamilton was right; the people are incapable. Who is going to contend for this? It is unfortunately true that the people as a whole are not of great learning or great intelligence. But they have average intelligence and the instinct of self-preservation; and through all their blundering they will tend toward the right goal. What is done by all with the approval of all cannot be hurtful to many, or if so, will be soon corrected. But what is done by a few for the good of a few is sure to be hurtful to many and if the governing power rests with a few there can be no remedy.

Government means power. It means power backed by force, and in spite of the claptrap of campaign oratory about the people governing, the people never have and do not now govern. They go like lambs to the slaughter, they are led by the nose, they are taxed, pillaged and plundered and government still rests, as it did in kingly days, with a few. They were then called nobles. Today they are called bosses and money-barons. Anything which even tends to break into the power of the dominant classes is good. Anything which tends to make the people think about themselves and know their rights and power is good. Nothing ever sprang perfect from its seed. All things must develop by the slow process of evolution, and our laws and institutions are no exception. The initiative and referendum law in its essence is right and good. It has come to stay. That political managers are hostile to it is, perhaps, no sign of fault in the law.

The Direct Primary is also a new machine and may need adjustment; but the very hostility of the practical politicians who made and dominated conventions is a tribute to its beneficial effect. It certainly does at present leave nominations at sea. It certainly does leave the gate wide open for "fools to rush in where angels fear to tread." (That is a quotation, the angel candidate is unknown.) It does not provide for a preliminary discussion of principles and platforms; but all these things can come and will come by the voluntary act of the people.

Conventions, themselves, are a growth. They were not created by law and there undoubtedly will be party conventions to discuss platforms and candidates; but just as the referendum is a most beneficial check upon "loaded" legislatures, so will the Direct Primary be a most beneficial check on "loaded" conventions.

DIRECT ELECTION OF UNITED STATES SENATOR

The *Oregonian* has been arguing that Statement Number One was never intended to mean that a Republican Legislature should send a Democratic Senator to the Congress and that such a result is impossible. I agree that such a result is impossible. It will not be done; but I do not agree that the Republican Legislature ought not to send a Democrat to the Senate if the Democratic candidate receives the mandate of the people to go to the Senate.

I perceive the force of the argument that the Legislature is clothed with the constitutional power and responsibility, that the Senate is a Chamber of National legislation and National policies, that a Republican Legislature ought not to be expected to weaken Republican ranks and Republican policies and Republican patronage by sending a member of the opposing party to the National Congress. But to my mind all these arguments fall before the one root question. Are the people themselves to govern or are they to be governed? Suppose the United States constitution was amended so that Senators were elected by the people, and suppose the people elected a Republican State Legislature and a Democratic Senator. There would be no doubt that he was intended by the people to be Senator in spite of the loss in Republican patronage and prestige. To my mind the true intent of the nomination by the people is simply to accomplish indirectly what the United States constitution prevents being done directly, that is, the actual election of Senators by the direct vote of the people. The great majority of the people of the United States wish for the amendment. No one doubts that. Now is the spirit or the letter to control? Are the people now living to be the judges of their own welfare and own desires or are these to be judged for them by a generation long since dead, the makers of the United States constitution? No generation ought to bind another. Each should be free to make its own mistakes and find its own remedies. We of today think the election of Senators by legislatures is a mistake. We desire to remedy it. We desire to elect them ourselves. We desire to abolish that part of the United States constitution. That is the real purpose and effect of the nomination of Senators by the people. If the people send the wrong man to the Senate, on their heads be it. They are the judges.

Introduction to "Why Strikes?"

Responding in an October "Impressions" to a telegraphers' strike in 1907, C. E. S. Wood took the side of the strikers and launched into a diatribe against the great corporations consistent with the trust-busting spirit of Teddy Roosevelt's administration. Wood went on to support socialism as an ideal because it uses government to correct the ills of government and hence is in touch with existing conditions. With his characteristically optimistic outlook, he sees socialism preparing the way for anarchism. Stock-jobbing, by the way, is a form of manipulating stock investments to the disadvantage of the buyer.

Why Strikes?

Why strikes? Are the demands of the laborers or the expectations of capital unreasonable? As I write the Telegraphers' strike is on. Their demands seem reasonable. Wages which will have the same purchasing power as former wages (for in these piping times of prosperity the price of everything but labor has gone up) and hours which do not overtax at a stretch brain and body. To these the Portland (Oregon) union adds a demand for ventilation and cleanliness in operating and toilet rooms—a demand which is a credit to those making it and a disgrace to the company which forces it to be made. There is one clear duty due from the great wealthy corporations to their armies of employees. That is to teach them the safety and morality of cleanliness, the self-respecting quality of decency, the ethics and aesthetics of life. The office and surroundings of the plutocratic corporation ought not to be below the level of the home of the drudging employee. It ought, rather, to set an example of beauty and cleanliness.

Why strikes? Clearly an effort to better the condition of the laborer —certainly we all want to see that done. It is a desirable end. Possibly the daughter of the railway or telegraph magnate is striving for the same end—through a free soup kitchen or free reading room, or free soap. Why strikes? Why are not the just demands of the laborer anticipated, and why is he not made a partaker in the unrivaled prosperity of his corporation? The corporation fails to better the condition of its employed either because the prosperity of the corporation really does not justify any betterment, or because the policy of the corporation is to give grudgingly, making a fight for all it can get, yielding only what it must. Because it regards its employees not as its partners, but as its natural foes.

Still, why strikes? If the profits on the actual, bona fide investment, or, better, if the profits on the actual market value of the plant are not sufficient to justify higher wages the employed can be easily made to see that. A frank, simple statement made honestly without bookkeeping —juggling or stock watering or inflated expenses, would soon be understood by the employed, would be accepted as a sufficient answer —and there would be no strike. No man expects to be paid to the loss of his employer: most men are reasonable. But the great corporations would consider it insolence to be asked to exhibit their true balance sheets to their hirelings, and folly to do it. It might also prevent stock-jobbing. They persist in the folly that they privately own the great public corporations. Whom the gods would destroy they first make mad. There would never have been any revolutions if the upper classes had foreseen justice and wisely administered it in advance. The great corporations do not see that the slow and stupid creature called the Public will one day ask "Why should I wait while these people fight out their troubles? Have I no rights? Shall I, who have created this public corporation to serve me, be servant to my own creature?" So the public, tired of waiting for its telegrams and cars and branch line railways; tired of fattening multimillionaires with the dollars which should build new lines, improve old ones, increase wages, or reduce rates, will oust these private owners and take possession. The government ownership predicted by Mr. Bryan [William Jennings Bryan, Nebraska Senator and perennial presidential candidate] is sure to come. Much as I disbelieve in it in principle, much as I fear the vast army of government employees in an elective republic, I cannot blind myself to the fact that no single problem has been resolved on the side of individual freedom. Every solution has been a socialistic one, and in socialistic solutions the state or local government is being ousted by the great central federal government. Its bureaus are controlling our forests and our grazing land, our fisheries and fish culture, our livestock shipments and slaughtering, our microbes and bacteria, our food and drugs, our bugs and pests, our rivers, railways, banks, and, under the whiphand of our dominant president, our senators, representatives and judges. This is to be expected. By natural processes only similar forms can be evolved from existing ones. From ideas of government can come only various forms of government.

My own theories are opposed to the governmental ownership of railways and telegraph lines, but by the laws of evolution that is the only possible next step, and the persistent folly of railroad and telegraph managements in refusing to see that they are trustees for the people will hasten the step as the obstinate folly of the privileged ones in all periods has hastened their overthrow. If the profits of a corporation do not justify the demands of the strikers, ordinary wisdom, policy or business shrewdness would impel the corporations to take the public into their confidence and enlist public sympathy on their side.

That they do not do so strongly implies that their profits are abundant and the demands of the strikers just. Either this, or that they consider it none of the public's business. In this last the corporations are mistaken, and it will be so proved to them.

The conscious attitude of the corporations is probably that they are paying the market value of labor such as they are using. This in every instance is a deceitful proposition. In the first place, labor is the only element in the production of wealth in which there is absolute free trade. Labor is absolutely unprotected. So long as babies are born there will be the competition to live, and this means a competition in labor, a competition pressing harder and harder as population increases. This gloomy outlook for the masses of men is what inspires and justifies both socialism and anarchism, both seeking the same end: the abolishing of monopoly or privilege. The first seeking to abolish competition among laborers and the privileges of capital by having the government the one great capitalist, the trustee for all—all for one and one for all; the government the sole benevolent monopolist, controlling the sources of production and the means of distribution. The second seeking to abolish monopoly and all privilege by abolishing the powers of government over the economic affairs of men. Every privilege is the creature of law, and laws are made by government, and government always has been and now is administered in the interest of the predatory few. Anarchism does not seek to abolish peace and order, or control of the vicious who forcibly interfere with others, nor courts or some boards of award to settle disputes. It does not set up a cut-and-dried plan; it simply says "laws give every privilege and monopoly; these are the claws of government; let us cut these claws," leaving the rest to natural evolution as society shall have the ability to meet its needs as they arise. And it suggests that when no power can give any man any privilege over another, self-interest will dictate a voluntary cooperation more effective than that of socialism.

Personally, I believe anarchism the ideal, because it permits individual freedom in an equal environment; but, as socialism uses government to correct the ills of government, it is nearest to existing conditions; it uses existing conditions, modified, to meet pressing ills. Therefore it seems to me natural that all our evolution should be toward socialism. It is, in my opinion, preparing the way for anarchism. But the corporations do not recognize that they are fattening on privilege and monopoly; that the fight between them and labor is not an equal one. They do not see that when they say "we believe in the open shop and individual freedom," they are setting every laborer free to compete with every other laborer, while they themselves are the creatures of special privilege and protected monopoly. The fight is unequal. This inequality has produced the union—an effort to combine labor, so that it will not cut its own throat by hungry competition. It is the protection given by law to the privileged corporations, or to capital generally, for it is all supported by legal privileges of various sorts, which necessitates unions. The union is full of tyranny of its own—full of ignorance; but so long as capital is protected as it is and enabled to farm labor and take an undue share of the product of labor, so long labor must, in self-defense, form its unions. The whole thing is wrong. Out of one stupid injustice comes another. Gradually the government will absorb first the functions of the privileged public service corporations; later those of other employments of labor, for there is no relief so long as capital is protected and there is free trade in labor and so long as babies are born. And finally, by natural evolution, government as a maker of privileges will be abolished and then the field will be open to individual effort and individual reward, always modest, for there never yet was great individual reward except by the channel of a legally protected monopoly.

IN HIS "IMPRESSIONS" for *Pacific Monthly*, August 1908, Erskine writes on the anarchist idea and creed, insisting that anarchists are not violent. He came to know Emma Goldman through their mutual sympathies with radical labor, and he defends her against unwarranted charges of inciting Leon Czolgoz, a Detroit anarchist, to assassinate President William McKinley in Buffalo, New York, on September 6, 1901. The President died of gunshot wounds eight days later. Czolgosz was tried, convicted, and sentenced to death. He was executed at Auburn, New York, in late October 1901.

Lithuanian-born Emma Goldman came to New York in 1889; she was an anarchist, an effective labor agitator, and a fiery speaker. Goldman published an anarchist magazine, *Mother Earth*, from 1906 to 1917. In her massive autobiography, *Living My Life*, she writes warmly of Wood as her friend and sponsor on her lecture tours to Portland. Both in writing and in speaking, Colonel Wood was wont to draw the distinction between what he called anarchism of the word and anarchism of the deed.

THE ANARCHIST CREED

Government has no right to use force against peaceable men, but government is an institution and it cannot be abolished by killing an individual. The individual has a right to his life unless it is taken in self-defense. To kill an official only strengthens the power he represents, for it seems to justify that power, even though it be tyranny. Possibly some misguided individual, insane over what he regards as the injustice of government, may be guilty of assassination and call himself an anarchist. But more likely this will be the newspaper designation. I know of no genuine anarchists who have advocated or attempted assassination. Booth was not an anarchist, nor Guiteau, nor Czolgoz. They were all insane, clearly; but the trial of the latter showed that he acted alone and did not even know what anarchy was.

When Kings or tyrants were assailed by assassins, the assailant was called an anarchist by the existing powers, who believed one who lifted his hands against the Lord's anointed must be opposed to all government, which in their eyes was synonymous with being opposed to peace and order. So the word has acquired a sanguinary meaning in the popular mind, suggesting murder, looting, chaos, and a general demoralization of society. For this reason I personally regret that the word anarchy was selected for the political and social theory. What it really means is personal liberty, the right of the quiet, peaceable citizen to live his life in his own way. The abolishment of all monopolies and special privileges; the preservation of peace and order and restraint of force; the settlement of disputes by a recognized tribunal; the right of the individual to own and control his property; the organization of society on a basis of voluntary co-operation; (a small instance is the sprinkling of their streets; also the policing of certain districts by the voluntary co-operation of certain Chicago property holders).

As Yet But a Theory

Anarchy does not pretend to describe in detail how anarchistic society will be organized and operated. It simply advances a theory, leaving evolution to determine how the theory shall be applied. All systems of society are evolved. You cannot cast them in a mould ready-made. It is folly to ask how will this be done, or how will that be done? The real question is: is government still a ruling of the many by a class? Do the few exact tribute from the many by the power of government? Is government the source of plutocracy of the few and poverty in the masses? If so, government ought to be abolished.

Anarchism expects organization for the preservation of the peace against those exceptional few who would forcibly invade the rights of others. Such criminals are the few even in our wretched state of society, but when society is free and poverty and wretchedness abolished, they will be still fewer. To those who say this is all the dreaming of visionaries, I have nothing to say. Unless a theory commends itself on the stating of it, it is not apt to be enforced by argument.

The Declaration of Independence was once a dream.

The Emancipation Proclamation was once a dream.

The steam engine was once a dream, and Christianity was once a dream. Very great in the eye of Heaven are the dreamers of dreams. One of these is Emma Goldman, a Russian Jewess, who has seen the wretched of the earth trampled under hoof and bleeding, kiss the hands of their masters, begging the right to work to earn a crust. Her sympathy has gone out to the oppressed of the earth, and for their sake she has endured persecution from the well-fed.

129

The Real Emma Goldman

When some crazed fanatic commits some political crime, the police, to prove their vigilance and justify their existence, arrest Emma Goldman. From her viewpoint it is laughable comedy, but as a display of American tyranny and ignorance, it is tragical. Emma Goldman never exhorted to violence in her life. She doesn't believe in violence. First, because it is against the tenets of the anarchistic creed, which condemns all force against peaceable men. Second, because it is useless and only begets a distrust and prejudice. It strengthens the side so attacked. Understand me. Emma Goldman does not believe the people should cower like sheep while the Cossacks gallop their horses over the breasts of women, neither do I, and if some grief-crazed wretch strikes at Czar or Governor he has her pity and mine. Emma Goldman has never advocated an act of violence. It is said she instigated the Haymarket bomb-throwing. She was seventeen years old at that time and knew nothing of the affair.

It is said she incited Czolgosz. She did not even know him. She was arrested at that time by the intelligent police and discharged with censure of the police for a wholly groundless arrest. Emma Goldman is a trained nurse—educated in Vienna—who all her life has gone about doing good, nursing the poor and seeking to lessen the distress of the wretched. If the half-baked fanatics of the pulpit and the press who shriek along the surface of things, would follow in her footsteps for a time, they might be of some real benefit to sad humanity. They would also discover that, as I have said, her whole discourse is an appeal to justice through the intellect, and she never said a syllable of violence in her life. They would also discover what would be more potent than truth to them, that she is the friend of Prince Kropotkin. Think of it! a real Prince, nearer in blood-right to the throne of Russia than the Czar himself. They would discover that this woman who, before she has uttered a word, is hauled off the stage by such cheap American thugs as Chief Shippey of Chicago, is met in England by Edward Carpenter, the poet, and taken to her lectures in his automobile; that the people she knows abroad are the dramatists, poets, literary men, musicians, people of brains who move the world. How Bernard Shaw would laugh that the Y.M.C.A. of Portland and the Arion Society refused her their halls under the belief that she is a murderess, a wild woman going up and down the land seeking whom she may devour.

HOW RIDICULOUS WE ARE!

I hope he will hear of it and give one more sarcastic illumination of our insular American ignorance—our provincialism. In England, Emma Goldman lectures as anyone else would, to a quiet audience, without a policeman in sight. In Free America she is dogged by detectives and hauled to jail by opera bouffe policemen till we are ridiculous in the eyes of the world. And this, too, after years and years of careful detective work and failure to convict her of an improper, dangerous, or unlawful word. It is a comedy. If she says anything contrary to the peace and dignity of society, why is she not arrested after each lecture? Why is she never tried? I repeat, the whole thing is so shallow and silly that if Miss Goldman had organized it as an advertising dodge she would make herself ridiculous. Portland has reason to congratulate herself on the sanity of her Mayor, Chief of Police and Police Commissioners, who in effect laughed at the hysterics of those who wanted this dangerous woman arrested and thrown into a dungeon in advance, and pointed to the Oregon constitution, which says: "Any person shall have the right to freely express himself on any subject whatsoever, being responsible for an abuse of such right." And they said wait till she abuses the right of free speech and violates the law, then we will act. The consequence was, her five lectures in Portland were as uneventful as prayer-meetings. Not a policeman was visible, and there was no need for one. The Rev. Mr. Eliot, too, in the interests of free speech and sanity of judgment, offered the Unitarian Church if necessary—but it was not needed. Plenty of halls were available. Compare Portland's sanity and American spirit of action with Butte, where all hall-owners were notified not to give her room "under penalty of the law," whatever that may mean. Curious law they must have in Montana. But the same spirit prevails in Chicago, where the police dare to prohibit hall-owners from letting their halls to her use. This, you will please remember, when her lectures are printed and may be read—when in all her addresses not a solitary charge can be brought against her. I heard lawyers say: "She is a damned anarchist and ought to be hung!"—without trial, I suppose. Nice lawyers. They only exposed their ignorance—this detestable, bourgeois ignorance of anything but money. They admitted they had never heard her speak nor read a line she had written. Her full five lectures in Portland were reported and nothing even sensational found in them. If you ask why does she have this reputation, then? I ask why did the Abolition Yankees have horns and hoofs? Why did the early Christians sacrifice infants and eat their flesh? Why do the Jews in Russia and Poland drink the blood of Christian babes? Why, in the early Christian times, were all murders, all fires, all plagues, all riots, laid at the door of the Christians? Why did Virgil give a recipe for breeding bees from carrion? Why was Dreyfus convicted? Why does the average reporter and average newspaper print a sensation rather than the truth? Why all the lies and superstitions of the world? A Portland paper gave an interview with Emma Goldman, commencing by calling her the "arch-priestess of dynamite,"—a thing utterly false, and for which no foundation existed in the interview or anywhere else. So this myth has gone from paper to paper, from mouth to mouth, simply because Emma Goldman is an "anarchist"—a misconception of what the word means. She is an anarchist as Tolstoy is, and Kropotkin, Prudhon, Shaw, Carpenter, and the Americans, Warren, Thoreau, Tucker, Bolton Hall, Byington, Lysander Spooner. Dynamite! Bombs! Assassination! Rubbish! I have called it comedy. But the colossal American ignorance and gullibility is too tiresome to be comic. Let some one convict Emma Goldman of encouraging violence before we talk any more about it. There are plenty able and willing to do it if it can be done. The fact that it is not done, and a horde of police camping on her trail, is conclusive evidence.

A Yellow-News Bugaboo

The identical lectures she gives are printed and may be read by any one. These are evidence. Her magazine, "Mother Earth," is evidence. Reporters haunt her, these are evidence. Why is nothing ever done? Only those who do not hear her, but speak from hearsay, keep alive this absurd bugaboo. That Emma Goldman advocates violence is a pure myth. That she was associated with the Haymarket bomb-throwing or with Czolgosz are pure myths. An instance of this pitiful ignorance and reckless assertion is an article by one Broughton Brandenburg in the June issue of the "Broadway Magazine," "The Menace of the Red Flag." His very title proclaims his ignorance. The anarchists have no flag, no organization. The red flag is the socialist's symbol, and when Jack London raised it at a gathering in California he was nearly mobbed. Ignorance again. For it means, as I have said, only the blood common to all men—brotherly love, universal brotherhood, Christianity made practical. It floats freely over every socialist gathering in Europe. A gentleman told me he had seen it waving over a large assemblage in Hyde Park, London—an orderly assemblage and no policemen visible.

Despotic Britain! Free America! Brandenburg's article is rather briefly and contemptuously reviewed in "Mother Earth."

He asserts that Michael Bakunin was a Frenchman; that he was the author of a code for assassination, and that a copy of the code was found among Czolgosz' effects. In truth Bakunin was a Russian. He wrote no such code, none was found among Czolgosz' effects, and the trial made manifest that Czolgosz had no effects.

These were the very things the police did not find, and which the prosecution could not produce. Not a scrap. Not one line or word. Czolgosz was a poor fellow, who brooded alone till he went insane. He testified that he was utterly alone, and the most rigorous investigation by willing detectives and in a time of high excitement, failed to disclose any associates or even friends. That Brandenburg does not know his subject, and has been too lazy to learn, is shown by his ignorance of names. He refers to William McQueen as Peter; Bresci as Brescia; classes socialists like Hunter (whose book was reviewed in this department last month), Patterson of Chicago, Phelps Stokes, the New York wealthy reformer, as anarchists; does not even mention such active and well known American anarchists as Josiah Warren, Stephen Pearl Andrews, Lysander Spooner, David Thoreau, Benjamin R. Tucker, Joseph Labadie, and others. Mr. Broughton Brandenburg is an ignorant writer of sensational space.

In our introduction to C. E. S. Wood's "Impressions" for April 1906, we sought to describe his connection with William S. U'Ren and their role in forging and promoting Progressive legislation such as the initiative, referendum, direct primary, and direct election of United States senators. In the process, we dealt briefly with Henry George's single tax, the primary motivation behind U'Ren's commitment to the "Oregon System" and one of the most complex and controversial economic, political, and social issues of the late nineteenth and early twentieth centuries. In one of his last "Impressions," that of November 1911, Wood devotes his entire column to an imaginary dialogue designed to explicate Henry George's single tax, a format he later used with marked success in *Heavenly Discourse.*

Henry George and Single Tax

Oregon and Washington are each agitating measures to exempt improvements and personal property from taxation and to limit taxation more closely to land values. Seattle is quite stirred by the examples in this direction of her northern neighbor, Vancouver, B.C., and I have myself often been asked by men who ought to know better, "What is this single tax?" I had thought to write a brief article some day for these columns but last week on the Mt. Tabor car I heard a conversation so much to the point that I reproduce it here from memory, in lieu of any exposition of my own:

A. Say, B., what is this single tax? They tell me you know all about it.

B. It isn't a tax at all, strictly; it's a ground rent, exacted from the owner of land by society on the theory that society creates the real value of raw unimproved land and is in the last analysis the owner. Or put it another way: Land in a wilderness without inhabitants is valueless. Its value increases only as population increases. The value of the raw land is therefore not created by any one individual, but by society as a whole, and this value may therefore be said to be unearned by the individual owner and may be called the unearned increment. Society takes for its purposes so much of this unearned increment as it needs.

A. That's what Lloyd-George has been arguing in England, isn't it?

B. Yes. Not straight single tax, but to take a small percentage of this unearned increment still leaving the larger part to the landlords.

A. According to your theory, the landlord doesn't earn any of it, so none of it rightfully belongs to him.

B. It doesn't.

A. I'm from Missouri; show me. Hasn't he paid for his land? Bought it and took his risks on it? It might have gone down in value; lots of it does. He's improved it and paid taxes on it. Seems to me whatever he gets out of it is his. Is Lloyd-George the man who invented this single tax ?

B. No. Henry George. He's dead. His son is in Congress from New York. Do you want me to answer you?

A. Sure, if you can.

B. My experience is that the best way is to begin at the beginning and then when we have thought it out to the end we can beat about the bush with all sorts of questions, if you like.

A. Fire away.

B. Do you believe every man has a right to the things he himself creates ?

A. Sure.

B. And what is true of each man is true of men taken together ?

A. Sure.

B. A man has a right to the things he himself creates. *A* corporation has the right to what it creates, and society divided into those corporations known as states, counties, cities, has a right to what it creates?

A. Sure.

B. Do you think a man ought to be punished for creating useful and valuable things?

A. Not unless he is a reformer. That's a joke. No; of course not.

B. Do you think a man ought to have the property he himself has created taken away from him without compensation?

A. No. Nonsense; it's against the law.

B. And these same principles apply to one man—a group of men—or all men collected as society?

135

A. Sure. Can't see any difference whether it's one man or a million. The principle is the same.

B. Then you are a single taxer.

A. All right. But I'm still from Missouri; show me.

B. What is the value of land without people? Let us, for example, stick to the city of Portland. What was the value of this townsite when it was a fir forest and only the passing Indians camped upon it?

A. Well, the land must have had some value, and the timber.

B. What value? It had a potential usefulness to come in the future. The land would raise crops when cultivated. The timber would build houses and other things when cut into lumber, but when the deer, the bear and the Indians roamed over the land, what was its value? To whom could you sell it? Where was the demand ? Did it have a market value ?

A. No. Without any one at all here wanting to use it, of course it couldn't have a market value.

B. Then if a man came and cleared a little farm, built a cabin and planted a garden and fields, what value did the land have?

A. Whose land, his or all of it around him ?

B. Both.

A. Well, the land around him didn't have any value because there was nobody wanting it, and there was lots of it, but suppose another fellow drifted in, don't you suppose he would pay more for the fields already in cultivation, rather than take a piece of wild land for nothing? Of course, the first settler put value into the land.

B. I don't know why it is the human mind finds it so hard to separate the value of raw wild land from the value given to it by man's labor. Now listen, once for all: The single tax does not propose to tax or lay claim to anything whatever created by man's labor or ingenuity. If he runs one furrow and plants one row of peas, that added value is his, not Society's. Every ditch, every fence, every rail, every house, every shingle, every flower bed or cabbage bed, every well, every conceivable thing created by man is exempt; for the reason that the single tax thinks it immoral as well as bad economic policy to take from a man what is truly his own. Every sheep, cow, horse, chicken is in the same category. They were reduced out of wildness ages ago by man's labor and ingenuity;

they are bred and cared for or created by his labor and ingenuity and are his as much as the plow or the wagon he makes. Now, once for all, eliminate from the single tax scheme everything created by man, either today or by his ancestors, and remember the single tax claims only the raw land. Not made by man or his ancestors, but created by Nature as the general inheritance for man, and claims it only as Nature left it, without claiming so much as a single ax-stroke done by man as improvement, and claims only on the theory that in the ultimate the land belongs to society for its uses, not to any one man, or group of men, and that society puts the value into it, as raw land, or as a site, or an opportunity. If you'll remember this it will save a lot of wobbly and confused thinking.

A. All right; raw land, or opportunity. Just the same, if I seize the opportunity, seems to me I have a right to the rise in value as much as I have to the loss in value, but go ahead.

B. Now, what the second settler would be paying for if he bought out the first settler—would be the first settler's labor. Just so long as there was plenty of land equally good and equally situated, the first settler's land as raw land would have no value over and above the rest of it. The settler's labor gave value in clearing and cultivating and that value is his own, but there is very little land that duplicates other land exactly in quality, situation, etc. Presently, as the social colony fills up, the land of equal value is gone and there commences a competition for the most favored land—the richer, the nearer the road, nearer the river, nearer to market—or it may have a fine spring, a hot spring, a gold mine, water power, and so on. Now, who put the richness into the land, or the spring, or the gold mine, or the location ? Certainly, the settlers did not, and as it is a convenient phrase we will say God did it. So it does not belong to any man as his creation, does it?

A. No.

B. Then the colony thickens up, a town begins, we will say again Portland, and the land in the favored location or townsite becomes town lots. What gives them their value?

A. Why, laying out the town.

B. Does it? I've seen lots of towns laid off on paper that remained on paper. So have you. You know it's the people coming in that makes the town.

137

A. Sure.

B. And the more the people the bigger the town, the bigger the lot values. Isn't that so?

A. Yes.

B. Lots on Washington Street around Fifth, Sixth and Seventh were a hundred dollars. Look at them now, at the hundreds of thousands. Did the owners make those values ?

A. No.

B. Who did ?

A. Oh, the growth of the town.

B. And what is the growth of the town?

A. The general increase in population.

B. So those values were made by no one man but by society in general?

A. Yes.

B. And on the principle we agreed on, that to each one belongs what he created, those raw land values belong to society, don't they?

A. Looks so. But the owners bought on speculation and paid the taxes.

B. That has nothing to do with who made the values. Some owners bought on speculation and some didn't, but fell into the ownership in spite of themselves. But no man can morally buy what the seller does not own, and no man can sell this unearned increment in raw land values because no man owns it. And as for paying taxes, that is a small part of what the owner should have paid as the price of the privilege of owning the lot. He has shuffled off a large part of his burden onto the personal property of the community, which really does belong to the owner and which the community has no right to tax at all. Single tax aims to set this right and exempt improvements.

A. Well, if he takes the loss oughtn't he to take the profit?

B. The single tax does not ask him to take either. It denies his right to the unearned increment whether it be in fact an increase or a loss. If his property shrinks in its raw land value, society or the single tax assumes that shrinkage and relieves him by that much; that is, lessens his tax or payment to society. If the value rises, naturally by the same reasoning, society assumes this also, and raises his tax or payment to society.

A. But where is the reward for his shrewdness in selecting his purchases?

B. We come back to the main question: Did his shrewdness create the land value? We know it did not. Why should his shrewdness be rewarded with a thing it did not create against those who came later and helped as much as he in the creation of the land value? Or against the unborn, who had no opportunity to select at all, but who will equally with him put value into the lot by the growth of the city? Why should men who gobble up power sites, for example, receive the whole unearned increment against society, which by its presence and growth and demand gives the entire value to the power site as a natural undeveloped force?

A. Well, I guess you've got me going.

B. The forestaller or gobbler may be likened to a pirate: By shrewdness and by force of law he seizes a piece of land and holds it while society is putting value into it. Then when another wants that site, the forestaller sells to him those very values he has not created. The whole question comes down to this: Who creates those raw land values which society seeks to appropriate for the general public uses? If the individual owners create them, they have a right to them. If society as a whole creates the values, society as a whole has a right to take them.

A. Oh, well, you know no one man makes land values.

B. Very well then, that's the end of it on the moral and economic side. But there is another side to it. You think it wrong to hale a man to the sheriff's office and fine him for creating great values.

A. Now you're talking nutty.

B. You know Portland has lately been tearing down old shacks all through the town and putting up fine six to fifteen-story buildings?

A. Yes.

B. Take the Yeon building. It went up where a lot of wooden shacks were.

A. Yes.

B. Don't you know the taxes on the Yeon building are enormously greater than they were on the old shacks.

A. Yes, of course.

B. So, Yeon has been fined. Actually dragged into the sheriff's office and fined for giving the town a splendid improvement. The lot he built on is precisely the same one that held the old shacks; his increased tax is his punishment for creating a great, fine building, and the speculators who leave their lots vacant are rewarded with low taxes.

A. But think of the increased rents Yeon gets.

B. Yes, I know. It's the same way in the country, a farmer imports a herd, or a stallion, or gets more ground under cultivation, or gets bigger crops. Up go his taxes, as a fine for his creative power. Are we to punish men because they can increase their rents or their crops? That is the present theory of taxation. Just old-fashioned blackmail. Take from every man a part of his increase, no matter how he gets it. Single tax says if it is really his let him keep it; all of it. Now, in morals and economics, the whole truth is, how does he get it? If by his own creative ability then it is his; every dime of it. If by the occupation of a favored site into which society puts the value, then so much as comes from the raw land value or site value belongs to society and is not his. For example, the annual rental or taxable value of the Yeon site belongs to society and if it needs it society can take it. The value of the building is Yeon's, every cent of it.

A. Then you would have him paying the same tax on the lots with the old shacks on them as with a fine building?

B. Just the same at the same period of time. Nothing whatever on improvements. All the tax on land values, that's the theory. It takes from no man what he has himself created. It punishes no man for his thrift or improvements.

A. How about the farmer?

B. Pshaw! That's an old scarecrow. The farmers have learned the single tax is a tax on land values, not on land, not on acres. And they know there is more value in a few acres of Portland than in all the farms in the county. The farmer having low land values and relatively high values on improvements would profit by it. And he is beginning to see this. There is no blinking the fact that the real burden would be on the cities, for the high land values are in the cities. And it would be just a balancing between the land values and the improvements. A man with more value in improvements than in site would gain. Site values would gradually fall, because sites held vacant for speculation would have to be improved by the owner or sold to some one who would improve. The single tax is really only a burden or penalty on the speculator who holds land out of use, waiting for society to create a heavy value which he can collect.

A. Your idea is, then, that a person who speculates in land sells values which he does not create and which do not belong to him ?

B. Yes.

A. But suppose he loses in the speculation ?

B. I have already told you whether the land values go up or down from any particular period does not alter the principle and a true application of the principle would never allow the individual to either lose or gain. Society as the landlord ought to be the loser or gainer.

A. So this is the single tax? I must say it's not as silly as I thought it was. But you say Oregon is not trying to apply the single tax?

B. No, not at all. The idea of making society the landlord, entitled to the rental value does not enter into any proposed law now pending in Oregon. All that any of these laws are attempting is to take the tax off of improvements and put it on land values. That is, like Lloyd-George in England, the Oregon reforms propose to take just a little of the land values by imposing a tax on them. If that proves to be a failure, it can be dropped. If it proves to be a success, the people can carry it as far as they please. In Vancouver, B. C., it is proving a great success.

At this point both gentlemen left the car and I have no doubt that the discussion is still going on.

INTRODUCTION TO *A Masque of Love*

WOOD'S SECOND BOOK, written as his first marriage eroded, *A Masque of Love* attempts to understand the relationship between love, marriage, and freedom. Written as a triptych, *A Masque of Love* begins with an idyllic, classical love story of Eve and Hubert, continues with a stormy, Shakespearean tale of adultery and murder featuring Magdalen and Edwin, and closes with a philosophical pastoral presenting Mary and Alfred living in conjugal joy, reminiscent of early Shakespearean comedies. The essential message of the idyllic, tragic, and bucolic sections of the masque (an elaborate form of entertainment popular in the Renaissance) is "all love is holy."

The masque originated in Italy and was quite popular in England during the reigns of Elizabeth I and James I. It combined poetic drama, music, dance, lavish costuming, and stage spectacle. A simple plot, usually mythological and allegorical, held together the various elements. The players were members of the court who, at the end, removed their masks and danced with the audience.

Wood liked this form, using it in one Christmas piece, *The Sleeping Child (A Masque)*, which family and friends performed on Christmas Eve of 1913. *A Masque of Love* was never performed. Wood uses masque elements, chiefly myth and song, and the pun on the word *mask* plays a powerful role in this exploration of the faces of true love.

A handsomely printed, letterpressed book of almost one hundred pages, *A Másque of Love* was published in 1904 by Walter M. Hill in Chicago for the Elston Press in New York in an edition of four hundred copies.

A Masque of Love

Scene VII. The Court Room
JUDGE, JURY, CLERK, BAILIFFS, PROSECUTING ATTORNEY and others.

JUDGE: Bring in the prisoner. [*Enter Sheriff with Edwin*]

ATTORNEY: One word. [*To Edwin*] Again I say, you stand in peril of
your life. A woman's presence oft is eloquent and pity puts to rout
the strongest proof. I pray you let me bid her come. 'Tis most
imperative.

EDWIN: Again I say I will not have her here. Let us go on.

ATTORNEY: I'm ready, please the Court.

JUDGE: Now call the jury roll.

[*Roll is called. All answer*]

CLERK: The jury is complete.

JUDGE: The trial may proceed.

PROSECUTING ATTORNEY: Let Benjamin Badeau resume the stand.
[*Benjamin stands forth*] Conclude your evidence.

BENJAMIN: Must I go on?

PROSECUTING ATTORNEY: You must.

BENJAMIN: The night my master died—it was a wild and dismal night—
I crept with silent steps and awe-held breath into the chamber of
the dead.

PROSECUTING ATTORNEY: For what?

BENJAMIN: To mend the fire.

PROSECUTING ATTORNEY: Go on.

BENJAMIN: There was no sound but slow death ticking of a clock and
on his bed my master slept—or what had been my master lay as if
asleep—and here, beside his bed, upon the floor—he could have
touched it—lay this handkerchief.

[*Enter Magdalen*]

PROSECUTING ATTORNEY: This handkerchief?

BENJAMIN: This handkerchief.

PROSECUTING ATTORNEY: Whose is this handkerchief?

BENJAMIN: It is the prisoner's.

MAGDALEN: I charge you stop! Why vex the world with all this tedious
circumstance when Truth stands ready at your hand? I killed my
husband—I—

EDWIN: For God's sake, Magdalen!

PROSECUTING ATTORNEY: May it please the Court, we do object.

MAGDALEN: Object! Object to truth!

PROSECUTING ATTORNEY: There will be a proper time for this; not now.

MAGDALEN: Forgive my ignorance. I did suppose all rules were meant to point the honest way and every rule would bend to save a life. I say 'twas I alone who killed my husband.

JUDGE: The law is tender of a life and will not let you, unadvised, proclaim your guilt and seek a shameful death.

MAGDALEN: Is law so tender of a life it will not let me tell the truth to save one innocent, but puts its shutters up and bars its doors? I say again, 'twas I alone who killed my husband. There's no power of God, or man, or long delay, or prison fare, or death will make me alter in this truth.

JUDGE: I do advise you all you say may on your trial be retold against you.

MAGDALEN: I do so understand. Why not? 'Tis true.

JUDGE: Let her be sworn.

PROSECUTING ATTORNEY: But we object. The prosecution has not closed.

JUDGE: Are you the advocate for truth or death? I say I'll hear her now. Let her be sworn.

CLERK: You, Magdalen McLane, do swear to tell the truth and all the truth and nothing but the truth, so help you God?

MAGDALEN: I do—so help me God. So help me God! Oh, I have need of help. My story is soon told. It is not new. I loved not when I wed. Therein was I to blame—but I was very young and after wedding I recoiled into some arctic, love-deserted place and pushed my husband out. And then I loved another man. Oh, I was bred religiously. I knelt beside my narrow bed and prayed for help. I clenched my fist against the far, dumb sky. I wept upon my arms and often knelt the long night through with sobbing moans beseeching God to tear this devil, love, from out my heart. It fed upon my tears. I was possessed of love. I have not seen another one who loved as I. It drew my very soul as is the battling and rebellious sea drawn into tides, or as the earth is drawn upon her wind-swept path. I could not more resist, and blind with happiness, and soothed, I said, "God's will be done." So lost myself in him who is the sun and center of my universe. I knew no shame. I felt a greater than a priest had blessed; a law, not made by man, had ratified. I told my husband all and begged release. He held me tighter in his lawful bond. His lawful bond! A madness seized my mind. "If I were free—if I were free—if only I were free. The home, the happiness, the child, the bliss as perfect as a half-wrecked vessel finds when out of all the wild tumultuous roar she rounds some sheltering cape and rides mid little, playful waves." Then came this sickness and I said unto myself, "He holds me by the law until Death do part. Then Death shall part." The poison, ready to my hand, I gave it him. But all for love. Indeed I did, I did it all for love. I would have been so glad to have him live. I hate not any one, but I did love too much. My love, my Edwin, was with me that night. It was a wild and terrible night, and when the thing was done by me alone I called him in and he stood fixed—displeased. My heart, like some spring flower which feels the frost, grew chill, for I did know that in that instant he had changed to me, and there he dropped his handkerchief and my poor life. Oh, God! Oh, God! Oh, God!

EDWIN: She is o'er wrought. Quick! She falls.

JUDGE: Call a physician.

EDWIN: See! Her spirit hath repented of its flight and now resumes its earthly tenement. She breathes. She opes her eyes. 'Tis I. 'Tis Edwin, Magdalen!

MAGDALEN: Nay, let me rise. I know you well. You are that ghost which dogs my heels and cries into my ear, False! False! False!

EDWIN: My God! Her looks! I'm Edwin. Look. I am your very Edwin!

MAGDALEN: My very Edwin! No—I know you, Edwin, and I am not mad. You are not my Edwin, for I am the bride of worms. I killed my husband. You do know that true—and so I killed your love— and so I die.

PHYSICIAN: She is not mad. She knows her words.

JUDGE: Then must she tread the gallows' step. Alas, the pigmy clumsiness of man—take her from hence. O, what a fragile ball we juggle with!

End of the second part

INTRODUCTION TO THE SHORT STORIES

C. E. S. WOOD WROTE A SPATE of short stories during the first decade of the twentieth century. Some of them he published in Louis Post's *Public* in Chicago or in Marion Reedy's *Mirror* in St. Louis or in Benjamin Tucker's *Liberty* in New York, all three outlets for radical writing. However, most of Erskine's short fiction, like much of his writing in this period, appeared in *Pacific Monthly*. The first of these bore the exotic signature Felix Benguiat and was submitted to *Pacific Monthly*'s new editor, Lute Pease. Wood published thirteen other stories in the magazine, all of them under pseudonyms.

The stories vary widely in atmosphere and setting. Some have an Arabian Nights flavor; some are realistic treatments of social problems such as poverty, exploitation of labor, and prostitution; some have a touch of the supernatural; some are whimsical; all stress the virtue of and need for individual freedom. Two of Erskine Wood's stories follow.

INTRODUCTION TO "THE TOAST"

"THE TOAST," FROM *Pacific Monthly* (November 1908) celebrates far western independence and freedom for men and women alike. Like much of Wood's writing, this story is marked by allusions and asides that display his wit and learning but impede the flow of the narrative. In fact, sometimes Erskine improvises and embellishes to the point of becoming lost in the digressions much as his friend Mark Twain was wont to do. The glittering banquet setting in "The Toast" allows the author ample opportunity to criticize the shallowness of the city's upper crust and the venality, boorishness, and cowardice of Senator Oldfield, the eastern tycoon.

THE TOAST

The dinner was given to Bertha Stillman, on her return from Europe, and it was such a dinner as San Francisco delighted to give when she sat in opulence upon her hills in the days before the earthquake. The table was under a pergola thick with passion-vine and jessamine. The stars and the moon peeped through, distant and pure. Luxurious rugs carpeted the white marble floor and there was nothing of that bourgeoise nickel-plated culture which renders the social board unsocial and turns a feast with pleasant conversation into a cheap concert. Only twice or thrice was music heard and then it stole from afar in soft strains, as if someone thought in music upon the night. The night air was as caressing as a bride's kiss and out beyond the radiance of the electric lights, which were concealed among the leaves, was the deep velvet blue of night, made deeper by contrast, and against the sky the fringes of stately palms made vague draperies. Some candles on the table gave still another light,—a mellow and convivial light, and their soft splendor was caught again and again by the glitter of glass. Nothing is or has been or will be more beautiful than glass; not the mechanic sparkle of cut-glass, heavy and meaningless, but glass, light and airy as breath itself, and in such exquisite forms as show the delight of the artist in throwing from his lips—nay, from his soul,—these fixed and brilliant bubbles. The glass of ancient Venice; when gondoliers in blood-red velvet and gold brocade sang to some window, or there was heard in the stillness of the night the sullen plunge of a corpse into the canal. The glass of ancient Greece; when every village loved beauty and even shepherds were instinctive in the forms of art. Temples have gone, and cities, but there have come down to us, without a crack, vessels fragile as air, vases from which Aspasia may have poured water and wine for Pericles, or oil for her own bright body, and so it is; bricks of the law-giver and the philosopher crumble, the arches of the conqueror decay, but the filmy vase of the poet survives, defying the greedy and gnawing tooth of Time and compelling its envious touch to gild the bubble with a rainbow radiance.

The table was brilliant with Venetian glass and the dinner was such as I would have been glad to have sat down to; a salad of alligator pears and tomatoes; the little native oysters on their thin, pearly-green shells; a bit of striped bass steamed in white wine with peppers and a sauce the subtlety of which, like that of all art, defies expression. I care not what kickshaws and trifles else, the essential being a great pie of mountain quail with fresh mushrooms and truffles; and at this point a glass of Burgundy.

Arma virumque cano. This dinner by Bertha Stillman's friend, Sally Walcott, (Walcott duly divorced) was intended to throw Bertha into the arms of Spencer Oldfield. Fortunate arms. She was the daughter of Gerald Stillman, the newspaper man: himself brilliant, captivating, with, for a heart, a butterfly. Peace to his ashes! He was as God made him. Her mother was never known in San Francisco, and Bertha was held doubtfully by those who found nothing in literature, art or the wonders of the universe more absorbing than bridge-whist and tattle of their neighbors' weaknesses or misfortunes. Until she grew beautiful and celebrated: then the world of convention was at her feet. As I think of her beauty I feel like saying, as old Winton did, "My God, but that woman is beautiful!" Her beauty gripped you by the throat; it made your soul ache and your mouth water. The figure of a dryad, full-chested, supple, tall.

She had written three novels, many stories and had come home to attend the presentation of her clever but impossible play, "In Love With His Wife." She lived well enough, but with that spice of economy which the rich—poor devils—are deprived of. She had small dressmakers' bills for she wore no corsets and draped herself softly. Still she was poor, as genius ought to be. No genius could possibly love money. No genius should ever be wealthy even by accident. I think I never heard of a wealthy genius. (I am poor myself).

Spencer Oldfield was in the very aristocracy of plutocracy. He was rich by inheritance. His money had lost the taint of the making. His father made his first stroke in floating, among his friends and the public, the stock of the Western Coal & Iron Company; floated it in its own water. But as his stealing was done according to law, by use of majority stock and directors, and the purchase of corrupt aldermen, he died worth millions and of course outside the penitentiary. Spencer was respectable. He had never done a day's work in his life and was almost religiously scrupulous not to flaunt his immoralities. Society is governed by fictions, superstitions and shams. You may do anything if you do not publish it. You may preach anything if you do not do it. One of the superstitions was that Spencer was respectable. He had barely enough hair to part sedately and accurately in the middle of his broad skull, brilliant steel-blue eyes, big teeth, a coarse mouth, thick lips, broad hands, stumpy fingers, and a habit of clearing his throat and pulling up his collar or adjusting his necktie when he was nervous. Though still young, the fit of his clothes suggested that his tailor would be a good maker of balloons. Such was Spencer Oldfield,—any woman's aversion. Such was Bertha Stillman,—any man's joy. Beauty and the beast. Yet Sallie Walcott in the space beneath her tiara which she called her mind, distinctly thought of selling her to him. She really believed she was Bertha's friend. The consideration—Money. She wished to give Bertha millions. Bertha knew her friend's intention perfectly well; not from conversation, but from observation, and as she surveyed her fate and thought of him as a bridegroom in the sweet mystery of willing love, she was sufficiently masculine-minded to have mental and moral goose-flesh,—or better, aesthetic goose-flesh; for the true, healthy, aesthetic feeling is surer and finer and purer than mere morals. But the Beast raped her with his eyes and would have her at any price, which shows that love does not always fly through the rosy sky, like twin butterflies caressing each other, but sometimes drives stupidly up to the door alone in a butcher's cart, with a club.

The conversation was becoming general. Buller, the artist, a self-satisfied, stout man with grey Vandyke beard, said in the ex-cathedra tone of the master among his worshipers, "Art is form and form is art." All stopped to listen. "If you discard form," continued he grandly, "you discard art." "Then why did you do it?" asked Johnny Winslow, the wit of the Bohemian Club,—which I will admit was small beer after all. "It discarded me," said the artist, casting an instantaneous glance over his comfortable proportions. "And," said he, raising his voice slightly, as he now had the company for an audience, "the object of art is to please, not to preach. A tragedy may preach a lesson in virtue, but the preaching is merely incidental. Its artistic object and result is pleasure; otherwise it is a sermon."

"Oh, I don't know," said Winslow. "How would you class a rapid tendency to baldness? or the daily tragedy of the divorce?"

"Divorce is cheap melodrama," interrupted Bertha.

"But the vitalizing soul of art," resumed Buller, bowing and smiling to the interruption, "is imagination. By it we conceive the beautiful, and the beautiful is the eternal."

"I agree with you," said Gerald Lincoln, the chestnut-bearded poet with rather long, wavy hair, who sat at the middle of the table. "In my opinion, there can be no poetry without imagination and no poetry

149

without beauty, and the greatest poetry has a perfection of form, though not necessarily the most artificial form; then it becomes mechanic. I hate Pope. Imagination," said the poet, his eye lighting and waving his hand with an elegant gesture at the company, "has lifted man from the brutes; made the world his treasurehouse and his playground; expanded its limits beyond the stars; decorated it with the wonders of day and night and the seasons, and has opened before man the endless avenues yet to be trod. Imagination distinguishes not only man from the brutes, but the genius who is a jewel of the world from the common man who is absolutely worthless."

"Ahem," said the wit, modestly behind his hand and bowing at the word "genius."

"I would rather have imagination than any other gift," said the poet in a more matter-of-fact tone, dropping suddenly out of the air.

"I knew a man," said slim Doctor Perkins, the distinguished alienist, "who imagined he was Mary, Queen of Scots."

"He had evidently lost his head," said Winslow, and at last everybody laughed.

"But, Doctor, you cannot say that he was not happier in this foolish dream, than if he had known the earth as we know it?" said Bertha, leaning forward earnestly.

"No," said the Doctor, "we cannot say. Who knows what dreams may come? Visions grander than ours, as well as terrors greater than ours. The mind is a sea which has no bounds. Shakespeare was in a sense a lunatic, living in realms of his own imagination; and that is why I believe that each one should have perfect liberty in this world to do exactly as he pleases. To follow his own chase, for joy, peace, contentment; and that there should be no limitations except to restrain the use of force by one against another."

Bertha Stillman had been watching the doctor intently and as he came to this period she said: "Good!" so heartily that all looked at her, and the Doctor, coming back to earth a little shamefacedly, as the poet had just done, added, "No; no one can say what is best for another."

"I can say for myself," said David Scott, a smooth-shaven lawyer on the happy side of middle age, with an orator's mouth and a handsome, straight nose, who sat opposite to Bertha, "that I am happier to know the earth as I know it tonight, with you opposite me, Miss Stillman; far happier." Bertha bowed and everybody smiled. Oldfield laughed aloud, but not with delightful heartiness.

"If I had imagination," said Wit Winslow hastily, for fear he was losing ground, "I would imagine the world a vast bed of roses, on which I would lie and view the stars which, as they came toward me, proved to be the beautiful eyes of beautiful women, and the foliage on the trees about me would be receipted bills,—mine own."

"Oh, there is a limit to the imagination, Winslow," said Scott. "If it were not so, I would like to imagine that Miss Stillman loved me." Bertha quickly quoted to him:

> Bold lover, never, never can'st thou kiss,
> Though winning near the goal;
> Yet do not grieve;
> She cannot fade, though thou hast not thy bliss;
> Forever wilt thou love, and she be fair.

"Mr. Scott also forgets that there is a limit to the imagination," said Spencer Oldfield, sarcastically.

"Oh, I don't know," laughed Bertha; and Nelly Bodie, a beautiful girl of the tropical type, with luxuriant red under the olive-brown of her cheeks, said, laughingly, "Why, to love Mr. Scott seems really not so difficult." "Great Scott!" said the wit, and again they laughed, except Spencer Oldfield who endeavored to look bored. Nellie Bodie laughed mischievously and ran her hand over the glossy black hair, which, falling in simple bands from her forehead, was coiled heavy and thick, low at the back of her neck. The hostess nodded to the poet, who slowly arose and after a few preliminary "ahs" finally got under headway and said he desired to propose the health of one upon whom Aphrodite and Athena had smiled in unison, one who had received from the gods bright visions of the air and deep yearnings of the ever-moaning sea; who was herself a goddess of the mind and of the soul and yet not the less a very Venus to gladden the eye; one who added to the charm of her charming sex, etc., etc., etc., the intellectual force supposed to be peculiar to men, etc., etc., etc., who by beauty of face, as well as of mind, etc., etc., etc., was the goddess of the Golden West and Aphrodite of the Orient sea, — Miss Stillman.

Mr. Oldfield shouted, "Hear! Hear!" vociferously and drank copiously. Bertha responded lightly, gracefully, wittily; and at the last, warmly and sincerely, and when she sat down Spencer Oldfield said with solemn emphasis: "Great! Great! Great!" three times and very seriously lifted his glass to her. She bowed and he swelled like the frog in the fable.

Mrs. Walcott saw this and felt all the thrills of the angler who feels the quick strike and nervous pull. Her fish was hooked. She was very glad. Dear Bertha could have now everything her heart desired—(except love and happiness). Thank Heaven it was settled. She could hardly wait for the evening to end and the intimate secret confab of the bedroom to begin.

Mr. Oldfield was saying to the lady next to him, but with half an eye for Bertha, "My idea of a gentleman, Miss Carter, is one who lives on his income. A man who has to work for a living may be honest in his way and a decent enough sort of a fellow, and all that, don't you know, but he is not what you would call a gentleman, don't you know."

Miss Carter having expressed her sympathy with this view added that this country was becoming fearfully democratic, but Mr. Oldfield comforted her by saying that the country would get over this evil tendency in time, for as wealth remained in the same family for many generations, there would gradually be bred a real gentleman class. Mr. Oldfield then felt he could properly leave Miss Carter to hug this comforting thought and he quickly turned to Bertha Stillman, saying: "I wonder, Miss Stillman, that you have not written a book or a play about the Western mining camps."

"Yes," she replied, "I wonder too, for I know nothing about them."

"How you surprise me," said he. "I wish we could make up a party this summer to visit my mine. There is awfully good hunting and fishing and good mountain roads."

"What is your mine, Mr. Oldfield?"

"It's the biggest gold quartz mine in the State," said he proudly, "the Grizzly Giant."

"The Grizzly Giant!" echoed Bertha, and studied his face a second or two and then with a sudden chill she added, as if to herself, "Oh, yes, yes; certainly."

"You know it?" he asked.

"Well, no, not exactly," she hesitated; "but I have heard of it."

"We could have a couple of motor cars taken up on the train," he went on, "the mine is only eighteen miles from the railroad spur which runs into Red Gulch. That's the name of the little mining town."

"Oh, yes," said Bertha; "I know Red Gulch."

"You do!" exclaimed Oldfield, looking at her with some surprise.

"Yes," she replied, "I have friends who have a ranch somewhere in that region."

"Well, I'll tell you what," said he, "I wish you would make up a party to be my guests up there any time you wish;" and lowering his voice to a confidential murmur he added: "it would make me the happiest man in the world if you would consider everything I have your own."

Bertha quickly interrupted, as if she had not heard fully: "Mr. Oldfield, I trust it is not impertinence to ask how you came by that scar on your forehead?"

"Oh," said he, pulling at his collar, "I got that in an accident up at the mine. I was up there with Jack Ingalls. You've heard of Jack. He owns Olympus, Olympiad, Olympic and all that strain of thoroughbreds, and he imported Blue Rocket and Meteor. He and I are going abroad this fall; unless," he added, again lowering his voice to a confidential tone, "you will let me do something for you," and he languished a look upon her such as only the animal man can give and which makes us long for the simple dignity of the brutes.

At this point the hostess, leaning forward a little, said to her: "Bertha, Mr. Winslow says that women can lecture in private, but cannot talk in public. Now I want you to propose a toast to the gentlemen."

"No, no," said Miss Stillman, shaking her head.

"Please, Bertha," said her hostess, appealingly.

"Oh, well," she consented, "I will propose the health of a gentleman. — Not any particular gentleman, but the ideal; and I'll tell you a story." She pushed the things away a little from in front of her and leaning her arms on the table, she told, most dramatically, this story:

"Three years ago I was visiting Mary Milliken. She married Tolliver Warrington, a good-looking, good-natured Englishman, who bought a ranch in Calaveras County, at an outrageous price, but he was to get rich, fabulously rich, raising sheep. He and the sheep are poorer than ever, but you love them both, for they make you welcome and leave you alone.

"One hot August morning Mary asked me to drive to Red Gulch, the railway station, and get Marian Greene, her cousin, who was coming from New York. Something had gone wrong with those blessed sheep and Mr. Warrington and the foreman had started for the mountains.

"If any of you have ever lived on a sheep ranch you will recognize the aptness of the Bible's allusions to lost sheep. A more helpless and naturally erring lot of creatures, from the cradle to the grave, I never saw, unless it be society women. There is certainly more excitement over one of the strayed imbeciles than over the ninety and nine which the dogs have kept safe, sane and moral. With women in society this is different.

"For two dry months the dust had been deepening in the yellow road till it was now eight inches deep, as fine as flour; and as irritating—as only alkali dust can be. The heat was fairly quivering across the plain where stretched the road. I put on a shabby duster, tied a straw hat over my head, drew on old gloves and started with a pair of mustangs that were fat, fresh and looking for trouble. But it was my own fault. I thought I was a complete horsewoman—I think so still—and I insisted on this team, for I had no desire to linger on fifteen miles of dusty desert. The buggy—well, you all know a California ranch buggy. It had never known water in its life. The mud of winter and the dust of summer had accumulated upon it, and like the tramps of humanity, it had got reckless in its shabbiness. The road from Warrington's ranch to Red Gulch is first about ten miles of sagebrush-and-greasewood desert; then a climb to a stony *mesa*, where the road is harder and better (Warrington having employed men to throw the rocks out of the road); then a sharp turn down into the river canyon, with the face of a rock precipice on your left and wild roses and death and destruction on your right. Then across the wide river bed, nearly dry at this time, up the long grade to the summit, and down four miles of winding grade, with Red Gulch under your hand all the time, with its little houses and locomotives looking like a toy." ("That's right," murmured Oldfield, to himself).

"I drove fast to keep ahead of the dust over the desert, and after climbing to the *mesa* I let the horses walk a little and in this time, overcome by the heat, I fell asleep. I slept most of the distance across the *mesa*, when I was awakened by a great jerk; the team was running away. Do not ask what made them run, for I don't know. Perhaps a loose strap; a horned toad running in the dust; the glint of an empty can; the buzz of a rattlesnake; the smell of a carcass; or perhaps the planets had predestined from the very beginning of time that it was to be and it was just their hour to run.

"I gathered the lines instinctively and in less than three seconds was doing my best, but we went like the forefront of a tempest and the buggy and I were but a leaf in the furious wake. I do not believe that people really think under such circumstances. I blessed Tolliver Warrington afterwards that he was an Englishman and despised American roads and insisted, out of his own slender substance, in keeping the *mesa* road smooth; but at the time I simply steered them instinctively, or, rather, they kept the road themselves, for out of it would have been very rocky going. The first brain work I was conscious of was the knowledge that we were approaching the canyon, with the sharp turn down into the river bed, which would inevitably hurl me over the beautiful sweetbriers down to the sharp rocks below, a torn and mangled bundle, in a wretched duster and a very unbecoming old straw hat. Not that I thought of this at the time. It was cause for gratitude afterward. But I did realize, with terror in my soul, that I was flying to certain death, and I know that to all the children of men death is horror. We recoil from it instinctively. So, in an agonized way, I began to meditate jumping from the wagon as flying from certain death to only possible death. I had not the courage to jump until the last moment, and so I waited. It was all instinct with me, not intelligence at all.

"Meanwhile, with the same blind instinct, I sawed desperately at the horses, but I was a pigmy pulling against a mountain, and I knew that I was helpless and alone. The fright and pathos of it made me sob a few short, dry sobs, as I saw death and the head of the canyon but a little way in front of me. Just then—though my over-occupied senses had heard nothing—a great dark mass, almost as if it was a gigantic bird, shot past me out of the road onto the lava rocks, something whirled before my eyes and in a moment the horses lay prostrate, half in the road and half on the rocks and on the very edge of the precipice. I jumped from the buggy immediately, not realizing what had happened, only knowing that my wild flight had stopped and I had a chance to escape; but I jumped right into the arms of a cowboy, who seated me on a great lava boulder, took off his grey felt *sombrero*, wiped his brow with the back of his hand and, alas, alas, spat some tobacco juice in the dust and said to me in an encouraging and amiable tone, 'Close shave. Set here a minute.' And he hurried off to the prostrate team.

"I need not tell you that I set. I did not, as a heroine should, look at my hero, or perhaps I did, for I became fascinated by a great powerful bay horse now black with sweat, who stood out on the rocks, his straight, powerful legs braced, his handsome neck arched and his great intelligent eyes fixed on the runaways, lying there panting. From the horn of the saddle on the bay to the neck of the farther runaway, stretched a rawhide lariat, tight as a bow-string, and the great bay made it his business to keep it tight. If the struggles of the captives loosened the tension, the captor backed away and restored it; the nearer horse lay somewhat under the other. Both finally ceased to struggle, but the vigilant bay never winked an eye, but stood there like a figure of victorious strength and relentless duty. How I did love him! I am ashamed to say I tried to buy him from his master.

"The other hero—the man hero—was busy among the harness, throwing off the traces and straps; then he ran the buggy back a little way, loosened the choking lariat from the throat which was breathing hoarsely and piteously, took both horses by their heads and motioning to the bay to come forward so as to relax the lariat, helped the runaways to their feet, where they stood quietly enough, frightened and trembling. The pole was split. He took a halter rope out of the buggy and lashed it, walked around the horses, petted them, looked the lines and harness all over, got some leather strings from his saddle and did a little repairing and then hitched the horses in again.

"He called to me: 'Would it bother you to stand over here and hold the horses?' I went, and I watched him as he moved about, skillful, self-reliant and quiet. He was tall and spare; a fine athletic figure, with rather a long face, powerful mouth and aquiline nose; a high-bred man physically; the hawk type of man, but with no cruelty in eyes or mouth. Indeed, the forgiving way in which he soothed the poor wicked runaways was a lesson for sinners. I am proud to say his name was not Bill. This is a true story. If it were not, I would feel obliged to call him Bill. All Western heroes are named Bill. His name was Curtin St. John."

Mr. Spencer Oldfield again fussed with his collar and tie and cleared his throat.

"St. John slowly coiled his *riatta*, tied it to his saddle, threw away his chew of tobacco, untied a coat from his saddle, slipped it on, adjusted his neckerchief of a terrible magenta color; then said, quite simply, 'I'll get in first, if you'll excuse me. It will be safer; I can handle them better.' He made room for me beside him, leaned over, gave me a strong hand and as I stepped into the buggy I felt the lift and thrill of great masculine power, so fascinating to a woman wherever she finds it, and it ought to be. It means energy, safety, attraction; life, eternity.

"As we started he whistled to the splendid bay and the statue broke into easy supple motion and trotted after us. St. John saw my admiration and looked as pleased as a mother.

"'He is a beauty,' said I, 'What is his name?'

"'His name is Baby. I went back to Kentucky about five years ago and brought out a carload of horses for the company and I got this little fellow for myself. He wasn't hardly old enough to be taken from his mother. It wasn't just right, but I couldn't buy both of them. In fact, she wasn't for sale at all. So I have made a pet of him and I got to calling him Baby, but it does seem a foolish name for him now, so I call him Bay,' and as he spoke St. John threw his arm back over the seat and the beautiful horse crowded up and poked his soft nose into his master's hand.

"'Well, you and Bay have saved my life,' I said. 'I won't try to thank you, because I can't. I just want you to know that I know it.'

"'Guess you're from San Francisco,' said he, with light in his eye. 'People out here don't bother about such little accidents. Where was you going?' he said, in a businesslike tone. I told him I was going to Red Gulch to meet the train. He glanced at the sun and hurried the team. I told him my name and that I was a visitor at the Warrington ranch, but I had to ask him his name.

"Some little distance before you enter the long grade up from the river, the road from Grizzly joins the main road, and coming down this branch road we saw a buggy with two men in it and they, seeing us, whipped up and entered the main road first. Their team and buggy threw out such thick volumes of dust that I could scarcely see or breathe. St. John slowed up till the air had cleared a little and then seeing the team ahead of us was at a walk he trotted up and tried to pass, but as he did so they whipped up again and, as we were out on the rocks, we had to fall back and take their heavy volumes of dust. This was repeated a number of times until it was perfectly evident that the men in the buggy intended to keep ahead of us and to go at a walk except when necessary to prevent our passing them.

"If you are suffering from nervous headache under a broiling sun, choking with dust and your eyes burning like coals, you can have a better appreciation of my feelings than you can possibly have under these present delightful surroundings."

Here Miss Stillman looked about the table and let her glance rest for a moment on Mr. Oldfield's scar. He coughed, arranged his tie and took a gulp of wine. Then she resumed:

"St. John turned to me and said, 'Would it bother you, Miss, if I chewed some tobacco?' 'Not at all,' said I, 'I wish I could chew something myself.' He looked off into the canyon, smiling at my vicious tone. We heard the men ahead laugh. St. John only chewed. Apparently the situation meant nothing to him. To me it was not only an insult of the most boorish character, but it was great physical discomfort also."

Mr. Oldfield became noticeably worried about his throat, but no one noticed him: all eyes were on the lovely speaker.

"'I never smoke,' said St. John, as if anxious to make conversation, 'even if a lady tells me to, for I know that ladies often lie to be good-natured, that's the woman of it; and I don't believe in taking advantage of it and being disagreeable.' He pointed his whip at a chipmunk and said, 'Innocent little fellows, ain't they? Them and horned toads and camp robbers has the brightest eyes of anything.' 'Camp robbers,' said I, at last becoming interested. 'Yes,' said he, 'little grey birds that as soon as you make camp in the mountains, come into the trees right over your head and pretty soon get down beside you and it won't take 'em long, if they get any encouragement, to be pecking out of your plate. Most every one likes to be doin' gun practice on 'em, and they certainly are regular thieves, but I don't allow it. No bird that shows that confidence in a man ought to be betrayed: it is sure treachery.' He passed the reins over to the other hand and continued: 'I ain't much on killing harmless things anyhow,' and after a silence of some minutes he continued, apparently oblivious of the time which had passed: 'Everything seems to like to live, don't it?' He looked at me for a reply, but I was not in the humor and I said to him abruptly, 'Ask those—those men, to let us pass.' He stopped the team and handed me the reins, saying, 'I hate to seem ornery to a lady, but this team is perfectly safe now and it's up-hill for three miles and I'd a little rather that you'd let me get out and you ask them yourself.' 'No,' said I, 'I will not ask them. They have seen us try to pass them a dozen times and words could say no more.' 'That's what I thought,' said he and we plodded on in silence, the great bay following with bowed head and I swallowing my wrath and the dust.

"After a progress of this kind which seemed ages, I noticed St. John begin to watch the road as if he were studying his position and gradually our horses pushed into the thick of the dust and walked close behind the other buggy, and I was about to suggest falling back into clearer atmosphere when St. John brought the whip down on the backs of our team with a vengeance and we sprang into a turn-out made to enable wagons to pass each other on a steep promontory. The men ahead of us whipped up also, but it was too late; down came St. John's whip again; he turned so sharply as nearly to upset us, thrust our team against the heads of the other horses and throwing them out of the road close to the edge of a fearful embankment. Our wheels cut their legs and made them rear. Both men jumped out of the buggy and one ran to the heads of their horses. We swung into the road amid a storm of curses, oaths and blasphemy. St. John never turned his head. Bay came thundering after us and we pushed on."

(Spencer Oldfield again adjusted his necktie).

"'Mountains are solemn things,' said my eagle-faced, calm charioteer, and I felt that if I tried to answer him I would cry hysterically. 'Life in the mountains is nice; they are so cool and quiet; but everything likes to live wherever it is: the lizzard out in the desert, just the same as the deer in the mountains, and the little Jenny-wren just as much as the grizzly. Everything likes to live, and life ought to be good to everybody. If it ain't, then something is wrong and against Nature.' I philosophized with him a little and then as it all came over me again, I thanked him once more fervently for saving my life. But he put the subject aside and for lack of anything better to say I asked him if he had been on his way to Red Gulch when my mad career engaged his attention The corners of his eyes wrinkled a little in a smile, as he said, 'No, ma'am. I was on my way to Warrington's ranch.' 'Oh,' said I, 'I am very sorry I did not know that.' 'What would you have done?' asked he. I felt like whimpering, but said as bravely as I could, 'Well, it's too bad to have caused you all this trouble.' 'It's been no trouble; one day is like another to me. If I don't get to a place today, I can tomorrow. Now, if you was a cowboy out here, and found a lady in trouble, what would you have done? You see there wasn't but one thing to do.' 'Well,' said I, 'I hope I may be able some day to show my gratitude.'

"We had been flying down the long grade and as soon as he had hitched the team for me in Red Gulch, he lifted his *sombrero* and sauntered away, his spurs jingling and that beautiful horse following him like a dog.

"I had the excitement of seeing the train come in and after some delay arranging about her baggage, Miss Greene and I were ready to start back. Just then a man in blue overalls and checked jumper called out from the platform to the man who was assisting us: 'Reddy, did you hear about Curt St. John?' 'What about him?' said Reddy. 'He pulled the two swells out of their buggy and licked 'em like hell with a cowhide he bought special. One of 'em drawed a gun, but Curt took it away from him and hit him over the forehead with it, so that he is having it sewed up now by Doc Ginty.' 'What's it all about?' 'God knows. The men say he just jumped 'em without any reason and they're going to arrest him and hang him maybe.' 'Guess again,' said our helper and he and his informant laughed. 'What does Curt say is the trouble?' bawled Reddy, handing us the reins. 'Oh, says he doesn't like their looks,' said the other man as he walked away.

"Our man laughed softly to himself. 'Will there be trouble about this?' I asked. 'Won't be no trouble for Curt St. John,' said Reddy. 'If you are interested in the other fellows you might worry a little,' and again he laughed his mysterious chuckle, as if the idea of Curt St. John getting into trouble had a decided streak of humor in it. 'Ever see Curt thrash a man?' said Reddy, as he stepped back with our fee in his pocket. 'No, we never had that pleasure.' 'Ever see him handle a gun?' 'No.' 'Ever see him ride?' 'No.' 'Well, of course, then you ain't never seen him use a lass rope.' 'Yes,' said I eagerly, 'I have, once.' 'Once! Guess you don't know Curt very well. Well, I wouldn't worry about him, ladies,' and he walked off, rattling the silver in his pocket.

"Just as we turned the summit and the heat of day was fading and out on the desert we could see the sun half-way down the sky, making golden the long lines of dust stirred up by cattle and vehicles, or the pillars of dust raised by the whirlwinds, we heard behind us the rhythmic beat of horse-hoofs and Bay overtook us, his nostrils distended and flecks of foam on his breast. St. John rode him straight up and like a feather.

"'I don't want to bother you ladies by seeming to hang on, but I'm going to Warrington's and I thought I better stay by you till you get back.'

"I thanked him very cordially and presented Miss Greene, and all the time I was looking him over for any signs of conflict, for I felt that he was my knight and my heart went out to him; but I saw none; he had been freshly shaved and his hair was wet as if from a bath. He remarked that sunrise and sunset were wonderful sights, and then he fell back, out of the dust, and we saw nothing more of him, except as our out-rider, until we reached the ranch.

"I told the Warringtons what he had done for me and they said I was in luck that Curt St. John happened to be on the spot. After he had transacted his business with Mr. Warrington and was about to depart, the next day, he standing beside Bay, with the bridle-rein hung over his arm, I felt that in saying goodbye I ought perhaps to show some interest in his combat in my behalf and I said, 'I hope I didn't involve you in a quarrel.' 'Oh, no,' said he. 'No, you didn't. I done what I did on principle.

Them things seems necessary to be done by somebody, but I always feel mean afterwards.'

"It was then that I made my great mistake and was guilty of inexcusable want of tact. I approached the subject as cautiously as I could, but finally hinted that I would like to buy Bay. He turned around and looked at Bay for a moment and Bay looked placidly and confidingly at him; then he turned back to me and smiled and said:

"'He never batted an eye, did he? I guess he didn't hear you. You can't buy love, can you?' said he. 'No, it ain't reasonable; love which is real love can't be bought, and you can't sell it. Have you a child, ma'am?'

"'No,' said I, 'I'm not married.'

"'Excuse me,' said he, looking awkward.

"'Oh, never mind,' I replied. 'Even that will be all right some day.'

"He stared a moment, bewildered, and then went on: 'Well, you're a woman and can guess what a child would be to its mother. Would you sell it?'

"'Forgive me,' I said, 'I have been very stupid; I really did not understand. To most people a horse is just a horse.'

"'That's so,' said he, 'and if I was to sell Bay he couldn't cry and he couldn't beg me not to let him go, and he couldn't tell me what he thought of me, and folks would think I had a right to sell him, but I'd feel just as bad as if I sold a little child who had sat on my knee till we learned to love each other.' Bay ran his velvet nose up to St. John's shoulder and gave an impatient nudge. 'I'll make my will tomorrow, Miss, and if ever you hear of Curt St. John going under, you can look to see Bay coming to you.'

"'God forbid,' said I, giving him my hand.

"We shook hands, he lifted his *sombrero* and walked away, slapping the glossy neck of Bay with especial affection as if the lost were found. I have never seen them since.

"Now, ladies and gentlemen, here's to a gentleman: one who is brave with the strong and tender with the weak; who exceeds a woman in gentleness where there is suffering or sin, and exceeds heroes where there is wrong to be righted or the helpless to be helped. Who forgets self. Who never forgets duty, and who believes his first duty is to make the world happier. Who is as honest as the mountains, or the sea, or the desert, with Nature's primeval honesty. Who is clean inside and out; fearless, truthful, brave, honest, gentle. And on whatever lonely *mesa* he may happen to be tonight, here is to Curtin St. John, Gentleman."

161

Brava! brava! brava! The toast was cheered and drunk enthusiastically, all rising with the subdued noise of chairs pushed back and the rustle of women's skirts. Spencer Oldfield was the last to his feet, arranging his necktie and pulling his collar desperately. Before they sat down, Nellie Bodie called out:

"And here's to Bay, that dear horse."

Amid the buzz of renewed demonstration, Mrs. Walcott said enthusiastically to Spencer Oldfield: "Isn't Bertha splendid? Didn't she tell that story dramatically?"

"Yes, indeed," said Oldfield, his hand starting toward his neck but hastily dropping, and the hostess led the way to the music-room, while the gentlemen finished their cigars.

Presently an old-time Spanish serenade floated in through the passion vines. The rich contralto voice poured the passion of the song upon the night. "That is Miss Stillman," said Winslow. "By all the gods she is a gifted woman," said the poet. Spencer Oldfield sat shrunk down in his chair, feeling the scar on his forehead; and the moon looked down.

INTRODUCTION TO "THE DESERTED CABIN"

"THE DESERTED CABIN," from *Pacific Monthly* (November 1910), is a tale within a tale set in the fir, spruce, and cedar forests of the Pacific Northwest. The story is romantic and calls for willing suspension of disbelief but it is notable for passages that evoke Oregon's forested wilderness as vividly and compellingly in prose as parts of Wood's poetry bring to life the state's high desert.

THE DESERTED CABIN

The man was found dead, with his head upon the last page of an unfinished manuscript, as if he had been overcome with sleep. This is the story he had written:

"Andy MacDonald is dead," said Herman Rasmussen, timber cruiser.

"Dead?" said I.

"Yes; killed in that last storm; a tree blew over onto him."

"Dead!" I repeated. "And only two weeks more to go!"

"What's the matter?" asked Herman.

"Do you believe in ghosts?" I asked him.

"No," he answered. "Certainly not."

"Neither do I, but neither do I believe that all manifestations of matter are understood. I notice," I continued, "that there is in Australia a medium, or some such professed controller of matter by so-called spirits, who, given darkness to work in, will fill a cage with birds."

"Doubtless," said Herman, lighting his pipe. "I have known persons who under the same conditions would empty a coop of birds."

"Given," I went on, ignoring the interruption, "the very probable wireless telegraphy between those batteries or automata we call John and Mary, add coincidence to this; add to this, credulity and imagination, and the wonder is that there are not more wonders. Listen, and I will tell you why poor Andy's death shocks me so; though mind you I don't believe what I am going to tell you was anything more than sleeplessness distorting natural incidents. Nothing in Nature can be supernatural, but Nature is still so unexplored that he is wisest who limits himself to saying, 'I believe,' and will not say, 'I know.'"

When I told my tale by the camp-fire, among the dark and solemn firs, they—Herman and the rest—all insisted that I ought to write it down as soon as we came in. So here I am, putting it down in black and white on this the last day of the year in which Andy and I were to die. He has gone, poor fellow, in curious fulfilment of the prophecy, and I, the survivor, feel a strong impulse to write the story. After all, it is not the supernatural in it which interests me, but its simple humanity. There is a queer dread in my heart, too, I admit. Shall I, also, die, according to the belief? If so, I have but a few hours to live.

I am a timber cruiser and, in the latter part of last November, I was cruising a body of land in the upper Nehalem Valley, Oregon, for a

Minneapolis syndicate. Timber cruising in the coast mountains of Oregon is a job only for a youngish and vigorous man. Your compassman must keep his course in order to traverse the ground on fairly parallel lines at fairly regular intervals and he must keep proper tally. Sometimes you are on a windfall, the trees piled thirty feet above the ground; you are always scrambling over giant fallen trunks and always you are in dense underbrush, often so dense that only the hatchet will let you through. Throughout this struggle in a jungle, the timber cruiser must make mental notes of the size of the trees, the varieties: yellow fir, red fir, bastard fir, cedar, hemlock, spruce; the number of feet of lumber they will produce and the number of piles, poles, and railroad ties; character of the ground for logging, etc. I will only say that an honest, intelligent timber cruiser deserves all he gets and more. Perhaps every honest man deserves more than he ever gets, for certainly as society is now organized the rich rewards go to the pirate and the liar—and the great daily, which is both.

Andy MacDonald was my compassman, and just a year ago we were leaving our old camp and going to operate lower down in the mountains. I had sent the camp-tender with his pack-horse to the new camp by the trail, and, with Andy, I was going to finish the last of the higher body of timber and go to the camp direct through the forest, by compass. Woe be to him who enters these dark primeval fastnesses without his compass. The giant trees stand so thick and reach so high that the sun never penetrates to the ground. Beneath the trees is a matted tangle of ferns, salal-bushes, laurel, and in the canyons the terrible devil's walking-stick. The smaller streams run in every direction, and the mountains are broken into ravines, one exactly like the other, and all difficult. Woodcraft is baffled. The long winter mists and the equal gloom cause the moss to grow the same on every side of the trees, and the bark is equally thick. The trunks rise to heaven, straight as monumental shafts, and far overhead their branches blot out the stars. No one, save from necessity, goes alone into these forests; a broken leg would mean death. The wretch would never be discovered, save by the cougars, bears, or timber wolves.

Andy, a Canadian, was as good a man as ever ran the line and called the tally. My watch and compass had been left by mistake in my best waterproof shirt at camp, an inexcusable and almost fatal neglect. Andy had the only compass.

We finished the piece to be done before two o'clock. As we headed for the new camp there was a grunt and a sniff right in front of us, and a huge brown bear rose on his haunches, his fore-paws hanging down in a seemingly helpless way. He shook his head at us and grinned, but not agreeably.

The folly of men who live in the woods is inconceivable. We had worked the whole season with no other weapons than our axes and jack-knives. The fact is the camp-tender does all the hunting. Usually game comes to your door, and the cruiser gets so accustomed to elk, cougar and bear crashing away from him, their bulk disappearing instantly in the underbrush, that he will not burden himself with arms.

So it was that Andy and I had only our hatchets and knives. After the first shock of surprise, I threw up my hands and yelled at the hairy monster, expecting him to dash away. Instead of fleeing, he dropped on all fours and commenced to walk around us, sniffing and grumbling. There seemed nothing else to do, so I broke off a dead fir limb of some size and hurled it at him. It was a mistake, for it bounded easily from his well-protected ribs, and he, accepting the challenge, lowered his head and charged. Fortunately, we were near a steep, bare hillside. We both fled down this rocky place, for there was not a tree a man could climb. You might as well have tried to climb a forest of factory-chimneys. Our flight was not directed by any sense or purpose, but by a blind instinct, and it was only by chance that we separated and took different directions. The bear fixed his pursuit on Andy and, either Andy stumbled, or, as he always claimed, the bear made a forward pass and caught one of his feet, but in some way or other, when they were at full speed and the bear right on top of him, they fell; the bear overshot him and hit the top edge of a steep incline of loose shell rock, leading down into a small canyon. The loose rock gave way and slid with the bear, gathering force and material as they went, until he went crashing through a thick border of wild-rose, accompanied by a small avalanche of stones, into a bed of devil's walking-stick at the bottom,—a devil of a bed even for a bear. That is the last we saw of him.

We were both badly frightened and struck off for camp, talking over the experience, and had gone a considerable distance when suddenly Andy said, "I've lost my compass!" To tell the truth, we didn't care to return to that neighborhood, especially on the slim chance of finding the compass. "Oh, we can make it," said I, and off we started.

The day had been one of those misty Oregon winter drizzles, which you can hardly call rain, but is more like a falling fog. The ground was strewed with the wreck of centuries. There were ravines to cross and windfalls to go around, or over, and it was impossible to keep course, with no semblance of sun to guide us.

We both soon realized that we were floundering in the forest like tenderfeet. "There is only one thing to do," said Andy. "Let's work down to a stream and follow it to the main river and so on down to some settlement."

"A fine theory in books," said I, "but don't you know the Nehalem River flows a hundred and fifty miles, and yet, in air line, there is only about twenty miles between its source and its mouth, and not a ranch till you get to tidewater, and the whole course is through this primeval forest?"

"It's the only go," growled Andy; so we went at it, and rough going it was.

As the day turned to evening, the mist became a soft, deliberate rain, which fell as quietly and relentlessly as fate. Had we been in a mood for beauty, the great forest was beautiful. The giant trunks, delicate lavender grey through the rain; the blue-green vistas between them; the carpet of giant ferns and every twig, every needle, every leaf gemmed with the diamonds of the rain. The stiff sword-ferns shone like beautiful green enamel, and as far as the eye could penetrate the forest they decorated the earth in a tropical luxuriance. The beds of moss, under the influence of the rain, shamed, in softness and wealth of color, any velvet woven by man, and the lichens clung to the trunks of the trees like a silken garment of the loveliest grey.

But we saw none of this then. It was only a vast, solemn jungle of forest, in which we were lost. That night we built a fire by a sheltering log, and under a hastily improvised roof of bark and boughs we submitted to Fate. In fact, a night out is no uncommon experience for a cruiser. We gathered some of those slimy-topped, yellow, spongy-looking toadstools, which look so poisonous, but which the elk and the bear love, and we roasted them for our supper with a very moderate pull from our pocket-flasks,—for he is a fool who drinks before he is out of the woods. There was certainly nothing to detain us in our beds, so at the earliest light which came to us down in our depths we struck out again, and during the day came to the Nehalem, down which, sometimes in the river and sometimes out of it, seemed the easiest path we had found.

Toward evening we saw signs of a clearing. True, it was partly a clearing, but chiefly a small natural meadow in the curve of the river.

Here it was much lighter than in the forest. At the upper edge of the opening was a large ancient beaver dam, over which the water splashed merrily, heedless of the changes of time,—the never-ceasing laughing of Nature. At the farthest edge of the meadow, on a little knoll, we could dimly see in the rainy twilight the outline of a house,—a pleasant sight, for on a rainy November night there is nothing really so important as a good roof. The house was dark and silent. There was no sound of dogs or cattle. Therefore, we were not surprised to find the place deserted.

Deserted it evidently had been for years. The fence around the house had fallen to decay and we noted with interest that it was a rustic fence, made with much state from cedar-roots and twisted limbs. Neat steps with a rustic hand-rail led from the lower side of the enclosed garden down a steep bank to the river below. These steps were decayed and broken. A neglected orchard filled a gentle slope back of the house. But Nature, ever struggling to be kind, had filled the moss-choked trees with fruit. Many apples still clung to the boughs, and were good. All things are good to the starving. Back of the orchard was a cedar hedge, now sprawling wildly, all uncared for. Everything showed that at some time here had been unusual taste and care. It was too dark now to see far, but fronting the neat front porch (also of rustic finish) was a huge fir tree, one of Nature's most royal monarchs. It was twenty-five feet, or more, in circumference and towered into the sky at least two hundred and fifty feet,—an hundred feet of straight, massive column, unbroken by a limb; Titan of an earlier world; living monument of nearly a thousand years of time; a great tree, and ancient when Columbus set sail. Its bark was broken into netted scars five inches deep. It was a cosmos in itself. The moss and lichens of centuries grew upon it. Ants and squirrels were dormant under its roots. Salal-bushes and vine-maples grew upon its knees and in the summer season birds dwelt safely in its branches. In its keeping, at its feet, were two graves, side by side. At the head of each was a plain cedar cross, and a great cross was cut in the bark of the venerable fir which had wept its balsam out of the wound in streaming tears.

The rain increased with the night. Deserted though it was, and melancholy as it now seemed, we turned to the house for shelter, oppressed with the solemnity of the evening, the forest, and the sight of a grave,—that reminder of what we all must come to—the unbroken silence; the eternal dark.

We found the door not locked, but in good order; the windows whole, except one pane. There were chairs and a table in the main room, which were beautifully made; some from the vine-maple in rustic form; some from cedar, finished and polished. The table was made of boards cut from cedar-roots and carefully fitted and polished. Some books and newspapers lay on the table; these we found to be in French. In the shed, which made part of the house, we found plenty of fir-roots and split stumps, full of pitch, from all of which we argued that the place could not have been deserted for as long as it seemed, or that it was in a most isolated spot.

It was not long till a blaze was roaring up the chimney-throat and we were steaming before it. Blessed is warmth after wet and cold, and comfort after toil. We found two easy rocking-chairs, and congratulated ourselves on the difference between our fortune of this night and the night before. The wind had suddenly increased to a tempest and made war upon the forest; the rain had increased and was pouring down with a heavy splash and hum. The trees wrestled together and groaned; sometimes there would be the artillery report of a great limb thrown as an offering to the storm, or the passing of a patriarch of the forest whose time had come.

We found one comfortable peculiarity in this house. The wood-shed, the store-room and the well were all grouped together with covered ways communicating, so there was no need to be exposed to the weather in getting either wood or water, and as we drew a bucket of sparkling water from the well, we remarked that the builder of this house was a man thoughtful for his own comfort. "Or his wife's," added Andy.

We could have dispensed with the books and papers, especially as they were in French, in return for biscuit and cheese, but there was not a scrap of food to be found, so we gathered some of the belated apples and, feeling safe, we treated ourselves to liberal grog, then lighted our pipes and fell to speculating as to the two sleepers out there in the rain and the storm, under the giant fir, themselves so much again a part of Nature that they now reveled in the rain and storm as did the ferns and wild rose-bushes which dripped the abundance of Heaven's dews upon them.

I want to tell the events of that night as accurately as I can, because I believe half the strange experiences related as ghost stories are either imagined afterward, or deliberately fabricated.

After looking through the three other rooms of the house and finding no beds, we settled into our comfortable rocking-chairs for the night. Those who have kept up a fire all night will understand how we dozed until the fire went down and then, roused by the chilliness, one of us threw on another chunk and we dozed again.

I say we found no beds, but in a large room, which fronted the east and a beautiful stretch of the river, there was built into one corner a heavy cedar bedstead with carved sideboards and posts and, against the wall, carved pilasters. The carving was of flowers and leaves, crudely done, but with real feeling and beauty. There was no mattress, however, so, as I have already stated, we betook ourselves to the chairs.

The wind blew hard all night, somewhat abating toward morning. About midnight I was awakened by a tapping on the window-pane. I looked up quickly, but saw nothing, and the tapping ceased. I did not think much of this, for an old house, in the midst of a forest, on a windy night, produces all manner of noises. I soon dozed off, but was again wakened by this tapping, and I found Andy also staring at the window. "What's the matter?" said I. "Nothing," he answered. "I thought I heard someone tapping at the window." We mended the fire and slept.

I was awakened by a sigh, right in my ear, as it seemed. The fire had burned down, and I was chilled. The mysterious sigh made my blood run cold, in spite of the fact that I put it down to the imagination of one just about to awake. Again I built up the fire and was in the delicious state of warmth and drowsiness, but not asleep, when there was the slight rustle of silk, or it might have been the papers on the table, and a long-drawn, sobbing sigh, about which there could be no mistake. I jumped to my feet, wide awake, and with a chill of terror. "Who's there?" said I. Andy started up, and in his turn asked, "What's the matter?" To which I replied, as he had, "Nothing," and began to persuade myself I was the victim of my own imagination.

I could not sleep after this, but kept up the fire while Andy dozed until dawn. Andy awoke as I threw a fresh stump on the fire, and I asked, "How do you feel?" "Fine," answered he. "Only between the tapping on that window and the sighing of the draught in my ear I haven't slept much at a stretch, but it beats the leeside of a wet log."

We had no breakfast to get and therefore as soon as the light was strong enough, we started. Before we left we took one last look at the deserted but beautiful spot, the neat cabin embowered in wild clematis, the tangled garden and orchard and the two graves with no letter or sign above them, save the sign of the cross.

We left the sleepers to their slumber and the place to silence, which Nature loves and man hates; for every step of his accomplishment is accompanied by increasing noise.

That day we came to our own camp and had breakfast, dinner and supper in one. I asked the camp-tender about the deserted cabin, but like ourselves he was new to the country and knew nothing about it.

After I had finished the job and had come out to Nehalem City, I found everyone knew. The first person I spoke to, rugged Captain Olafson, did not answer, but looked at me curiously and then asked in a voice of awe, "Did you for true sleep there?"

"Certainly," I answered.

"I would not have done it for ten million dollars," he said. "I would rather have slept in the woods if it had been raining hell-fire. Didn't you hear something?"

"Hear what?" I asked, with something of a clutch at my heart.

"A tapping at the window and sighs," whispered the captain, at which my blood ran cold, but the old captain would not discuss the question further than to say, "The house is haunted." But what the captain would not tell, others with less tact hastened to say.

The house was haunted and any one who slept in it would die within the year. What creatures of superstition we are in the face of the great unsolved mystery we all shrink from. I admit I have never quite forgotten this prediction, and it has been an anxious year, and now, just as I was prepared to laugh at the credulous and point to a denial of the prophecy, Andy has been killed in just such another storm, and as for myself, well, I am frightened. I do not want to die.

* * * *

This is the tale of the cabin as it was given me.

Jack Reno (originally Jacque Renaut) was a French-Canadian, who trapped fur through the mountains: bear, mink, otter, and when the law allowed, or when the place was solitary enough, beaver. Reno had a contempt for the law, saying, "What is it? Who made it? The people? Yes, I have seen the people. Some cheap lawyers and sharp fellows, loud mouthed, except when sucking a cigar or looking through the bottom of a glass. A peaceable man who does not steal can make his own law. Why not?" Therefore, Reno settled at that beautiful bend in the river where we found the cabin, because it was a solitary spot with beaver-dams above and below. He built himself a small cabin of one room and prospered, being of good habits and of a thrifty race.

Rita Jansen was a daughter of the Northland, and of Jan Jansen, a fisherman, who cast his nets into the all-devouring sea once too often and left Rita toddling about as indifferent to death and what she should eat and wherewithal she should be clothed as ever were the sparrows. Had she been of the age of reason, she would have been glad—no, probably not, being a woman. But she ought to have been glad that some maid of the sea reached up out of those depths and gently dragged Jan Jansen to her bower. He only fished for drink; which is one reason why, added to the scarcity of unowned females, he had not provided Rita with a second mother immediately on the death of her own,—a timid woman, of sweet face and so frail you marveled how she could stand Jan's beatings.

Thus Rita fell heir to the town and *vice versa*.

There is one trait man still holds in common with his fellow-monkeys: He is not willing to see a helpless one of his race starve to death before his eyes. He is perfectly willing to starve them by the million, under pretense that they have a chance to work; but he is still so much the monkey that he cannot endure the cries of pain in his ears, or the sight of infant starvation in his very eyes. So Rita passed into the custody of Mother Simpson, to whom the county made an allowance for Rita's care and keep.

Man has still another monkey-trait, shared also by that noblest and most Christian animal, the dog, in that his sympathies are in direct proportion to the helplessness of the subject. Therefore, infants left on doorsteps by their careless parents are taken in and cherished, but a man seeking the same sanctuary is sent to the police-station.

When Mother Simpson died and her married daughter came down, like the Assyrian, and took possession of the humble shack with hop-vines over the little porch, Rita, being now fifteen, was sent out to earn her own living and make her own way in the world. The Lord had gilded her with a gift which he meant should be a bait and temptation unto all men forever, but which the monkey, man, in his folly, has determined shall be a curse unto woman,—beauty. Rita was marvelously beautiful; the beauty of the pink rose. Pale gold was her hair; her eyes the green of the sea with the bloom of the sky upon it; her skin, milk and roses; her nose straight and fine. And over all this sweet blossoming was a spirituality to be marveled at, considering her origin. She was undoubtedly burly Jan Jansen's daughter, but how came this flower from such a soil? A world-old question which Mother Earth delights in.

Perhaps her mother was from the Vikings, or perhaps Jan himself. He had some qualities which, with a good capacious skull as goblet, would have placed him high among the Vikings in Valhalla.

Rita gave promise in height and bust and shoulders of a woman of queenly mould. Partly by her youth, partly by her isolation, she was one of the fortunate, or unfortunate, waifs of beauty who escape the penalty of it. Jack Reno found her as waitress and maid of any and all work in the Astor House, a two-story land-wreck which may have derived its name because of the usual American lack of originality, or because Tim McGurth, the proprietor, was from Astoria, at the mouth of the Columbia. The hotel was not in any way connected with the Astor family.

Here, lending grace to her occupation by her sweetness, and pleasure to the guests by her beauty, Reno found her pure and dewy as a morning rosebud in the mountains, and as she handed him his coffee he fell in love.

It is no lengthy siege, this falling in love. Tut! A slip—a splash—and you are in all over. The trouble is nowadays in getting out.

It was springtime. Jack Reno had sold his winter catch and his buckskin-sack was heavy with gold. He had bought what new traps and clothes he needed, flour, meal, sugar, coffee, soap, matches, beans and bacon for the summer, and still the buckskin-sack was very heavy. He felt happy and proud. He was a success. The world was before him and his cabin was in the sweetest spot in all the world, with beaver, mink, otter and bear in abundance around him, delightfully ready to lend him their hides. They were to him as labor is to capital.

Frankness and honesty are trademarks. They speak for themselves, and Rita, like all women unspoiled by hot-house falsities, had the woman's natural instinct for true manhood. In two days they were in cordial and trustful relations, as she never would have been to the end of time with the smart drummers who attempted to make love to her. She and Jack walked by the ever-angry sea, watched its teeth and heard its roar. Shall I say they drank of its majesty and eternity? I cannot tell. They were looking deeply into each other's eyes, and there, also, lay eternal depths.

On a warm, clear evening, when her work was done, they sat on the dry sand, near the line of stunted spruce-trees, which for centuries had been so savagely blown back by the storms that they had taken the fixed pose of trees bent in the very teeth of a gale. They were like hair blown back from the brow of Earth. Shall I say they noted the rich velvet green of these spruce walls and the lines which marked the persistent struggle for existence? No. Because I do not think they noticed these little dwarfed trees, all distorted, each rising a little higher than its forward protector. They noticed nothing, for they, also, were victims of the struggle for existence. The Evening Star came up and hung like a lantern in the East and said, "Lo, I am indifferent to all your loves and hates. I have looked, and shall look, upon many, many millions such poor moths of an hour."

Rita did indeed notice the star and, for something to say, whispered, "How bright is that star." But Jack drew her closer to him and murmured, "You are warmer." His arms gathered her in and she felt the womanly deliciousness of being mastered. The hypnotism of love, which made her happy to yield to him.

He told her that he loved her, and he told of the beautiful spot where, overlooking the river, he would build her the most perfect cabin ever offered to a bride, in the solemn solitude of the wilderness. He had known her fully three days. Why not? Leave the long and calculating siege and threadbare dalliance to love kid-gloved and corseted, alert for profit. There should be in love no cold calculation. The ecstasy of it is the freshness of it; the avalanche of it; the surge and madness of it; the youth of it. It is man's superstition and slavishness which blots the divine spark and makes necessary the caution to buy well and be bought well.

Calculating thoughts did not touch them. He had found his mate of all the world, and she hers. She had no doubt of him, nor of herself. She lay in his arms without fear and took his kisses deliciously,—stunned, as the lion's victim is dulled to the things of the world by the first blow of the all-powerful paw.

The resistless paw had struck her. She lay in Jack's arms without question, thrilled with wonderful thrills and glad that he found her sweet.

It was springtime. The Earth harkened unto a mysterious voice and awoke. She called to her children, "Live again." The Nehalem ran full and turbulent, muttering and mumbling incoherently to its stones, as it plunged toward the great devourer. The shining salmon, gilt with love, flashed like bolts of silver from salty abysses up to the clear and rippling fountain-heads, never to return; there to die as votaries of Love and Life and Death. These three always inseparable. So the queen-bee whirls to the upper empyrean, her wooers in mad pursuit of Death, through the flash of Love. To the fortunate victor, in the instant of his fortune, comes death. So it is eternally: Death that there may be Life. The polished wheat-kernel, with its vital germinal point, yields its existence to the Earth, that the tiny green spear may prick upward to flourish its lovely ribbons for that supreme wooer, the Sun. Out of the one are made many and the Earth is replenished many fold. Make me a wheat-grain, priest or philosopher, but one tiny grain, which will keep watch and ward on the swift race of the Earth in the Zodiac, sleeping undeceived through the rains and sunshine of autumn and of winter, but recognizing instantly the voice of the bridegroom in springtime, awaking at his touch and hastening, in satiny green, to meet him. By what mysterious alchemy does it draw life and strength from Earth's bosom and at last model many images of itself, each, also, pregnant with the inscrutable mystery of Life and the wisdom of multiplication? Make me but one such grain of wheat, O priest, or philosopher, and I will then listen to you when you prate of human love and the mating and destiny of man. I will harken when you profess to know exclusively what are the petty rules pleasing to Nature and Nature's God. Make me an egg, O lawgiver, but the tiniest egg of the dragon-fly—that angel of the air and the reedy pool; or of the life-tenacious frog, and teach that speck to inevitably grow into the tadpole, and the tadpole into the frog; or check, if you can, the irresistible destiny of the wriggling lizard to become a frog. Keep him always a tadpole, if you can. Or make me but one bud, which will unfold itself toward the sun and enter upon its wizardry of bottling the heat and light of the great Sun-God, or tell me why the bud of the pear, on the stem of the quince, will produce pears, not quinces; nay, make me but one grain of the golden pollen of the dandelion, with its life-giving power, and I will bow to you, O, inestimable ass, in your efforts to regulate the lives and loves of mankind.

It was springtime. A faint sparkle of green overspread the ruddy wildrose-thicket. The alders and ash trees in the bottoms wove a veil of shimmering greenery across the pearly-grey background. The skunk-cabbage rejoiced at the summons and reached a golden hand up from the black bog where all winter it had lain drowned. The dogwoods spread their great bouquets of star-blossoms against the dark hillside, and the vine-maples, with pink buds and wine-colored blossoms, were tipped as with fire. Suddenly all the birds had appeared, by one wave of the magician's wand; larks whistled from tree-tops; and blackbirds from the willows and in the low places trilled their melodious tinkle.

It was springtime. The Sun worked his mastery. It was good to live. The breast of Earth sent up an opalescent mist; lilies, purple pansies and dogtooth violets decorated the aisles of the forest; aisles which led deeper to the shrine of silence and great peace. This was the first spring the world had ever known. Creation was just dawning. Life was new-made. The world was now fresh from the Creator's hand, and this was the birth hour of Jack and Rita. They thought neither of the limitless past, nor of the limitless future. Life for them, too, had just begun. Eternity was with them. Silence was eloquent. They touched hands and lips. They drew close to each other and were comforted. They paused to kiss and search each other's eyes, walking through a pregnant world jeweled with buds and joyous with song. So they passed through the Earth and found it Paradise.

It is very difficult for lovers to part. Thanks be to God that it is so. —Wonderful frenzy! Jack Reno was helped by the thought that the sooner he began work on that cabin, the sooner would he have her for his very own, so one day he kissed her for the last time and set out up river.

It is not necessary to follow precisely his ardent exertions in selecting the beautiful promontory, hewing and fitting the logs for the Cabin of the Heart, arranging woodshed and well and store-house all under one roof, tight and dry, so that his beloved need not be blown of the winds, nor even wet her pretty feet: an inspiration of love which made him often laugh softly to himself, thinking how surprised and pleased she would be. At night he made rustic furniture for her delight. He had a natural gift for carving and carved lovingly the fixed bedstead which he built into the corner of their room—their room. It was a thought which thrilled him. He hung in this room the crucifix his mother had given him when he left home in upper Quebec. He had grown much away from it himself, but it was a womanly thing,—his mother's—and he had a happy feeling of love and superstition in placing it above the spot where the head of his wife was to rest. He worked with the enthusiasm of a nest-building bird, feverishly, to make ready the nest. Several times he could not endure absence longer and hurried down to Nehalem City to see his beloved. Not Carthage and Dido were so dear to Aeneas as this rickety town and Rita were to him. Each time he brought back with him a load of things for the cabin. Finally came the last trip before the last, the last time he would go solitary and unaccompanied up the silver pathway to the forest home,—the love-built nest.

Nature had dipped her garments into dyes of orange and red and gold. She was scattering jewels upon the winds. The young and lusty winter was despoiling her and days were near when it would be good to sit by the fire and watch the slant of the pearly rain. The woodshed was well-stored with a full winter's supply of stumps and roots for the fireplace and split wood for the stove. The nest was well-built and well-lined. The day for the wedding was set and Jack was hastening the last touches. He had brought up grapevines and apple-trees in the spring and they were flourishing. He had set wild clematis about the porch and had set out a hedge of cedar to fence in the orchard close. How surprised she would be, the gentle-hearted Rita. He carried the joy of it with him. How happy they both would be here in this true home in the great silence, alone with love. In three days more he would start. He knew how she longed for him. Every day she walked up to the long reach of the river whence she could see his coming for a great distance. Every morning she prayed for him and said, "This is one day nearer to his coming." Every night she prayed for him and said, "This day has brought us one day nearer to each other." She adored him. She was ready to die for him. That is why man's love can never measure itself against woman's love, for the love of man is a passing thing at best, but the love of a woman says always, "If need be, I will die for the love of thee. I am ready."

In three days more Jack Reno would start down the river. He built a fire in the great fireplace and he sat before it, thinking of her: How tall she was and her crown of golden hair. How sad and true were her eyes. How soft and warm her lips. How beautiful she was. How honest and how pure. He grew drowsy before the fire and fancied himself still sitting there with her beside him, gently stroking his cheek, and a child of theirs upon each knee, boy and girl. Why was God so good to him?

Just then there was a tapping at the window and looking up he saw a bird fluttering at the window-pane, tap, tapping with its bill. He grew cold and pale in an instant. In the superstition in which he had been reared, this was the certain call of death. It was the spirit of some loved one come to salute the living and calling to him. He arose from his chair, the sweat starting on his brow. The bird disappeared into the night, but only for an instant. It returned, fluttering and tapping at the pane. Again it disappeared. Again it returned. And Reno, with his staring eyes fixed upon it, said solemnly, aloud, "I will come. I will come." Then it disappeared and returned no more.

With terror gripping his heart, Jack Reno went into the darkness, untied his skiff, and with Dread for his companion, he pulled long and strong down the sobbing pathway to the sea.

It was bright day when he came to the long reach of the river where she used to watch for him. Worn and wearied, he still swept his oars with long strong stroke; his head bowed; his eyes seeing nothing. Suddenly there was a shout from the shore and he saw Nels Kesterson, on horseback, beckoning to him. He swerved in to the shore, knowing that he was now to hear the evil tidings.

"I was just going for you," said Nels, swinging down from the foaming horse. "Here, ride in. I will bring the boat. Rita is awful sick. She wants you."

"I know it," said Jack, and that was all he said. He lifted himself into the saddle and was off like a mad rider. But ride fast as he may, there is a swifter rider.

When he threw himself to earth at the little cottage, there was a group of weeping women to meet him. One of them took him by the hand and said, "She is dead." They led him into the room and he knelt by the bedside, calling, "Rita! Rita!" so that it seemed even the dead must hear. But the calm, sweet face changed not.

"Leave me with her," he prayed, wringing his hands. And they left him.

All that night and all the next day he stayed by her side. Then he came out and said, "I am hungry. I want to eat and sleep. Tomorrow I shall take her home."

On the morrow he laid her in his skiff so tenderly, so gently, as indeed he would have laid her. He would have none with him. With slow and measured strokes he passed on, up the sliding liquid pathway, with his beloved, to their home. They two alone, as it was to be. Up the murmurous and shining pathway, into the great silence.

Those who fearing for him went after him two days later found them lying side by side, under the great fir tree, his own knife in his heart.

They buried them where they lay and set the crosses above them. There was no one to inherit the cabin and it was left reverently alone for some time, and then some people undertook to move into it, but they were driven away after the first night by the strange noises and sights and sighs which made the place terrible, and it was noticed that one by one they died, until at the end of the year not one was living. So superstition shrouded the house until an old trapper, not knowing of the circumstances, undertook to make his home there, and he, too, was driven out, and he was found tangled in one of his own traps, drowned. Since then superstitious fear had been a perfect protection to it and it was well believed that whoever should sleep in the Deserted Cabin would have his death summons surely before the year is out.

So ends the tale. Andy has gone and I confess I have lived in something of superstitious fear. But now, as I write, the hand of the dial is almost upon the very last hour of the year and I —

Introduction to "The Christmas Burden"

Wood's romance with occasional pieces flourished most ferociously around Christmas. Soon after the turn of the century, he began the custom of sending out Christmas missives, often exquisitely printed, to friends and family. His ire at human hypocrisy found Christmas particularly fertile ground.

For the next fifteen years, Wood printed and distributed something nearly every Christmas. In later years in California, he periodically resurrected the custom. The central target of Wood's Christmas pieces, achieved, as was his way, in various forms—a lyric with olde English spelling, several ballads, a fairy tale, a masque, a one-act play, and even a cantata—is the hypocrisy of Christmas. Whether simply or elaborately, Wood never fails to make the point that social justice, feeding and helping the poor, is the true spirit of Christmas, of Christ, and should not be an annual occurrence but a daily one.

The theme of Christ returning to earth unrecognized and persecuted once again is one of Wood's favorites, weaving its way through his Christmas pieces and various other works.

THE CHRISTMAS BURDEN

Merry Christmas! I have reformed. All times are good for repentance, but surely there is none better than Christmas. Repentance suits the season, and how much nobler it is to reform before Christmas than a week after, when good resolutions are cheap as rain in spring, or snow in winter, or falling leaves in autumn. I have reformed and I am proud of it. Repentance and pride are twins. No man can truly repent and not feel proud of that fact. Thus it is that in this Merry Christmas season I thank God I am not as other men, and I wish you Merry Christmas.

To reform is almost to confess a former state of error—but not always, for it is possible to reform from too much goodness or what is mistaken for goodness. There is something also to be said about error. To err is human and it is a great thing to be natural in anything. What is sin? It is difficult to define and very elusive. The more you try to answer this question the more it will be borne in on you that sin is what you do not care to do yourself. Christmas and Christmas festivities used to be sin, and music and kissing—which still is, if the right person be the wrong one. To keep Ramadan religiously would be a sin to some Christians, yet it is a very solemn religious fast to other people. But the great beauty inseparable from sin is that without it there could be no repentance. Repentance is the most precious of all things. It means struggle, and struggle means growth.

What a world if every one lived the perfect life! Nature abhors monotony. The daisy and the apple tree shun it, as well as man. If all men were perfect there could be no comparison. No strong to help the weak and no weak to help the strong. No sinners, in the contemplation of whom the righteous could feel more righteous. No righteous, in the contemplation of whom the sinner could feel content. If there were no sin, there could be no righteousness. It would be as dull as Heaven. Sin is necessary, for it marks goodness and permits repentance; and repentance is beautiful, if it be really sincere, for it suggests the possibility of sinning again, like fitful music heard half dreaming. To have sinned splendidly and repented sincerely is really a soulful life.

Narrow people, who insist that the world was made yesterday and will perish tomorrow and that wisdom will die with them, believe that reform must be permanent. This is desirable, if the reform be not worse than the sin, but the essential quality of repentance is that it be sincere at the time. The truth of the matter was stated by the severely religious old captain of infantry who, being reproached for his frequent lapses into drunkenness, said: "The Lord Jesus Christ does not ask men not to fall. All he asks is that every time they get up they keep coming toward him."

I hope with the help of my good friends to make my reform permanent, but be that as it may, I am at present sincerely determined not to give Christmas gifts. There are many causes which have brought about my repentance. In the first place, I have given away nearly everything I do not care for, and I am so confused as to who gave me the remaining things which I would be glad to be rid of, that I fear I might give them back to the donors, and this would not be in the true spirit of Christmas or Christianity. For we ought to return good for evil.

In the next place, the art of giving is so difficult that a drama could be written or the cellar cleaned with less expense of strength and thought and time than is required to determine the very thing fit to be given to each person. The lady who gave her husband eighteen yards of maroon silk as a Christmas gift did not comprehend the whole art of giving—or perhaps she did. To give a child the new shoes he has much needed is, to my mind, obtaining Christmas under false pretenses. A Christmas gift ought not to be that which we are in duty bound to furnish, and it ought to be that which will give pleasure and surprise. For example, this epistle. But it is impossible for any mind less omnipotent than that of all-seeing Jove, the cloud-compelling, or of our worthy President, to do all things well at all times, with never a nod toward the mortal march of error. The following unfilial letter will show that even I have slipped:

Dear Father: As you always give me books for Christmas, which are nice to have unless you prefer to send money and save your time, I write to say not to send me this year the Ballad of Reading Gaol. I have read what you said, or what you said Wilde said, about its being the cry of Marsyas and not the song of Apollo, and I guess that's right, but as you have sent me a copy for four Christmases, I don't believe any more will do me any good.

A feeling of shame causes me to suppress the name of this ingrate.

A careful study of the letter has aroused in me a suspicion that it hints at sending money instead of books. I will not do it. Money is (in a sense) the cheapest and easiest gift of all. It is a labor-saving device. It contains no flavor of thought or warmth of individuality. For these (and other) reasons I never send checks.

No gift should be so valuable as to beget an obligation or start a race on the debit and credit plan. In the expenditure of time and thought and care and strength and money; in the creation of an endless chain of obligation and in the remorse of Christmas bills; Christmas has become a burden, and instead of a restful season, with peace on earth, good will toward men, it has become a season of exhaustion and worry, with a hatred for mankind and a mad longing for solitude. So I have reformed. I shall give no more Christmas gifts. If there be showered upon me the treasures of Ormus and of Ind, I shall accept them, but I will give nothing back.

And lastly, for even a Christmas sermon must come to an end, I will tell two out of many experiences to show why I have repented of giving to him that hath.

Last Christmas afternoon I was walking down North Fourth Street, when my attention was attracted to two little girls in the squalid yard of a squalid house, in the window of which was a sign "Lodgings to let." They were around a small branch of evergreen stuck in a corner of the grassless yard, the bough evidently borrowed from a scanty hedge which graced the sidewalk in front of a saloon next door. The arms of the little girls were too thin, their faces too white, and there were blue, semi-transparent circles under their eyes. They looked shabby and neglected, and yet an effort to be gay showed through the neglect, each having a new bright blue ribbon in her hair. They were fussing about the branch of evergreen like a couple of sparrows, and had decorated it with two pieces of tobacco tinfoil, three cigar ribbons (one red and two yellow), several gilt paper cigar bands—all evidently spoils from the saloon—and three pink tissue paper parcels, the tissue paper being orange-wrappers from the fruit stand opposite, the bulging contents, dirt from the yard—cheap and probably nutritious. As they fluttered about their scrawny bush with an air partly suggestive of nest-building and partly of an artist stepping back to view his work, they chattered to themselves, and I gathered that father would be greatly pleased with their tree when he returned and they hoped he would have money enough to take them out to a Christmas dinner at twenty-five cents each. Presently a mechanic, in a suit of threadbare best clothes, came slowly up the street, walking like a sick man and looking so white it seemed a pity that he had cleaned himself up for Christmas day. This was father, and as he entered the yard, of course he had to admire the Christmas tree, which he did as might a dying man. He took from his pockets two small oranges and handed one to each of the little girls, and then the smaller piped up, "Are we going to have any Christmas dinner, dad?" I didn't hear what he answered, but he climbed the rickety steps and went into the cheerless house, shutting the dirty unpainted door behind him and somehow leaving the impression that he might never come out again. The little girls began trying to tie their oranges on to their tree, finding great difficulty in doing so. While thus engaged, some seafaring gentlemen suddenly erupted from the neighboring saloon, clinging together like swarming bees. They had evidently had their land legs on for some time and began tacking down the street toward the children. They, or some one of them, saw the Christmas tree and the swarm settled on the fence and began quarreling as to whether it wasn't a pretty little tree or wasn't a shame (more or less qualified) that such pretty and decent little girls should have for their Christmas tree such a wretched scavenger's swab, as one of the gentlemen termed it. He tossed a half dollar into the yard, and then, with spontaneous unanimity, Danae's shower of gold was imitated in silver, in a modest way. Having done this act of Christmas charity, the marine swarm drifted down the street. The little girls quickly gathered up two dollars and seventy-five cents, and first plucking their oranges from the tree, they hastily disappeared in glad excitement behind the sad-looking door.

The tree remained a monument to the truth that those who have little are easily pleased. Indeed, it seemed to me, as I looked at this Christmas tree, that when it takes so little to please, it is a pity that such as these should not have at least one happy day in the year.

The other experience I shall mention is taken from this joyous month of December, 1906. There came to my office a worn woman with the unmistakable look of the underfed and the gentle timidity which in a pushing world means failure. Her garments were faded, mended and turned. She wore a poor thin wrap and clutched an invalid umbrella, her fingers sticking out at the ends of her despairing gloves. She and the umbrella were dripping wet. She was looking for work. Anything to keep body and soul together. Life was just a struggle to live and not a struggle for love of life, but for love of her children; and she the daughter of a musician, herself fond of music and good books and knowing good from evil. There were five children, hourly illustrating to her Nature's great truth that to live we must eat. Five children to be fed, clothed and, if possible, protected. I asked what had become of her husband. "Gone," she said. "But it doesn't make any difference. He has given us nothing for a long time. It wouldn't be so bad if I had my health, but I have been sick so much and Nelly has nursed me. You don't know how bad it makes me feel to see her so thin and worn before she is even grown," and her eyes filled with tears, which she put aside in quite a matter of fact way. "Why don't you lay the law on your husband's back?" said I. "Get a decree from the court commanding him to return and be a man, ordering him to do his duty and help care for these children?" "I didn't know there was such a law," she said. "What? Didn't you know that there is a law for everything? That the law will cure every evil and is omnipotent? You may thank your stars that no legislature has seen fit to pass a law declaring the moon to be green cheese." "Oh, well," she said, very simply, "I don't know where he is, anyway. They tell me you are fond of pictures, so I brought one, hoping you might buy it or get some one to buy it. We always considered it very fine, but I don't know its value and will be glad to get anything, for I must pay the rent and get some flour." I saw at once that I would be doing art a great service if I bought the picture and burned it. I would be ashamed to tell what I paid for it. When I think of the hopeless face, the shabby gloves and the five children, I am ashamed that it was so little, and when I think of the picture, I am ashamed that it was so much. So I said to her, and also to myself to excuse my insult to art, "This will help toward Christmas," but she said without any bitterness, speaking listlessly as one who has accepted fate and given up hope, "Oh, we never think of that; we don't have any Christmas," and she thanked me and went out. Five children in the house and no Christmas, and Christmas day is the feast day of him who said, "Suffer little children to come unto me." Childhood, the time, if ever, for joy and gladness, and no Christmas! It really seems to me that if Christ kept his own day, we of the swallow-tailed coats and brilliant overloaded tables would not even see him. He would not choose to be with us, but would be scattering gladness among the children of the poor, and if we met him perhaps we would not know him. Perhaps we do meet him and never guess it.

But I have reformed. What I have to give I shall give to the soup-kettles of the Salvation Army and to other soup-kettles. It must be almost as much satisfaction to discover for one's self a worthy soup-kettle and make it boil over as to fail to discover the North Pole.

Hunting for game may be replaced by the excitement of a search for him who, but for the discovery, would have passed a cheerless Christmas day. He might perhaps be found in the hospital or in jail, and there is precedent for this. On Christmas Day, too, I confess to the weakness of thinking of the degenerates; for example, the confirmed drunkards. It is not for me to say how they came to be drunkards and why they are not governors or bishops or editors. It is not for me to say why I am not a drunkard; but I, by grace of fate, not being a drunkard, feel tempted to hand to my brother, who by curse of fate is a drunkard, the means to a Merry Christmas in his own way. If not, how shall I, without hypocrisy, wish him a Merry Christmas, as I do to you, my more sober friends?

But I have reformed, and I give fair warning that no one need expect a Christmas gift from me, except that if the best of a Christmas gift be the thought which prompts it and the feeling which goes with it, you have it here from me, and I wish you in truth a Merry Christmas.

INTRODUCTION TO "PORTLAND'S FEAST OF ROSES"

IN JUNE 1908, Wood contributed to *Pacific Monthly*'s promotional dimension with Portland's "Feast of Roses,"an essay celebrating what was later to be known as The Rose Festival. In an impressive display of erudition he looks back three thousand years to ancient Rhodes, the original Rose City, and then reels off a series of literary quotations concerning roses by Homer, Horace, Spenser, Herrick, and Hafiz. Coming up to his own times (the section excerpted here), he reminds his readers what early Portland was like and then strikes a remarkably modern note by decrying the rape of the ancient forests by the timber tycoons. This was a time of prodigal timber cutting with little concern for the forests of the future. The "sweet breathing space" Erskine mentions at the close of his piece refers to Portland's west hills, often called "The Heights," and has been preserved in the form of handsome residences of the wealthy. The accompanying sonnet is Wood's own.

Wood's knowledge of both world and regional history, his sensitive descriptions of nature, his foreboding as to the ultimate fate of Oregon's forests, all combine to raise this essay a good cut above the promotional prose so typical of the first quarter of the twentieth century.

FROM PORTLAND'S "FEAST OF ROSES"

If Portland seems to me to have burst the bud like a rose touched by the summer sun, how must it seem to those still living who remember the Rose City as, in 1847, a forest of firs out of the shadows of which stole a few frame shacks along the edge of the Willamette; a bakery on the north side of Morrison Street, which street was named for J. L. Morrison, who had a little store at the foot of it. Pettygrove's store, at the foot of Washington Street, a log cabin at the foot of Burnside (on Captain Couch's donation land claim), Job McNamee's log house at Front and Alder, Terwilliger's blacksmith shop on Main Street, between First and Second; the salmon fishery at the foot of Salmon Street, and on the corner of Taylor and Front the most superb structure in Portland. Waymire's double log cabin. On the bank of the river was his sawmill, a whip-saw operated by two men, one in the sawpit and one on the log. Humble beginning for the city which today manufactures more lumber than any city in the world: chief city of a state which holds one-sixth of the timber of the United States, more than three hundred billion feet, with twenty-three billion feet additional from that part of Washington tributary to the Columbia. Metropolis of a territory two hundred and twenty-five thousand square miles in extent. If only Tallantyre and Waymire, the two whip-saw lumber mill men of Portland sixty years ago, could stand as I have stood on the heights above the city on a sparkling autumn morning and mark the straight columns of steam rising all along the river like great altar-fires, blending with the pearly clouds and reflected in the river so that earth and sky mingled in one vaporous mystery, what a dream it would seem. To the silence of these heights rises the constant drone of the great band-saws which are slicing up five hundred and fifty million feet of lumber a year. Perhaps to these pioneer sawyers it would seem even more a dream if they were brought face to face with one of these great mills with its acres of stored lumber, its wilderness of electric lights at night, the scream of its saws, and the rumble of its chains and rollers; its giant log-ways, the Titanic power which snatches from the river, as a monster seizing its prey, logs five feet, even six feet and more in diameter, and rolls, shifts and adjusts them to its maw as if they were straws.

Like our great counterparts the Romans, we are, as I have said, a commercial and a utilitarian, not a poetic or artistic people. Our genius, too, is for construction; construction in institutions as well as in stone and mortar. Our art finds its place in skyscrapers and bridges. The dreamer has no place with us, though all which truly lives forever has begun as a dream. Three hundred billion feet of timber in Oregon are impossible figures to count on the fingers, but they are easily grasped by arithmetic. It is no trouble to divide them by Portland's own cut of lumber (which is only a part of the total cut), five hundred and fifty million feet a year, and to guess at the day when the Oregon forests shall not be. The City of Roses carved from that forest will have to take its visitors even now far to show them so much as a few acres of an unbroken forest, and it is so everywhere. The dollar rules, and except for the Government reservations there has been no thought of preserving a specimen of what mysterious Nature was a thousand years in building into infinite beauty with infinite patience. When I see a dead giant rising from the river and placed dripping and naked before the saw, stripped of its armor of rugged bark to which the lichens and mosses clung lovingly till the last, I am foolish enough to think of the past ages and the future, and to believe that it is not necessary all should be wiped off clean, and when I hear the shriek of the log at the first bite of the saw I am Greek enough to think of Daphne and the dryads and the hamadryads, and I like to think of the shadowy aisles of an untouched Oregon forest, where the sky is blotted out by the dark and over-arching roof of green and into the sky, smooth and clear and round, for one hundred, two hundred feet rise the great solemn columns of this cathedral, I smell the balsam and feel the soft carpet of needles and of moss and look into those bluish depths where the giant trunks become almost ghostly and, behind that veil, it seems to me still lingers the Great Spirit of Creation. There brooding Silence shuts out the world and in these temples there is perfect rest. It seems to me that this great beauty and solemnity is perhaps as valuable as the shriek and clamor of the mill. It is a pity to have all this majesty of antiquity wholly destroyed. Man cannot restore it. It cannot be rebuilt by Nature herself in less than a thousand years, nor indeed ever, for it never is renewed the same. Nor do the Government reservations preserve this to us; they, too, are wholly utilitarian and their plan contemplates the gradual sale and destruction of these Titans. There is no spot where the primeval forest is assured from the attack of that worst of all microbes, the dollar.

But Portland in her Feast of Roses is to throw commerce and the dollar to the winds. For one week at least she invites you to joy and beauty. To open your eyes and see the world you live in. King Rex—

which sounds tautological to say the least, but perhaps it is spelling Wrecks as Thompson spelled wrinkles—is to lead the festal procession, and with him it will be as with Browning's patriot:

> It was roses, roses all the way
> And myrtle mixed in my path like mad;
> The house-roofs seemed to heave and sway,
> The church spires flamed the flags they had.

And no veering of the fickle populace with King Rex on the scaffold at the end of his journey.

The city will be gay. It is a good thing, for tomorrow we die. The wise and inscrutable Celestial will hang out his great diaphanous lanterns with splendid red letters and invite you to his Orient-smelling shop, or serve you chop-suey, delicious tea, almonds and ginger and kumquhats in syrup on the balcony of his restaurant. The ships which carry wheat and flour and canned salmon to feed the world will flutter their many-colored buntings and perhaps the battleships—those wastrels of the Nation in which the people persist in taking delight—will sit upon the bosom of the Willamette like sacred swans. *Themmes* had his Spenser and the Willamette, its Sam Simpson. Get his beautiful *Willamette* and read it, if you read poetry. No one does. The Willamette is one of her jewels which Portland will show you. Her very own. She shares it not with other states or even other nations, as she must the Columbia. The Willamette, more gentle than the mighty Columbia, sings sweetly to its banks of green as it comes from the Southland.

Today (the end of April) the maples, hazels, alders and willows make a bright, bright new green with their young leaves, so that the river is all emerald and sapphire. The wild currant bushes make spots of coral pink along the bank and the hills are gay with dogwood blossoms scattered like stars. Sylvan, crystal and beautiful, like a bride pacing down an avenue of blossoms, the Willamette comes to Oregon City and there, wild and disheveled, plunges over, scattering for our uses in its plunge one and a half times the power given by the Mississippi at the Falls of St. Anthony; and then, as if subdued, our beautiful river flows more broadly to Portland, decorated with verdant islands and guarded by hills of bluish green which cast their reflections into the water, giving it where it mingles with the sky, the liquid and changeful beauty of the peacock's breast.

Portland will decorate her streets for her Feast of Roses, but if you would truly see the beauty she has to offer, go upon her hills. The city lies in an amphitheatre surrounded by hills seven hundred and a thousand feet high, soft with green of many hues. From these hills the city itself takes its place as only a bright and scattered spot in the landscape; its spires and towers rising above the common level; its smoke and steam wreathing about it; its houses half-concealed in trees and shrubbery, and the river lying like a silver ribbon through this house-clustered area which lies like a dotted rug upon the scene. Blue to the south is the valley of the Willamette; blue to the north the valley of the Columbia; blue to the east the great Cascade range, toward which roll the lesser hills, paling as they go and bright with villas and villages. Set into this blue, like pearls upon a sapphire girdle, glow the great snow mountains: Jefferson to the south; Hood full in front, sometimes it seems just across the river; St. Helens, also, full before us, like a pearly bubble of the world, and above the horizon the peaks of Rainier on the Sound and Adams away up in the Yakima country. This is a picture never the same, nor ever was from Time's beginning, nor ever will be, and not the same hour by hour. I have watched Mt. Hood and, all in a single hour in the evening, have seen it pearly white afloat in blue; then delicate rose upon amethyst; then, when all the earth had fallen into deep purple shadow, above it, against a rosy sky, flamed the great snow-peak, glorious in the rays of the sun, which it alone of all the earth still caught in full effulgence. At such a moment the great mountain seems to glow with an internal fire, as if it were a molten mass of metal sending out light: straw color, orange, cherry red; and then in a moment it is gone. The shadows have climbed quickly to the summit and the cold mountain becomes a sentinel of the night. And cool caressing night comes with gentle step and healing finger tips, the earth vanishes and fairy land appears. Far as the eye can reach the lights of the city glitter like a lower heaven, and on clear nights it is as if the sky had fallen or the world was one vast starry and sparkling space. To these hills the birds resort in the evening, making a carnival of song till slumber hushes them. Here are leafy thickets of hazel, wild currant, plumy spirea, the orange-blossom syringa and wild rose. Groups of dogwood trees, white in the spring and red in the fall. Wide-spreading maples and young firs with aromatic smell. But the giants are all gone. In the middle distance, down the Willamette River, is a small white block with a black line of smokestack. It is one of the boasts of Portland, the Portland Flouring Mills which grinds for that wise people we are pleased to call the heathen, three-quarters of a million barrels of flour a year, and is the head of a system which grinds nearly two million barrels. But among these hills, with the plaintive warble of a thrush sounding from a grove and the great snow-peaks looming into the sky, the mill seems only a very small white speck on the face of Nature.

Here is a sweet breathing-place which should be secured for the toilers and the moilers before the city is too large.

> *Upon these heights lies Peace, with parted lips*
> *And far-fixed eyes. Here at her feet I lie*
> *And watch the silent pictures of the ships*
> *Which float upon the mirror of the sky*
> *Down by the city's wharves. Columns of steam*
> *Which everywhere, like giant incense white,*
> *Up from the busy hives straight godward stream*
> *Or on the winds take soft and curling flight.*
> *And far across the city, heaven-kissed*
> *The snow-crowned mountains, so serenely pure,*
> *Afloat upon a sea of amethyst,*
> *There to remain while Time shall yet endure.*
> *When I and all this city, too, shall cease,*
> *Still on these heights shall dream eternal Peace.*

And yet it is good to come down from the heights to the haunts of men; good to strike hands together; to laugh and if need be weep together. But there shall be no place for weeping in Portland's rose festival. It shall all be gladness and fragrance and roses, roses all the way; rose-chaplets and rose-bowers and rose-wreaths and if any have not a rosy wreath to send to his fair one, let him read to her old Ben Jonson's "Song to Celia," which I give in the original spelling, not only as a protest against the worthless art of spelling, but as carrying with it somewhat of the flavor of the time:

> *Drink to me onely with thine eyes*
> *And I will pledge with mine,*
> *Or leave a kisse but in the cup*
> *And I'le not looke for wine.*
> *The thirst that from the soul doth rise*
> *Doth aske a drinke divine,*

But might I of Jove's nectar sup,
I would not change for thine.
I sent thee late a rosie wreath,
Not so much honoring thee
As giving it a hope that there
It could not withered bee.
But thou thereon didst onely breathe,
And sent'st it backe to mee.
Since when it grows, and smells, I sweare,
Not of it selfe, but thee.

INTRODUCTION TO
"THE EXHIBITION OF PAINTINGS OF EASTERN OREGON
BY CHILDE HASSAM"

IT IS NOT SURPRISING that one of the earliest pieces "Ces" Wood
wrote for *Pacific Monthly* was called "Art, a Threadbare Subject."
He was an artist himself with both pencil and brush. He arranged
for Olin Warner, sculptor of the doors of Congress, to design and
sculpt the Skidmore Fountain in Portland. He was in continual
touch with the circle of avant garde New York artists he had met
as an officer on leave in 1882, through his ongoing
correspondence with J. Alden Weir and through brokering the
sale of their work among his wealthy Portland friends and
colleagues.

In 1908, with the promise of good fishing and the incredible
light and air of eastern Oregon, Erskine lured the American
impressionist Childe Hassam out to the Harney desert. Hassam
stayed in Oregon for two months, part of the time as a guest of
Wood's good friend Bill Hanley at Hanley's P Ranch. Hassam
painted 27 canvases that were exhibited at the Portland Art
Museum. Wood's commentary on that exhibition in the *Pacific
Monthly* of February 1909, which was illustrated with
reproductions of some of the paintings, includes his ideas on what
constitutes good art.

The Exhibition of Paintings of Eastern Oregon by Childe Hassam

Childe Hassam is an American artist and takes pride in that fact. He contends that the best painting produced in the world today comes from America. He received his training first in Boston and then in Paris.

Every man is in character and style the composite result of native qualities, environment and special influence. What of these ingredients can be weighed out in Mr. Hassam's case, or in any other man's, it is impossible to say. Some men are distinctly influenced by others and the influence is visible. Hassam is individual. In painting light and air he undoubtedly owes something to the perceptions of the French Impressionists, and in suggesting all the shimmer and vibration of open air and full sunlight he owes something to their technique, just as they owed something to their predecessors—for art, like every other thing in the universe, is evolutionary.

When all is said and done, however, Hassam is strikingly original—not only in style, but in concept. What makes him valuable to the world is that he was born a colorist,—born with a keen sense of beauty and a power for arrangement, and has mastered a technique quite his own which gives a wonderful facility. In the two months spent in Eastern Oregon, he painted (as I remember the number) the twenty-seven canvases recently exhibited at the Portland Art Museum, some very important in size (thirty by forty inches), besides some ten or a dozen small panels. His landscapes, even the largest, are painted in one "go" —say from two to five hours, with possibly some reconsideration or additional touches next day; but essentially the picture is done at once.

Hassam fulfills his own criterion of a painter; one who can paint what he sees, and who paints it as he sees it—seeing it beautiful. Portraits, nudes, still life, landscape, idyls, mural decorations. He is the omnivorous painter and always the artist. Unfortunately there are many skillful painters who are not artists. The artist is born, not made.

To those curious in hereditary traits, it is interesting to note that Albert P. Ryder, great colorist and poet dreamer in paint, and William Gedney Bunce, a great colorist, and Hassam are all of Puritan New England extraction. That is to say, men peculiarly sensuous and gifted with extreme sensitiveness to beauty are derived from Puritan stock. To them may be added Olin L. Warner, decidedly the greatest artist in sculpture this country has produced.

*"Afternoon Sky,
Harney Desert"
by Childe Hassam*

*Oil on canvas. 1908.
Reproduced by permission of
Portland Art Museum, Oregon.*

I have been awaiting the arrival of a catalogue giving details of Mr. Hassam's life and achievements, but now the printer is pressing so I can only add that Mr. Hassam was born in Boston and is represented in the principal permanent collections of the country and has been awarded all the honors to be secured in this country. This is well, for not often is genius recognized in its own day. But the important thing is that the people should appreciate him, and that I believe they do. The cowboys and stockmen seemed to find a delight in the beauty of the canvases he painted among them, quite as genuine though more picturesquely expressed than that of the cultured amateur. These men of the desert saw without exception what the more conventionally minded do not always see; that is, Hassam's power as a draughtsman, his insistence on form. Those who are schooled to believe drawing consists of a hard, continuous, well-defined line, fail to appreciate Hassam's really exquisite drawing, in which the line is lost at points and its value varies exactly as it does in Nature. It is this subtlety which aids so much toward the effect of light and air and the poetry of the picture. I have only time to add that nearly all the pictures exhibited in Portland were painted in Harney County, Oregon, the high, so-called desert plateau. One was done in Catlow Valley, and three of Malheur Butte, in Malheur County. They all express the clear air and brilliant, blazing light of these high dry altitudes. They are all done with an infallible instinct for decorative arrangement. They are all beautiful, all works of art. I am sorry I cannot describe them in detail. The reproductions give only an idea of the composition. The reader will have to imagine instead of these dull grays, the brilliant skies, luminous clouds, bright yellow foregrounds, or delicate light gray when it is sage brush, and the opalescent, far distant hills in the horizon.

A general introduction to Wood's poetry is provided in the section on the Third Stage of his life and work, beginning on page 212, since this is when his most masterful work in this genre was written. Here we present four earlier poems in a variety of styles.

INTRODUCTION TO "THE CHANT OF EL DORADO"

THIS IS AN EXAMPLE OF Wood's western verse, published in *Pacific Monthly* in 1909 under the nom de plume of William Maxwell, his father's first and middle names. It is a ballad of love and betrayal in the gold mining camps in the days of '49. Wood was writing in a popular mode: western verse that presented the lives and loves and landscapes of western America in ballad or ballad-like forms and in a romantic way was quite popular in this era. Both Wood and the editor of *Pacific Monthly*, Lute Pease, quite liked this form and Wood, writing under the same name, had a number of other ballads published in the monthly, with such titles as "A Song of Cowboys," "The Rancher," "Pulque," and "The Dance at Silver Valley."

THE CHANT OF EL DORADO

In my ears a song is singing
Of the lusty days of old,
When the blood ran hot and stinging
In the yellow camps of gold;
O, the days were all of glory
And the nights were wild and free,
And the pulsing of the story
Is like surges of the sea.

'Twas the blood of three and twenty
And it fired the veins like wine;
All the world was wide and plenty,
There was music in the pine.

There was music in the river,
There was gladness in the breath,
And we shook the leaden quiver
Of the silent archer—Death.

Then a tent was more than palace
There the stars in splendor shone,
And the red drops from the chalice
By a spendthrift hand were thrown;
Then we smote the hills with laughter,
And we reck'd not life a span,
With no dream of a hereafter,
And no care for God or man.

Those were days when, like the thistle,
Love came floating down the wind,
And with lilting lure and whistle
We beguiled him—Love is blind.
In the cabin in the canyon,
With the tall pines sighing down,
Lay my love, my doe, my Manon,
With the eyes so tender brown.

Soft her lips, as crimson roses,
And her soul was like the dew
When the morning mist discloses
The bright day-dawn showing through.
And I kissed her nightly, kneeling
To her crucifix in prayer;
All her loveliness revealing,
And I swore that she was fair.

By the love of God and human,
She made beautiful the spot.
O, the love of loving woman
Is the love which changeth not.
And we laughed and loved together
To the sobbing of the pines,
In the days of summer weather,
At the El Dorado Mines.

'Tis a boy will crush a sparrow
And throw wide the broken nest.
'Tis a man will drive an arrow
Through a loving, throbbing breast.
And I left her, though she loved me,
And I left her and I lied.
By the living God above me,
For the love of me she died!

Give me back my days of madness
When we made the golden quest;
Give me back the brimming gladness
In that canyon of the West.
Where the breezes fell to sighing
Through the tufted, tasseled pine,
And her kisses were replying
To the every kiss of mine.

Give me back the days of wonder
When young life was on the wing,
When our hearts beat deep as thunder
And a man was all a king;
When the days were full of glory
And the nights were wild and free.
O, the pulsing of the story
Is like surging of the sea!

This is the last of ten sonnets of a sequence that appeared in *Pacific Monthly* in 1910. These sonnets deal with the eastern Oregon desert and seem to be groundwork for *The Poet in the Desert*. The prologue, in particular, employs the same heavy personification and transcendental sense of the desert's significance and power.

Sonnet X from "Desert Sonnets"

Lean, barren Desert, gray as any nun,
Up-riven rocks and silver leagues of sage;
The scarred old Mother, sere in countless age,
With naked breast parched dry beneath the sun.
As so it was when Time was first begun;
No blot of Man, no change upon thy page;
No cry for pity, since God in his rage
Set Desolation's seal thy brow upon.
Brave solitude, there's Freedom in thy breath
Which kissed eternity, and sweet release
From teasing strife and heart-corroding cares.
From out thy temples, stealing unawares,
There comes unto my troubled soul a peace
Wide as thy grandeur and as deep as Death.

THIS ELABORATELY DESIGNED lyric poem expresses a characteristic Wood sentiment, criticizing wealth and position as un-Christian. The typeface (closely linked to the one he used in *Maia*) is Cloister Black, also called Old English, and was used for the first setting of the King James Bible, which is perhaps the reason Wood employed it here in his 1910 Christmas message. A facsimile of the original appears on page 330.

FRIEND, LET THIS BE MY VOICE TO THEE

Friend, let this be my voice to thee
To wish thee Merry Christmas.
May all the year rejoice to thee
And be a Merry Christmas,
But not alone in Song and Wine;
Let Peace and Love for all Mankind
Make every day more choice to thee
And bring thee Merry Christmas.

They say that Christ was nailed on Cross
To give thee Merry Christmas;
A saddened world bewailed the Loss,
Ah, Bitter was the Christmas.
For those Men shame, Christ bled and died,
For Sorrow sake was Crucified;
High place and Wealth he hailed as Dross.
'Tis Love makes Merry Christmas.

Now Christmas comes the Poor to cheer.
Glad, Merry, Merry Christmas.
If Christmas might endure the year
Ah, what a Merry Christmas.
Nor Christ forgets the Ones who sin;
He opes the Door to let them in.
Wilt thou, also, make fewer the Tears?
I wish thee Merry Christmas.

INTRODUCTION TO "IRRIGATING"

PUBLISHED IN *Pacific Monthly* in 1911 under the pseudonym William Maxwell, this satirical poem reflects Wood's sense of irony about the beauties of agricultural development, rising out of his years working for the promotion of eastern Oregon with Bill Hanley and others.

IRRIGATING

The ditch runs full, the sky ablaze,
    A pure and perfect blue;
The mountains sleep in purple haze;
And I just lie around and laze.
      With not a thing to do
        But lift the gate;
          The waters run
      To thirsty Earth
        Beneath the sun.
      I hear it gurgle slow:
        Money, money,
        Plenty money;
      Money where I go.
        Hay and honey,
        Money, money,
      Money in my flow.

I lie beneath a willow-tree,
    Up by the main headgate.
The desert-breeze feels good to me,
And shining run the waters free
      Where fields and orchards wait.
        I lift the gate;
          The waters splash.
      Out in the field
        The shovels flash.
        Hark to the gurgle slow.
        Money, money,

Plenty money.
Money where I go.
Fields all sunny,
Grapes and honey,
Money in my flow.

INTRODUCTION TO "ON THE MAKING OF BOOKS"

C. E. S. WOOD LOVED BOOKS. He grew up surrounded by them at home. He collected them. He read them. He wrote them. He wrote about them. In this essay, "On the Making of Books," from *Pacific Monthly* (September 1911), under the guise of Felix Benguiat, Erskine defends the enduring value of the classics and decries the superficiality of the general public's taste in reading.

ON THE MAKING OF BOOKS

Of the making of many books there is no end. To consider their number is like attempting to grasp stellar distances, or the possible number of worlds within the uttermost verge of space. Millions of tons of paper every year go into the making of new books. What becomes of them? They are like the carpet of flowers which is spread in the desert by the cunning hands of spring, but in midsummer not a leaf, not a dry stem, remains to tell that once they were.

Of the reading of many books there is no end. These literary ephemera are read and forgotten. If so soon forgotten, why read? They are read for a certain brain-tickling and to avoid thought. Brain vacancy may be at times as restful as sleep; at such times a trifling book may be an opiate, a sugar-plum. But why live on opiates, or sugar-plums? The book which leaves not a mark behind is worse than valueless; it is enervating, dissipating, demoralizing. "Reading maketh a full man," sayeth the great Elizabethan, the "wisest of mankind;" but certainly the reading of the six best sellers of today and all the intermediates down to the thousand worst would not make a full man, unless flatulency be mistaken for fullness. There is not a book worth reading in this too short life which is "light reading" in the sense that it glides over the mind, requiring no effort on the part of the reader. Speaking with a thought toward our own immediate development and the evolution possible within us, there is not a book worth reading which does not exact from the reader thought, and thought means work. This work does not lessen the value of the book as an amusement. On the contrary, there is no real amusement, or true recreation without a sense of accomplishment, and this means labor though it may be pleasurable labor. When Burns came from the plough, filled with creative joy, and wrote the lines on upturning the nest of a field-mouse, or on uprooting a mountain-daisy, he labored and yet he was recreating himself. So the man who turns from sordid drudgery to read Hamlet for the twentieth time, wondering whether the melancholy young prince was mad or not, is finding recreation, and the more earnest his thought, the more he is lifted out of himself and recreated. He feels a pleasure which does not easily fade. He remembers his discoveries of beauty of language, beauty of thought, and intimacy with living characters as one of the memories of his life, and he derives a permanent pleasure from his reading, all the more if he has trained his memory and enriched his mind by memorizing the most beautiful passages. Young people should practice this memorizing of jewels. In other words, there is no real pleasure where there is no sense of progress made and profit taken. The book which can be poured through the mind like water through a sieve will make no impression and time spent on it is time wasted, unless in exceptional cases it be the temporary toy for a sick mind, and I doubt even that exception.

Tested by the standard of real value obtained by mental effort on the part of the reader, what book worth reading is easy or vacant reading. Homer? No, though he tells of battles wherein the gods mingled; of adventures by flood and field; of heroes and heroines; even she whose face launched a thousand ships and burnt the topless towers of Ilium. Beneath the walls of Troy the chariots flash amid the dust of conflict; smoke rises from the altars of sacrifice, ships crash and are overwhelmed of old Poseidon; bright-cheeked Briseis is torn weeping from her lover and the fate of the war hangs upon his resentment. Andromache swoons at the death of Hector. Ah, the old blind Greek beat Shakespeare there. No long speeches or exquisite rhetoric; no poetic drama; only when they tell her her idol is dead she faints and her women gather about her. It is the supreme dramatic touch, perfect in its simplicity and humanity. Odysseus dreams with Calypso, and Thersites laughs. But do people today read Homer ? No, they may pick out some of the episodic tales, as plums from a pudding. I admit he belongs to a past age and a past poetry. His perpetual slaughter, the unceasing gashing, hacking, biting of dust and gushing out of bowels—belong to a primitive heroic age; the Homeric catalogues mean nothing to us today. But to his auditors, hanging eagerly upon his words, depend upon it, every personal combat and every name in the interminable list of ships meant something and fired the imagination. The continual slaughter and duel upon duel is not for this age, but the knowledge of Nature and Human Nature is for all ages. Then there are Aeschylus, Sophocles, Euripides, and Aristophanes, the mocker. What cleverer satire and humor than "The Birds"? It is something, even in these days of two-year runs, for a comedy to have run more than two thousand years. Doctor Eliot has put "The Frogs" of Aristophanes on his five-foot book-shelf, so the old comedian has a chance for greater longevity. (I think I would have put "The Birds.") But even this laughter demands study and thought. It would not have lasted two thousand months if it did not. There is a dignity, a simple human naturalness combined with great sublimity, in Aeschylus, which makes much of Shakespeare verge on bombast, yet I may say, in these Baconian days, with his friend, rare Ben: "I do honor the man, this side idolatry, as much as any." According to George Bernard Shaw this marks me a "Duffer."

But if you say the ancients are too ancient—and I admit they are not of our mode and habit and each age has its own taste. Let us make a long jump over the Roman civilization to the Renaissance. Rome gave to the world only echoes of Greek art, literature and philosophy. Like ourselves, Rome was essentially commercial. She originated notes and bills, corporations, jurisprudence and good roads. She was utilitarian. Who reads Dante? or Rabelais? True Rabelais is very indecent in spots. He was so for a purpose, and the purpose has passed, and the spots may profitably be cut out. They were always excrescences, and formed no part of the work itself. But even Anthony Comstock cannot cut out Rabelais, for Rabelais made the French language, and he has made millions laugh. The world will never have so playful and so keen a satire on the courts and the course of justice as the impeachment of Justice Bridlegoose (who shook dice to decide his cases), and the earnest defense of the worthy justice, that he only went wrong when failing eyesight

201

caused him to mistake trey for deuce. *Gulliver's Travels* is Rabelais warmed over. There is an edition of Rabelais by John Morley, with the rotten spots cut out, so it is not necessary that disgust at his vulgarity should deter readers. It is more likely that his insight and satire, even when lighted by his humor, are so profound that he cannot be read lightly and therefore is not read at all. So, also, of Spain's one book. She has only one, but it is enough. Who reads "Don Quixote"? Friends have said to me, "After hearing you talk about Don Quixote, I tried to read it, but could not get on. It was deadly dull." After all, it is a question of taste in which each person has a right to be the final judge. To me, "Don Quixote" for subtle humor, satire and pathos commingled is the book of the world. Don Quixote, the Knight of the Ideal, living in the imagination, always striving for the highest and always falling short in the pursuit; laughed at by the common herd because of his failure, with no conception of the beauty of his ideal. Sancho Panza, squire to reality, the prosaic, the practical, the common man, never long forgetful of his belly and his bed. Don Quixote dwelling in the skies; Sancho Panza hugging the earth. To me they are a wonderful pair and if I visited Spain I would travel the roads they traveled and certainly would make diligent inquiry for their burial-places. After all, it is not the great people of history who really live; not Caesar or Napoleon: the immortal ones are the children of the poets' brains: Hector and Odysseus; Falstaff and Pantagruel. You would certainly expect to find Falstaff's grave somewhere in England. It requires an effort of the mind to realize that he never lived.

England's great ones who are equally kith and kin to us are known to scholars but they are not read. Perhaps they never were. Perhaps since the days of the bards and the reciters who gave to the brain-hungry audience their only pleasure, poetry has been caviare to the general. We know that in Shakespeare's time bull-baiting and cock-fighting were the amusements of the common people and there is much buffoonery and cheap word-play in Shakespeare for the benefit of the pit. We cannot be sure—at least I am not—how great a proportion of London was eager for Marlowe, Shakespeare, Jonson, Beaumont, and Fletcher except that we may be sure there were more than there are in New York today, for the Globe and the Bankside were profitable properties. I am not railing at a generation which has outgrown Homer and Shakespeare, because growth is inevitable and desirable, but I regret that to the world's salad we of the United States have added so little.

It seems to my possibly erroneous vision that when our history is written we will not occupy a very proud position in the realm of human art and culture. We will be great in science and in commerce and we will have done our part, a good, solid pioneer part in human progress, but it seems as if it were not our destiny to add to the world's joy in the immortal creations of poetry, whether in words, paint or stone.

I would say that our popular form of drama is the vaudeville. It flourishes everywhere and it flourishes where other forms of the drama will not live, whether the place be New York City or a small Western town. People say they do not go to the theatre to look at sorrows, or to be made to think. Certainly no one can accuse the vaudeville of thought, and the sorrow it occasions is not intentional. To my mind it still remains true that unless our profounder emotions are stirred and we are made to think, we have gone down, not up. We may have passed the hour, but we have gained nothing from the flight of time. The going-down habit is so easy that presently even sustained attention becomes a bore, and that probably is another reason the vaudeville flourishes. It has a fresh shock every five minutes; or, as some of the play-bills are fond of saying, "a laugh every minute," which seems to be the measure of successful drama today. You may go down the "Great White Way" of that raw, provincial town, New York, and you may try every city from there to San Francisco and you will find that what is popularly wanted is the most elementary amusement; the kind which appeals to childish minds; buffoonery; topical songs, with shrill, nasal, threadbare voices; shopworn women, under-dressed or over-dressed, and much horseplay, often coarse. In this medley there are spots of real humor, real character sketching and honest athletic skill, but giving these fragments due credit I think it remains true that our most profitable and popular form of theatrical entertainment (it is hardly fair to call it dramatic), is not stimulating, nor poetical. Take a step higher and you wonder if it is a step higher: Musical comedy is the next most insistent, popular and profitable theatrical amusement, a meaningless thing of legs and spangles and low comedy—very low—shallow music and a plot so disjointed that one would like to become acquainted with the brain which conceived it, in order to study the phenomenon. The most serious and purposeful form of the modern drama is the problem play, where the stage does resume one of its proper functions, that of the preacher, and this dramatic form is a natural outgrowth of our age, which is wrestling with the problems of social life as no age ever has. The United States has added little true literature to this higher form of the modern drama. It has seemed to me that the audiences attracted to these plays for the words of the play itself are not large. Curiosity as to the play, or as to the actress, fills the theatre, but if you want a run of two years you must drop to musical comedy or farce. I am a great believer in the problem play, as I am in every form of preaching and teaching the truth; but I doubt if any particular play will outlive its purpose. When the evils it aims at are gone; it will go. There will be no reason for its existence because it deals not with the ideal, the beautiful and the profound. In short, it does not seem to me it is imaginative poetry either in wording or in action, and nothing but poetry will live to another age. I submit that the fact that there can be a theatrical trust and that there can be runs of the same play for one, two and three years indicate our thorough commercialism and show that there is no true art either in the stage as an institution, or in the actor, and certainly there is no training-school for the young actor. Shakespeare produced a new play every week or so. Fancy Shakespeare and his company being content to run "Romeo and Juliet" for six hundred consecutive afternoons, or fancy Garrick consenting to play even "Hamlet" for two years without interruption.

One of our great publishers said to me, "There is no money in publishing poetry. People will not read it." He did not mean rhyme. He meant poetry, which reaches up into the skies and gives to airy nothing a local habitation and a name; which peoples the world with beings who might be, but, alas, are not, which stirs our every emotion to its profoundest depths. And just there is the reason, I take it, why poetry is not popular. It does not tell the whole story, but leaves much to the imagination of the reader. It compels thought to grasp its inner meaning or many meanings. It makes of the reader a worker to a degree even as the writer was, and the people today have no patience or liking for this. They want to be amused with a tale. They do not want to be compelled to step out of themselves and complete the creation out of their own imagination. In fact, about the only people today who have imagination are children and newspaper men. It is stamped out of the one. Alas! And should be out of the other. Alas!

We of the United States are engaged in a tremendous material struggle. Our masses are demanding economic justice; a more equal opportunity and a more just reward. It is a life-and-death struggle, far more important than poetry or art, and while it goes on it is perhaps too much to expect that we will produce dreamers to dream and dreamers to listen to the dreams. No genius ever came from a hostile soil, and those who talk of "American Art" (meaning a great gift to the world which after-ages will cherish, pointing to us as a luminous spot in history), talk of that which does not exist and for which there is no atmosphere. You can no more kill the imagination wholly among any people than you can kill hope itself, and there are, of course, some poetically-minded persons who crop up here and there and devote themselves to art, but our real popular taste as a people is for the comic supplement, rag-time and vaudeville. We worship technique and skill, rather than feeling, and, as I have said, we need not expect a place in literature and art, for you cannot make something out of nothing. No people ever produces what is not in it. We will produce scientific truths and economic truths and a better conception of justice (I mean we with the rest of the world), and after-ages will be happier and more comfortable for the labor we passed through, and then perhaps our art will be born. Or, it may be that we, like Rome, are destined never to be originals in art. I am referring to our own country (the United States). I do not forget that in Wagner our age has probably touched high-water mark in music, and that Monet in painting and Rodin in sculpture have opened doors in the temple of art—which lead out into sunlight and air—I do not forget we of the United States have given Whitman to posterity, a great mountain, rugged but beautiful—not polished as a jewel but of Nature's own grandeur. I do not think we can boast another great original, and I do not think these men are accepted by the popular mind.

Our children start with imagination, but our age and misguided parents take it out of them. All are turned in the same lathe. It is wonderful how little is enough for the imagination to build its immortal fabric upon. Greece, which peopled the skies with gods and every mountain, every stream, every strip of woods, with maenads, nymphs and dryads, which gave to its rivers, gods guarding their fountain-heads and made every spot the place of a drama, Greece upon whose philosophy and art our civilization rests, was a small, rugged country with not one great river in it, and the splendid Ilium, around whose tragic walls the generations have gathered breathless for more than two thousand years, was, according to scientific, unimaginative modern research, but a small town of a few acres in area. And that wonderful fleet of warships was a collection of small craft, more insignificant than the Gloucester fishing-fleet. But, after all, size is so insignificant, except with us. With us it is everything, be it an apple or a purse. Columbus and Drake and Magellan voyaged in cockle-shells.

Reading began with story-telling, the reciter holding his audience upon his words, and this mode will never be improved upon. The best reading will always be that of a reader to a sympathetic circle. It is wonderful what new color and interest is given to any book by reading it aloud to attentive listeners; say "Don Quixote." Each mind sees each incident from a different angle and the exchange of views is both delightful and instructive. Reading aloud used to be a common amusement with our grandfathers, but with us it is a lost art, like letter-writing. Of course, there are special classes for special studies, but I mean the reading-aloud *habit*, the impromptu and sociable reading aloud. I would also again urge that the old fashion be revived, of committing fine poems and splendid passages to memory. It is good gymnastics for the mind and it is good for culture. Who reads the Bible today, for its wonderful poetry and drama? Who reads the great poets, the great tellers of great tales, or, for the matter of that, speaking of wide general popular reading, who reads Fielding, Scott, Dickens, Thackeray, Meredith, Hugo, Balzac, Daudet, Zola, Stendhal, Manzoni? These should be easy reading, for they tell amusing tales in prose. I ask for information. A library record would tell. But I wonder if they are much read.

An essayist cannot change the times. He is the helpless cicada shrilling in autumnal days over the summer which has passed. Not all the essays in the world will make "Othello" or "As You Like It" pay as against "A Texas Steer" or "Seven Days." The public schools and the newspapers, if they felt their educational duty, might possibly scratch the surface, but the newspapers at least make black blacker by educating the baby mind on the comic supplement. What we need is the Modern School.

I have said we are wrestling with tremendous problems, more important to the masses of men than art or poetry; the problems of human life; of human happiness. But it is a sordid combat, with sordid forces, in a sordid arena. It is as intensely practical as trying to reach a life-raft after shipwreck. We are searching for Truth. We have killed that credulity which peopled the thickets with fauns and made of the murmurous rivulets the voices of nymphs. We have even killed Hell and Heaven as particular retreats for particular people, but a knowledge of truth need not and cannot kill the imagination. Imagination is not synonymous with credulity or superstition. It is the vital spark of the human mind and it remains for us to speculate upon what wonderful forms it will flame into when again it leaps upward. If I could leave a phrase to stimulate those who are upward-minded, I would say not only is there "no profit where is no pleasure ta'en. In brief, sir, study what you most affect." But, also, there is no pleasure where there is no profit taken. In brief, sir, read what is worth studying. Only that is worth reading.

In considering the question of mental cultivation, I often think of De Quincey's simile of the pearl-necklace which has been broken and the wearer sits in a boat in calmest sea, unconscious of the fact. One by one, the precious jewels slip off and hasten back to the eternal depths. The necklace is Life and the pearls are the hours which make it.

INTRODUCTION TO "THE DESERTER"

THIS BALLAD, PUBLISHED in *Pacific Monthly* under the name of William Maxwell, mixes Wood's anti-war feelings with his western-style verse. We see Wood advocating a version of the 1960s political slogan, "Make love not war."

THE DESERTER

It was in the gay September,
And the sun was burning down
On the great Nevada desert far away,
Where the yellow whirling whirlwinds
Waltzed their tall and ghostly round,
And the desert danced and shimmered where it lay.

There was smell of sage and summer,
It was hot as hot could be,
And the blood was hot as summer in my veins;
When she stood among the aspens

And she weeping said to me,
"Don't you go with them across the sunset plains."

Oh, her bosom bare was heaving,
And the aspen-leaves were gold;
Her voice it sobbed her girlish hopes and fears,
And her little hands they clutched me
Till they hurt where she did hold,
And her eyes were brimming o'er with salty tears.

"Don't you leave me, for I love you."
For I love you!—'Twas a prayer.
O! her eyes, they looked as I had been her God.
"Don't you leave me," sighed the aspens
As they whispered shivering there;
"Don't you leave me," pale the mountains seemed to nod.

Then I hung upon my saddle
Both my carbine and my sword,
And I doffed my chevroned jacket, bright and blue,
And I bade old grey go follow,
And I broke my soldier word,
For I didn't know what else a man could do.

Third Stage
(1912—1920)

1n 1912, C. E. S. Wood, almost 60 years old, entered his most productive period as a writer. A number of circumstances contributed to his late blooming. True, the demise of *Pacific Monthly* deprived him of a major outlet, but his creative drive did not depend on publication. He wrote largely for the love of it and out of his longing to leave the law for literature. Moreover, his passionate belief in social justice and his hatred of the approaching war lent impetus to his powerful pen.

However, far and away the most important factor in Erskine's literary efflorescence was his meeting Sara Bard Field Ehrgott in October 1910, at the instigation of their mutual friend, defense attorney Clarence Darrow. It turned out to be a true meeting of minds and hearts. By spring of 1911, although both living in Portland, they were deep into a prolific, clandestine correspondence with letters every day, sometimes twice a day. The letters were poetic, extravagant, inventive, witty, calling for both poets to draw deeply on their creative powers. Some of Sara's and Erskine's best literary expression went into their correspondence.

Throughout this decade, Sara's influence permeated Wood's poetry. That influence was clearly evident in *Sonnets* (1918); in the change from *Civilization* (1914) to *The Poet in the Desert* (1915); in *Maia* (1918); in a revision of *The Poet in the Desert* (1918) that cut the propaganda in the poem substantially; and in *Circe* (1919).

The second decade of the twentieth century was a transitional period in United States history. Progressive reform was very much alive during President Woodrow Wilson's first term but the war in Europe, threatening to involve the United States, caused a sharp shift in the nation's attention from the domestic to the international scene. Although the slogan, "He kept us out of war," helped Wilson win a narrow victory over Republican Charles Evans Hughes in 1916, Germany's submarine policy, among other provocations, brought the United States into war in the spring of

1917. Wood campaigned for Wilson, condemning World War I as a struggle among "privileged and governing classes who exploit the peoples." He played variations on this theme in correspondence, in poetry, in editorials, in Christmas messages, and in satire.

On the domestic scene Wood invariably wrote in support of radical or extremely liberal causes. He was a consistent champion of labor and he believed, along with William "Big Bill" Haywood, that labor should be organized in one grand union without regard to race, color, or gender. However, he declined to join Clarence Darrow in defending the McNamara brothers, labor leaders who were accused of dynamiting the building of the anti-union *Los Angeles Times*, because he believed, rightly, that Darrow would resort to illegal tactics in preparing for the trial. Erskine was committed to the defense of civil liberties as in the case, for example, of Margaret Sanger, who was charged with disseminating literature on birth control. Wood defended Sanger in court and the incident gave him a chance to satirize Anthony Comstock, New York's watchdog over public morals, in a heavenly discourse published in *The Masses*.

In this second decade of the twentieth century, C. E. S. Wood reacted in different ways to three amendments to the U. S. constitution. As anarchist and libertarian, he deplored the ratification in 1913 of the 16th amendment authorizing a federal income tax. More than ten years later, Wood won a suit against the federal government for recovery of taxes assessed against commissions paid him by Lazard Freres for the sale of the Willamette Valley and Cascade Mountain Wagon Road Grant. Wood also vehemently opposed the 18th amendment that established prohibition and gave him a superb subject for satire. Finally, he hailed the long-overdue adoption of the 19th amendment giving women the vote. Sara had been active in this crusade as a prominent member of Alice Paul's National Woman's Party.

By 1920, then, Erskine had retired from the practice of the law, left his wife and children financially secure through a series of trust funds, and joined his companion Sara in California in a new life of writing and support of liberal causes.

Introduction to "Thanksgiving at the House of Ayer"

THIS POEM WAS SENT on November 25, 1914, as a telegram from Paso Robles, California, on the occasion of the Thanksgiving dinner the Wood family traditionally shared at the home of Mr. and Mrs. William B. Ayer ("Uncle Dudley and Daisy"). "Mississippi" is a version of Wood's nickname for Nanny, "Sippy."

Wood was in Paso Robles for several weeks at this time receiving treatments at a health spa for an old knee injury. Sara was with him much of the time.

Thanksgiving at the House of Ayer

I would that I were there, at the famous House of Ayer
On the day of our Thanksgiving unto Daisy and the Lord.
Oh, the flow of wine and fancy! oh, the little Dave and Nancy,
Uncle Dudley and the turkey both a smoking on the board!
And the dear delightful Daisy! Pshaw! It almost sets me crazy,
When I think some other duffer will usurp my life-time place.
Will it be another Erskine, or, if possible, a worse one??
Jeff, Kirk, Dave, Uncle Neddo, or some other dark disgrace?

While you in wine are toasting, I am boiling, steaming, roasting;
And the sulphur fumes around me give the old, familiar smell.
Mud throwing is my training—worse than all my damned
    campaigning.
Please excuse the heated language—I am writing you from Hell.
Don't forget me in your thinking; don't forget me in your
    drinking.
Old wine, but just remember the good days when we were
    young.
If you can find a Lazarus, although the journey's hazardous.
Just give him one small bottle, start him down to cool my
    tongue.

Drink the health of Mississippi—she is far from an Xantippe—
All the Nans and both Rebeccas, Mona Lisa and that goose,
Old Jeff, who Joy enhances with his down East fancy dances
When he hits 'er down the middle and is full of apple juice.

211

Jack dear and dearest Justios—but the price of this will bust us!
I must end it in a hurry and I wish you all delight.
Here's to all the stars above us! Here's to all who really love us:
Here's to all at Daisy's table my love and my goodnight:
　　　C. E. S. Wood

Introduction to Poetry

THE SECOND DECADE of the twentieth century was Wood's most
tumultuous and most prolific. As he turned sixty, he came into his
own as a poet, publishing two books of high merit, *The Poet in the
Desert* and *Maia*. These and other works of this period reflect the
versatility and fluidity that distinguish Wood as a poet and a writer.

Poetry, it seems, was his favorite genre, possibly because it
suited his life style. He could dash off a poem in a moment stolen
from his crowded days or fill pages of his journal in the intervals
when time opened up. Sara Bard Field writes that he wrote a
number of racy ballads when on horseback during his Indian
campaigns. He also wrote on the train when crossing the
continent, which he frequently did for business, or in the summer
when overseeing the eastern Oregon wagon road grant for the
Lazard Freres firm.

Wood loved words and he loved people. He seems to have
written for pleasure and to please, though he was not terribly
interested in publication and, like his drama, much of his poetry
remains unpublished. His work was, however, published regularly
in certain magazines after the turn of the century. In his early
years, a good portion of his published poems (not reprinted here)
were blatant anti-imperialist propaganda pieces, a number of
which appeared in *The Public*. His poetry also appeared in Marion
Reedy's *Mirror*, Harriet Monroe's *Poetry*, *The Overland Monthly*,
and, of course, *Pacific Monthly*. When Wood submitted his poems
for publication, it was usually to places sympathetic to his view or
by request. He was more interested in how his poems were
presented than where. His published books of poems, almost all of
them self published, are notable for their fine press work,

particularly *Maia* (1919), *Poems from the Ranges* (1929), and *Sonnets to Sappho* (1939). Wood worked with two of the finest printing houses on the west coast, F. W. Baltes of Portland and the Grabhorn Press of San Francisco.

Wood's Renaissance gifts apply to his poetry. He wrote lyric, epic, occasional, formal, political, pastoral, satirical, rollicking, and contemplative poems. He was, however, quite fond of received forms—the rondeaux, the ballad, and, especially, the sonnet. Besides *Maia* and *Sonnets to Sappho*, he published *The Mill Race Sonnets* (1911) and *Sonnets* (1918).

As a sonneteer, Wood moved easily between the tightly structured and cerebral Petrarchan sonnet and the more malleable and epigrammatic Shakespearean form, favoring the latter in *Maia* and the former in *Sonnets to Sappho*. Though at times burdened by archaisms, revealing perhaps too much love of the Shakespearean mode, Wood adapted the sonnet to his vision, praising nature, exalting love, marking occasions, and censuring society for its failings. *Mill Race Sonnets* contains nine poems that move from *carpe diem* to social criticism. The exquisitely printed *Maia* follows the cycle of the seasons, sprinkling in prose meditations and brief lyrics, a structure suggested by Sara. Occasional works dominate *Sonnets,* while *Sonnets to Sappho*, published as Wood's robust health faltered, treats his failing potency as a farewell to Sappho, the Greek erotic poet.

Wood was also at home with free verse, which he employs with great power in *The Poet in the Desert* and some of the longer lyrics in his *Collected Poems* such as "Vagabond's Song" and "But Still There Shall Be Gods." Though he gained critical acclaim for his verse epic, Wood favored rhyme, returning to it in a relaxed, western way in *Poems from the Ranges*. In *Selected Poems by Charles Erskine Scott Wood and Sara Bard Field*, a lovely book printed in 1937 by the Grabhorn Press, the thirteen poems by Wood are mostly rhymed but not dominated by received forms.

Beyond his technical gifts, two strengths inform Wood's poetic vision, empowering his poetry. The first is a love of the physical world. His poems abound in the sensuous appreciation of incarnation—flowers, trees, gems, weather, seasons, animals, anything beautiful, exotic, vital, natural. This gusto for the colors and textures, the phenomenality of life, and the relish of naming them, connects Wood with Whitman, with whom he has often been compared.

213

Portrait of Sara Bard Field Wood by Johan Hagemeyer

Wood was not attracted to irony in poetry. He was, rather, moved by indignation at the lack of social justice he saw around him. This is the second strength in Wood's poetry and, of course, his work in general. More often than not, Wood's poems, especially his lyrics, engage the mode of praise. Inequity so rankled him, however, that relishing the beauties of the world would sometimes lead him to recognize that privilege prevents many from appreciating that beauty. This realization is fundamental to *The Poet in the Desert* and surfaces again in poems such as "Aliens" and "A Thought." Wood strives to define the nature of freedom and asserts that freedom and nature are the same, in *The Poet in the Desert* and poems such as "Vagabond's Song," and "Billy Craddock in Rome."

Personification flourishes in Wood's poetry, usually in the shape of a woman. Testifying to his passion for things Greek and Elizabethan, his poems are populated with a variety of mythological beings, dryads and wood nymphs and Dianas. Though somewhat old-fashioned, these elements combine with his enthusiasm and what Horace Gregory called, "Wood's ability to write poetry in simple, well-wrought images," making a poetry, at its best, of charm, power, and persuasive beauty.

To read Wood's poetry sympathetically, it helps to see him as a poet with a nineteenth-century sense of rhetoric and symbolism, a Progressive Era sense of justice, and a love of the physical world. It takes a shift in expectations for the contemporary reader; however, Wood's humanity and sympathy are robustly seductive enough to have gained him a reputation as the most original poet of the Pacific Northwest in the first decade of the twentieth century. In *Empire of the Columbia,* Johanson and Gates describe him as "Oregon's chief contribution to the 'New Poetry.'" In *The American Northwest*, Gordon Dodds writes that "The only distinguished poet of 'the turn of the century' was Charles Erskine Scott Wood."

WOOD'S CLOSE RELATIONSHIP with far eastern Oregon, Harney Valley, and the Blitzen Oasis, are reflected here. He and his children spent many summers here but by the time this poem was written on September 9, 1912, he was around sixty and his youngest, Berwick, had left the roost.

ONCE MORE I LIE UPON THE GRASSY SPOT

Once more I lie upon the grassy spot
 Where, years gone by, we pitched our summer tent,
 My sons and I; it cannot be forgot;
Here was the shaded path by which we went
 Down to the little beach and rippled pool
Of our friendly river; strokes our axes left
 Where we chopped out a bower in willows cool;
Now silent, of their restless youth bereft
 The sun still shines as bright; the river flows
As murmurous as when it soothed our sleep;
 Here was their bed, where the rose-brier grows,
Not anything for long our impress keeps.
 They all have gone their ways, and, close to tears,
 I muse upon the veiled and hurrying years.

THE CHRIST IN THIS Christmas piece, like the Christ Wood portrayed in other works, particularly *Heavenly Discourse*, is a revolutionary who stands for social justice, a true anarchist. In this ballad, Wood makes one of his favorite points—Christ goes unseen amongst us because we are too greedy and self-absorbed to recognize true Christian principles.

How Christ Spent His Christmas

Prologue

A friend asked me why my Christmas verses were always so dismal—so unsuited to the season. But are they? If Christmas were the fine old Pagan festival from which it came, celebrating the sun's remotest straying from his love and the beginning of his passionate return, I, too, could shout "Merry Christmas" with a pure and, I hope, uncontrite heart. If Christmas meant only the Pagan vision of buds and flowers to come, warm, poetic days of mystery, and the unveiling by Mother Earth of her abundant bosom, which should be open unto all, I, too, could laugh joyously, "Merry Christmas," as my expression of a world gladness. But when the Winter Festival has become the birthday of the Man of Sorrows, how can I celebrate it and not celebrate his message to Men? How can I, or ought I, to forget his teachings and their reward? Was he merry? Do those who have taken his name religiously carry out his clear injunctions? Is his message alive, putting forth fresh branches, or dead as a fossilized tree?

If I celebrate his birthday, I must celebrate his soul; and when I think how utterly despairing and dejected he would be should he return among us, I am not joyful. If you will have it out—when I permit my mind to wander from my own little fortunate circle into the great world, Christmas is a melancholy season, a day which celebrates a failure. The day as a date is nothing. Of course no one knows when Christ was born. German critics are denying that he ever lived. It is the province of critics to deny, especially German critics. I expect some day they will be denying that I ever lived. They are so thorough. It is immaterial when Christ was born, or whether he ever lived; it is sufficient that out of the years a brave and pathetic figure has come to us, who loved children, flowers and the poor; and though, indeed, he said the poor would be always with us, he could not have meant eternally—that the world was to stand still; and he was careful to insist, not once but many times, that the acquisition of great riches was a dangerous business, and did not fit a soul to enter the kingdom of heaven. He was even bitter against the oppressors of the poor, many, many times; and he castigated the bankers. You don't believe he was crucified, because he claimed to be a son of God, do you? Why, the Jews had been accustomed to such claims from the days of the prophets. He was crucified because he was a soap-box orator, a socialist, who was attacking the rich, defending the poor, making the poor restless, and his face was set against the existing order of things. That was his crime. He was hurting property and attacking society. He repeated the injunctions of Buddha and Socrates. "Return good for evil." "Love your enemies." "Regard all men as brothers." "Build the world on love, not on force." "Do unto others as you would have them do to you" under like circumstances. He was one of the earliest anarchists.

What more do we know of Buddha or Socrates than we know of Christ? It is the message that lives. Who cares who wrote Homer, or who wrote Shakespeare? We have Homer and we have Shakespeare.

If Christ be a pure fiction of the early centuries, he is still for us a living figure because of the utterances for which his name stands; and what possible difference can it make on what day he happened to be born?

So I accept quite gladly that Christ actually lived, a Galilean peasant bred to his father's trade; and that he rejected the drudgery of carpentry, refused his mother's entreaties to come home and be respectable, but persisted in giving expression to his own soul. I daresay he was called the equivalent in that day for "crank" and "hobo," but certainly he was unflinchingly a revolutionist, though the way led up Calvary to the Place of Skulls; as it always will for those who are cursed or blessed to see beyond the mole-tunnel in which we are born. The revolution he urged was so great that it has not yet been accomplished—no, not even begun. If you think of him as the Prince of Peace, look at Europe; or, if you are especially self-righteous, look at what we so nearly escaped in Mexico. It is useless to raise a great smoke about who started this war. It has the same root as every modern war. It was bound to come. Greed,

217

mines, investments, ports, boundaries, power, power, power—and for what? For profit; for competition in profit. It is vain to preach brotherly love among nations while they cut each others' throats in trade competition.

Do you think of Christ as tender toward the children who are to become men and women? Look at the factories, the canneries, the sweat-shops, where children's lives are blotted out of their ill-fed little bodies! Why? Greed! Competition for profit demands it.

Do you think of Christ as a lover of the poor and a hater of the idle oppressors? Look at our slums, reeking with degradation, and then shout "Merry Christmas!" if you can. But as for me, I feel like saying: "Christ, this is your birthday, and I would say 'Merry Christmas,' except that I see all your gospels rejected and crucified, and after two thousand years there remains only hypocrisy. I will do as the others: I will fool you with a prayer and then go out and kill my brother. I will go to church once a week to drug my sanctimonious heart, and six days will I labor in and for a system you condemned but failed to conquer, which sets mass against class, creates the poor and then starves them, massacres little children, and builds jails instead of temples, but this one day, for your sake, I will give the poor a dinner, out of charity. I will never seek justice. I will never use my brains in your cause. But I will give an annual meal to the poor, who, but for this plan of society, need not be poor."

My unuttered Christmas greeting is always:

Merry Christmas, all you slums and prisons.
Merry Christmas, you lean little factory girls.
Merry Christmas, you beggars and social vermin.
Merry Christmas, you Magdalens and bastards.
Merry Christmas, by all means, Merry Christmas!
Merry Christmas, you idolaters of property and of a system which
keeps you on the backs of the people. I think you are the poorest of
all, for, having power, you see not the possibility and beauty of a
povertyless world serene. "Father, forgive them, for they know not
what they do."

You see, when I think of the world, the Christian world, something of which I must be a part, not blinded by the happiness at my own fireside, I cannot shout: "Merry Christmas and a free dinner to the poor!"

HOW CHRIST SPENT HIS CHRISTMAS

Come listen, children, small and great,
    While I the mystery tell;
How Christ left his sublime estate
    And plunged once more to Hell.

The avenues of Heaven led from star to star,
    All lighted by the flash of angels' wings.
Against the celestial firmament afar
    The throne of God blazed its blue lightnings;
    And chorus of the seraphim encircling sings.

Christ stood before the throne, his haloed face
    Still sad for bitter failure of the years,
And prayed to leave the glad harmonious place
    To tread once more the stony path of tears—
    To wrestle with earth's agonies and fears.

Said Christ: "Tomorrow is my own birthday.
    "O, Father, let me go once more to them
"Who like lost sheep continually do stray;
    "My fellow men who see my diadem,
    "But do not stoop to kiss my garment's hem.

"They think they see, but, Father, they are blind.
    "They wear my name large on their Sabbath brows.
"Their prayers are emptier than desert wind,
    "Dry as a puff-ball their pretended vows,
    "And misery abideth in their house."

The Father nodded and the good Christ flew
    Down through the deep abysses of the air;
Unto this earth he came as comes the dew,
    So sweet and healingly, so pure and fair.
    He sought his proper home, his house of prayer.

But it was shut. "'Twill open be tomorrow,"
    An old man said before the iron grate.
"What, only once a week comes want and sorrow?"
    Said Christ. "But now I have no time to wait.
    "This is my house and I am at its gate."

"He's crazy," said the sexton, "Ragamuffin,
  "Be off," and Christ turned meekly to obey.
'Tis true Christ's coat was but a common rough one;
  His hands were hard, his dark hair streaked with grey.
  He smiled, and took his melancholy way.

The owner of a factory, whose wheels
  Ground up the lives of children as their grist,
Sat in his office. Suddenly Christ reveals
  Himself, a workman, grey and hard of fist,
  Leading a thin, wan child whom no one kissed.

"Suffer little children unto me to come.
  "Childhood is ruddy, gay and soon to pass;
"Youth is a dancer with a flute and drum.
  "Even the lambs do frolic in the grass.
  "Will you deny the children joy, alas?

"I know what you would say: 'The strife of greed
  "'Compels the slaughter of the children's lives.'
"But I say unto you, there's no such need,
  "But men should live in fair and flowery hives
  "Where none claims all, but each for other strives."

"Put out this lunatic! How got he in?"
  And Christ was hustled through the leering door.
The spinning-wheels sneered on in dismal din;
  The grim machines shook the insensate floor.
  The little child was weeping as before.

Christ the Redeemer, Jesus the Divine,
  So pale of face, so sinless of his soul,
Stood by the mouth of the black, tomb-like mine
  And said unto the masters in control:
  "Who gave you right to measure out a dole?

"O, not how little but how much the wages.
  "Give them their share. They have God's right of birth.
"I say to you, the sin of all the ages
  "Is lordship of the treasures of the earth—
  "To few abundance, and to millions dearth."

The miners listened. O how pale their faces;
　　The miners' wives, how lean their starved breasts!
The miners' children gathered in the places;
　　How thin the cheeks their mothers had caressed!
　　And everywhere were wistful eyes, distressed.

"Down with the agitator!" shout the landlords.
　　"Call out our special agents, paid for blood;
"Loose murder, rape and rapine, fire and sword;
　　"Destruction sweep the toilers in its flood;
　　"But we'll not budge an inch from where we stood."

They struck at Christ and opened new his wounds.
　　His blood once more ran down the pallid face;
They tramped him in the mire until he swooned.
　　They carried him unto the gibbet place
　　And flung him in, a thing of vile disgrace.

But when the servile jailer grimly came
　　To put the prisoner through the third degree,
Behold, the cell was empty, save a flame
　　Which for a moment flashed too splendidly,
　　Blinding the jailer so he could not see.

That selfsame hour, half-naked, grimy, dark,
　　Christ sweated in a furious fiery mill
Where molten iron shot its dazzling sparks,
　　And life was hopeless in a burning hell,
　　And sad men moved like dead things, to a bell.

Christ cried, throwing down the red-hot rod:
　　"Were you all born to helpless slavery?
"How long will you mistake for will of God
　　"The greedy laws of man's shrewd knavery?
　　"Rebellion is God's chosen bravery.

"For I am sick of all this cant and whine
　　"Which pollutes Heaven in my holy name;
"This smug veneering with a phrase divine
　　"What is in truth but man's own sordid shame.
　　"Rebellion is Truth's purest, whitest flame."

They seized him; haled him into court in a trice;
   Beat and abused him, knocked him down.
"Do you not understand that I am Christ?"
   He said. "See where I wore the thorny crown,
   "And in my side the Roman soldier's wound.

"I purged the temple—" Then their fears were fled.
   They mocked at him. One struck him with a stick.
That he would wake rebellion was their dread;
   They did not fear a crazy lunatic.
   They walled him in with those whose minds are sick.

'Twas Christmas day, a glad and golden morn.
   To celebrate the coming of God's Son,
The day the Man of Peace and Tears was born,
   The gentle and the brave, rebellious one
   By whom our earthly woes shall be undone.

He healed those, melancholy, of their plight,
   There in that place where he imprisoned was;
Then, through the guards, unseen of mortal sight
   He passed into the world, nor would he pause
   To listen to the Christmas morn's applause.

Cathedral towers shook with the voice of bells.
   The air was laggard with its incense load.
Singing and laughter, merriment foretells.
   A deep-toned organ the sacred manger showed.
   Christ entered in. It was his own abode.

He stood beside the preacher in the stall,
   And said "Beloved, I have come again
"To tell the newer truths. I told not all
   "When first I came, Redeemer unto men.
   "What now I know, indeed I knew not then.

"I said 'give to the Poor,' but now I say
   "'Give Justice to the Poor, not Charity;'
"Get off their backs before you kneel to pray.
   "Let none withhold Life's opportunity.
   "Who drains the toilers crucifieth Me."

"I see the silks and satins of these pews.
  "Mill and mine owners, smug and satisfied;
"But O, I see the foul and fetid stews;
    "The gaunt, depraved Poor; and O, you lied
    "Who said for such a world I lived and died.

"'Tis not my world where millions rot in shame;
    "Where starving children die like summer flies.
"'Tis not a world to which I give my name
    "Where war exalts its bloody agonies,
    "A world of robbery and greed and lies."

"Who is this anarchist? Call the police.
    "Who dares to desecrate our temple, fair,
"And blasphemes Christ, the Prince of Love and Peace?"
    They hurry Christ into the outer air,
    And then serenely offer up a prayer.

Christ rises, by street-mud and filth defiled,
    And listens while the choir superbly sings
Hail lowly Jesus, Heavenly Child.
    "Ah, slaves to lust for base, material things,
    "I should have worn my halo and my wings."

Up from the groans of the slums toward the stars
    From wailing want and genius all undone,
From bloodless slaughter and from bloody wars,
    Christ flew. "And did they know you there, dear Son?"
    The Father said. And Christ replied, "Not one."

INTRODUCTION TO *The Poet in the Desert*

The Poet in the Desert was the work for which C. E. S. Wood
wanted to be remembered. Harriet Monroe, editor of *Poetry
Magazine*, said of it, "This is enough to prove that the Far West
has produced a poet who, though somewhat burdened with his
message, is capable of rapture, a poet of large vision, of profound
sympathy and faith, whose verses sometimes attain orchestral
richness." The poem was widely praised by reviewers with
progressive sympathies and gained Wood modest national
recognition as a poet. Excerpts from the various editions of it were
printed in a number of anthologies during the 1920s and 1930s.

The epic-length poem of over one hundred pages is a rolling,
Whitmanesque pastoral organized, after the prologue, as a
dialogue between Truth and the Poet and set in a richly
personified and emblematic desert, clearly the Harney Valley area
of eastern Oregon. The poem contains sections resembling
psalms that alternate between rhapsody and recrimination,
lyricism and propaganda, the religious and the revolutionary,
orthodoxy and heresy. Incorporating Christian archetypes,
biblical rhetoric, and a transcendental cosmology grounded in the
efficacy of freedom and love in redeeming a misguided humanity,
The Poet in the Desert calls for a world informed by freedom
where justice and joy belong to everyone.

Wood claims to have written the first drafts of *The Poet in the
Desert* while staying at Bill Hanley's P Ranch in the Blitzen Valley
in eastern Oregon. In a letter to Max Hayek, his German
translator, Wood describes the origins of the poem.

> *Here in the willow banks of the Blitzen River flowing out of the
> Steens Mountain I used to camp with my sons—sometimes my
> daughters ... in the summer of 1912 "The Poet in the Desert" was
> written, sometimes on the river bank, where the shallows of the
> river warbled, sometimes out in the lonely silence of the desert
> among the sagebrush, sometimes in the shadows of a great rock
> overlooking the oasis. I was full of my life-long meditations that
> this is a world distorted by man and founded on injustice, and
> with little thought of art I expressed my soul.*

Wood may have romanticized the creation of the poem, though
it would seem that the strategy of contrasting nature and

224

civilization, the former offering beauty and freedom, the latter suffering and bondage, came to him that summer in eastern Oregon, shaping itself as a dialogue between Truth and the Poet. It is almost certain, though, that some of the material that became the poem was written over many years, as "Desert Sonnets" would suggest. It is quite likely, also, that without Sara's influence the poem would never have emerged from his other manuscript material.

Part of the reason, beyond her intelligence, political stance, and beauty, that Wood fell so deeply in love with Sara Bard Field was that she was a fine poet, better versed in it than he and a superior craftsperson. She had studied poetry briefly with Professor Thomas Lounsbury at Yale. As they became more involved, Wood asked Sara to look through a chest of his writing. She leafed through pages of manuscripts, finding, as she remembers in an article she published in *Saturday Review* in 1945:

> *too many trifles, too much vers de societé, too many lines of occasion, too much imitative style. Then I came to a yellow sheeted, paper-covered notebook containing free verse sketches of the desert, written long before the school of free verse had become articulate.*

Sara encouraged Erskine to work on these notes and in the summer of 1912 Wood found the strategy for this free-verse vision of nature's wisdom and humanity's folly. Over the next several years, with Sara's close, careful assistance, he revised what at first he called "Civilization" (printed and distributed in Portland in 1914 with this afterword: "Only for private distribution to personal friends. Not for publication"). When F. W. Baltes, a fine-press printer in Portland, published the second edition in 1915, it was called *The Poet in the Desert*.

As Wood's sense of his poetry developed, he battled the question of craft and message, of art and propaganda. This second edition (1915), from which we reprint the prologue, was criticized by some (including Harriet Monroe) for having too much propaganda and too little poetry. Wood set about revising it, encouraged by Sara and Max Eastman, one of the editors of *The Masses*. Wood published the third edition of *The Poet in the Desert* in 1918 in two forms. Most of this version was printed as a cheap paperback for Emma Goldman, who sold it at her rallies until she was deported to Russia. A smaller edition was printed on handmade linen paper and bound in boards. Sara called them the "prince and the pauper" editions. An inexpensive reprint of this 1918 edition was published in London by C. W. Daniel at around this same time.

The 1918 version removes much of the dialogue format, replacing it with numbered passages in which quotation marks suggest a dialogue, and increases the number of sections from twenty-four to fifty-two. Wood reduced the length of the lines dramatically, removing much of the prolix prose statement, and improving the cadence. In addition, he changed the ending to "And the little children be born into joy," a significant improvement. Originally, the poem ended with Truth saying of Justice and Freedom, "They are written in blood." In the end, according to Sara, Wood felt the 1918 version of the poem to be the superior version. His *Collected Poems* (1949), edited by Sara, contain this version and, with two exceptions (the prologue to the 1915 edition and section 53 of the 1929 edition), it is the version reprinted here.

Ten years later, in an anti-imperialist mood, Wood made substantial changes and additions to the poem, especially to the climactic anti-war portions, lengthening the poem by three sections, one of which is included in this selection. Vanguard published this version, the fourth and last, in 1929. It adds interpretive lines to virtually every section, lengthens some lines, inserts specific names, and shows a more modern sense of diction by dramatically reducing the Victorian poeticisms.

In his introduction to this edition, Wood writes: "One whose genius for constructive criticism I greatly revere has begged for this final edition of *The Poet in the Desert*—that all preaching be omitted. . . that the greatest poets have failed to successfully mix poetry and propaganda." Wood agrees but justifies his revision with these words: "If the urge to preaching interrupts the urge to poetry, still it is myself and if art be violated I like to think our indulgent old Mother Earth will tread her sunward path undisturbed." The 1918 edition is perhaps more unified, more of a piece, but there are aspects and parts, especially the new ones, of the 1929 edition that lend it a singular integrity and power.

The Poet in the Desert

Prologue

POET:

I have entered into the Desert, the place of desolation.
The Desert confronts me haughtily and assails me with solitude.
She sits on a throne of light,
Her hands clasped, her eyes solemnly questioning.
I have come into the lean and stricken land
Which fears not God, that I may meet my soul
Face to face, naked as the Desert is naked;
Bare as the great silence is bare:

I will question the Silent Ones who have gone before and are
    forgotten,
And the great host which shall come after,
By whom I also shall be forgot.
As the Desert is defiant unto all gods,
So am I defiant of all gods,
Shadows of Man cast upon the fogs of his ignorance.
As a helpless child follows the hand of its mother,
So I put my hand into the hand of the Eternal.

I have come to lose myself in the wide immensity and know my
    littleness.
I have come to lie in the lap of my mother and be comforted.
I am alone but not alone—I am with myself.
My soul is my companion above all companions.

Behold the signs of the Desert:
A buzzard, afloat on airy seas,
Alone, between the two immensities, as I am alone between two
    immensities;
A juniper-tree on a rocky hillside;
A dark signal from afar off, where the weary may rest in the
    shade;
A monastery for the flocks of little birds which by night hurry
    across the Desert and hide in the heat of the day;
A basaltic-cliff, embroidered with lichens and illuminated by
    the sun, orange and yellow,

The work of a great painter, careless in the splash of his brush.
In its shadow lie timid antelope, which flit through the
sage-brush and are gone;
But easily they become fearless unto love.
The sea of sage-brush, breaking against the purple hills far
away.
And the white alkali-flats which shimmer in the mirage as
beautiful blue lakes, constantly retreating.
The mirage paints upon the sky, rivers with cool, willowy banks;
You can almost hear the lapping of the water,
But they flee mockingly, leaving the thirsty to perish.
I lie down upon the warm sand of the Desert and it seems to me
Life has its mirages, also.
I sift the sand through my fingers.

Behold the signs of the Desert:
The stagnant water-hole, trampled with hoofs;
About it shine the white bones of those who came too late.
The whirling dust-pillar, waltz of Wind and Earth,
The dust carried up to the sky in the hot, furious arms of the
wind, as I also am lifted up.
The glistening black wall of obsidian, where the wild tribes
came to fashion their arrows, knives, spearheads.
The ground is strewn with the fragments, just as they dropped
them, the strokes of the maker undimmed through the
desperate years.
But the hunters have gone forever.

The Desert cares no more for the death of the tribes than for
the death of the armies of black crawling crickets.
Silence. Invincible. Impregnable. Compelling the soul to stand
forth to be questioned.
Dazzling in the sun, whiter than snow, I see the bones
Of those who have existed as I now exist. The bones are here;
where are they who lived?
Like a thin veil, I see a crowd of gnats, buzzing their hour.
I know that they are my brethren, I am less than the shadow of
this rock,
For the shadow returneth forever.
Night overwhelms me. The coyotes bark to the stars.

Upon the warm midnight sand I lie thoughtfully sifting the
    earth through my fingers. I am that dust.
I look up unto the stars, knowing that to them my life is not
    more valuable than that of the flowers;
The little, delicate flowers of the Desert,
Which, like a breath, catch at the hem of Spring and are gone.

I have come into the Desert because my soul is athirst as the
    Desert is athirst;
My soul which is the soul of all; universal; not different.
We are athirst for the waters which make beautiful the path
And entice the grass, the willows and poplars,
So that in the heat of the day we may lie in a cool shadow,
Soothed as by the hands of quiet women, listening to the
    discourse of running waters as the voices of women,
    exchanging the confidences of love.
The little rivers run away from the rugged Titans who are
    wrapped in cloaks of azure.
They steal out from the mountains into the bosom of the
    Desert;
And the willows follow after them, waving their hands, calling
    that they run not so fast away.

The river builds a safe fortress where the birds hide and the
    antelopes come for shelter.
The carpet is a weaving of sweet grasses;
But at last the impatient life-givers marry
The marshes which in the Springtime are green with tule-rush
    and in Autumn copper-red;
Vast sanctuaries for the herons, ducks, pelicans and plover.
Here breed the stately cranes which in the fading year mount
    high to the cloudless heavens and circle about calling for the
    Southland.
Who is their monitor? Who is their pilot?

The mountains afar girdle the Desert as a zone of amethyst;
Pale, translucent walls of opal,   .
Girdling the Desert as Life is girt by Eternity.
They lift their heads high above our tribulation
Into the azure vault of Time;
Theirs are the airy castles which are set upon foundations of
    sapphire.

My soul goes out to them as the bird to her secret nest.
They are the abode of peace. The vexed soul's brooding place.
Behind them, Creation slumbers, a naked god;
His head pillowed on a rock, molten in the fires of chaos;
He dreams of gods to come.
Who shall awake him?
Shall the flowers awake him with their tender fingers, or with
　　the fairy music of their tremulous bells?
Larkspur and blue-bells, lupine, spikes of lapislazuli;
Wild sweet-william, pink as Aurora's bed?
Sunflowers which on rocky hillsides flaunt the banners of their
　　conquest?
And golden seas of rabbit-brush which roll to the sunset,
　　commingling?

The flowers bloom in the Desert joyously.
They do not weary themselves with questioning;
They are careless whether they be seen, or praised.
They blossom unto life perfectly and unto death perfectly,
　　leaving nothing unsaid.
They spread a voluptuous carpet for the feet of the Wind
And to the frolic Breezes which overleap them, they whisper:
"Stay a moment, Brother; plunder us of our passion;
"Our day is short, but our beauty is eternal."

Never have I found a place, or a season, without beauty.
Neither the sea, where the white stallions champ their bits and
　　rear against their bridles,
Nor the Desert, bride of the Sun, which sits scornful, apart,
Like an unwooed Princess, careless; indifferent.
She spreads her garments, wonderful beyond estimation,
And embroiders continually her mantle.
She is a queen, seated on a throne of gold
In the Hall of Silence.
She insists upon humility.
She insists upon meditation.
She insists that the soul be free.
She requires an answer.
She demands the final reply to thoughts which cannot be
　　answered.

She lights the Sun for a torch
And sets up the great cliffs as sentinels;
The morning and the evening are curtains before her
    chambers.
She displays the stars as her coronet.
She is cruel and invites victims,
Restlessly moving her wrists and ankles,
Which are loaded with sapphires.
Her brown breasts flash with opals.
She slays those who fear her,
But runs her hand lovingly over the brow of those who know
    her,
Soothing with a voluptuous caress.
She is a courtesan, wearing jewels,
Enticing, smiling a bold smile;
Adjusting her brilliant raiment negligently,
Lying brooding upon her floor which is richly carpeted;
Her brown thighs beautiful and naked.
She toys with the dazzlry of her diadems,
Smiling inscrutably.
She is a nun, withdrawing behind her veil;
Gray, subdued, silent, mysterious, meditative; unapproachable.
She is fair as a goddess sitting beneath a flowering peach tree,
    beside a clear river.
Her body is tawny with the eagerness of the Sun
And her eyes are like pools which shine in deep canyons.
She is beautiful as a swart woman, with opals at her throat,
Rubies on her wrists and topaz about her ankles.
Her breasts are like the evening and the day stars;
She sits upon her throne of light, proud and silent, indifferent
    to her wooers.
The Sun is her servitor, the Stars are her attendants; running
    before her.
She sings a song unto her own ears, solitary, but it is sufficient.
It is the song of her being. O if I may sing the song of my being
    it will be sufficient.
She is like a jeweled dancer, dancing upon a pavement of gold;
Dazzling, so that the eyes must be shaded.
She wears the stars upon her bosom and braids her hair with
    the constellations.

I know the Desert is beautiful, for I have lain in her arms and
  she has kissed me.
I have come to her, that I may know Freedom;
That I may lie upon the breast of the Mother and breathe the
  air of primal conditions.
I have come out from the haunts of men;
From the struggle of wolves upon a carcass,
To be melted in Creation's crucible and be made clean;
To know that the law of Nature is freedom.

These are the signs of the Desert:
Light, brilliant and blinding.
Sky and earth; the pale rim of mountains; and here, by my feet,
The skull of him that was.
I will go out from the Desert while yet I am.
I will cast off my fetters and even in rags
I will, like a street singer, sing my song.
I will sing my song of meditation and defiance;
But even as I go I look back and see the Desert smiling
  scornfully.
I hear her mocking whisper.

Only Man has enforced his brother;
Only Man has compelled servitude.
Only Man has dwarfed his own godhood, cherished Poverty and
  exalted Ugliness.
Only Man has defied Nature and set up the idols of his
  ignorance.
He has denied Freedom and Beauty.

I will not climb unto the Morning peaks and, like a lark,
Shoot my exultant song down into the shadows where the
  millions drudge and the children are born unto Labor,
But I will lie like a mourner upon the bare and barren bosom
  of the Great Mother.
I will chant a dirge unto Civilization.
I cannot sing a song of Beauty, for Man has put a scar upon her
  forehead and twisted her exquisite limbs.
I cannot sing a song of Truth, for Man has never yet perceived
  the flashing of her eyes.

I cannot sing a song of Justice, for Justice stands on a great
    height, scornful, like a thunder-cloud brooding on a dark
    mountain.
I cannot sing a song of Freedom, for Freedom is beyond this
    present Night, like a distant star kissing the edge of the
    world.
Poets have sung of Freedom, but never has Freedom pressed
    Man's pale lips.
Poets have sung of Justice, but Justice has not dwelt in the
    haunts of men.
Poets have sung of Beauty, but who has perceived her, or been
    folded to the resilient perfection of her bosom?
Unless all rejoice in beauty, there is no beauty.
A palace is not beautiful if it rest upon a sewer which defiles its
    pavements.
The gilding gildeth not a charnel-house.
Poets have sung of Truth, but who has been burned by the
    lightnings of his eyes, or swept by the rushing of his wings?

I have come into the primal solitude to seek Truth;
To lie at ease upon the breast of my Mother,
And to be athirst amid the primal conditions.
Nothing will I sing of quaint conceit or purring softness,
Wresting my thought unto a rhyming word,
But I will sing a dirge unto Civilization.
It is a brazen mirror wherein all is distorted;
A chattering of monkeys who are foolish proud
Because they have put on clothes.
They imitate each other in the follies of their ignorance;
And all is falsity. They mould all to a false pattern.
The blind correcting the blind.
The more ignorant compelling the less ignorant.
The dumb sheep ordered not with a shepherd's crook, but with
    a sword;
The souls of the Rare Ones ruled by the drooling Many,
Or the souls of the hungry hordes ruled by their Oppressors.
Neither the freedom of the primal struggle,
Nor the freedom of the ultimate peace.
Society, a hoofed monster, trampling to death the race.

Truth, dweller in the starry places,
More elusive than moonlight upon the sea, tremulous.
Let me behold your brow which is vague as night, infinite.
Let me look into your eyes which are deeper than the skies of
    this Desert.

Where are you, Truth, where are you?
Shadowy, appearing, disappearing, ever retreating,
As the mirage of the Desert which lures to the glittering
Death-spaces; always advancing, never overtaken.
Your smile is serene as death,
And your hand is comforting.
Where are you, Truth, where are you?
The Desert is empty, vague, vast and terrifying;
Its stillness is as the spaces between the stars,
So that I hear the murmur of my own heart and am afraid.
I look up to the sky, which is eternal,
And down to the hot sand, which is eternal,
And I am afraid of my littleness.
I know the brevity of my existence,
Which is like the passing of the shadow of a cloud.
I salute the little mottled lizard which intently watches me;
I salute you, Brother;
Yet I know I am greater than you; greater than all else.
I am to myself greater than the Desert, or the world,
Or the curiously peering stars.
I feel that I am, in a mysterious way,
Part of Time; part of Eternity.
When I have saluted Death and taken him by the hand,
I shall be absolved and know no more;
Even as these white skulls and ribs know no more.
Nevertheless, I am now a part of Time and I shall then be
As fully as the sun or the stars.
Indestructibly a part of Eternity.

Where are you, Truth, where are you?
The Desert is pitiless.
I am frightened of its bigness and its indifference.
I am alone, an atom thrown out from Eternity,
Allotted to do my part.

I will do my part, and it shall be my own.
I refuse to be moulded in the common mould,
None different from another.
I refuse to step regularly according to custom;
To measure myself among the monotonous patterns laid
out before me.
I will be myself and obey the voice within me
Which impetuously cries to be free;
To wander imperiously, destroying the paths,
The moulds and the patterns.
O Truth discover yourself unto me.
[*Enter Truth, with shining wings.*]
TRUTH:
Ask, and I will answer.

IX

Man declares a sanctity in cloth,
But not in the flesh of babes.
The Patriot bares his head before a flag,
But in its fluttering shadow he
Is stricken down with clubs.
Authority, Authority! O Authority!
The garments of the Rich are a passport;
But the rags of the Poor are friendless.
Holier to me than any flag, the tatters of her
Who should be a full-bosomed mother;
More eloquent to me than banners,
The pathetic patches of Labor;
I had rather keep in my heart
The sacraments of Freedom
Than dull my questioning mind
With blind idolatry.
Why should I, who soon will drink
The comfortable cup,
Shower rose-petal words upon the backs

Of toil-bowed men and women
Whose ears are stopped by Grief?
Shall I twitter a morning song
While millions lie cold in darkness,
Or sing the rhapsodies of love
While my unhappy sisters barter
For bitter bread, or brittle pleasure,
That sacred fire, more elder than the Sun,
Lit in Eternity, purer than Purity,
Sheltered by the old, dead gods?
I will respect no idols.
I will examine all things.
I will fear nothing,
But fearless I will grip
The hands of the gods and cry,
"Hail, Comrades, I am your fellow."

XV

Behold the silver-kirtled Dawn
Life-renewer; Harvester of gloom;
Bright Bringer of good hope.
The skies are listening to Earth's silence.
The Desert sleeps, but her wild children,
Like fretful babies, stir upon her bosom,
And the Comforter casts abroad her gossamer mantle.
The prowler of the night,
The lean coyote,
Slips to his rocky fastnesses,
And noiselessly, through the gray sage,
Jack-rabbits shuttle.
Now, from the castellated cliffs,
Rock-ravens launch their proud black sails.
Wild horses neigh and toss their manes,
Trooping back to pasture;
Orioles begin to twitter.

All shy things, breathless, watch
The thin, white skirts of Dawn,
The Dancer of the sky,
Tripping daintily down the roseate mountain,
Emptying a golden basin.
A red-bird, dipped in sunrise,
Cracks from a poplar top
His exultant whip above a silver world.

XIX

I see my white-faced sisters of the foul tenements
Stooping over their needles,
Which flash faster than the wings of the dragon-fly,
Or the fangs of the quick-coiling serpent.
Their fingers are yellow, the fingers of the dead;
The thin fingers of those who have died of hunger.
Without pause, not daring to lose a moment,
They snatch at the crust of their starvation;
Bending close above the garments,
And the murmur of their hearts is continually:
"Lest we starve! Lest we starve!"
I see my haggard sisters of the prisoning factories;
Their eyes sunken and their mouths chiseled by grief.
Their yellow hands are the talons of an eagle.
The clamorous looms catch up the souls of the workers
And weave them into cloth;
The souls of submissive women woven into cloth;
The woman, left a husk before the loom.
O, the din of the mind-madding looms.

The devil-dance of the shuttles.
They weave up the freshness of Youth,
The silver thread of children's lives,
The morning roses of maidens' cheeks,
The whiteness of mothers' breasts:

Pure ivory bowls of far Eternity
Which should be beautiful.

FROM XXIX
This is the pedigree of Degradation:
Authority, father of Laws;
Laws, father of Privilege;
Privilege, father of Poverty;
Poverty, father of Degradation.
I am a reaper of disordered fields,
And the sheaves which I gather are
Despair, drunkenness, crime, hate, ugliness,
Churches, jails, palaces of the idle rich,
And filthy nests of the debased poor;
Tormenting pain, unsatisfied longings,
A killing hunger of the body;
The hunger of the soul denied.

XLIX
I have lived with my brown brothers
Of the wilderness
And found them a mystery.
The cunning of the swift-starting trout
A mystery, also;
The wisdom of voyaging birds;
The gophers' winter-sleep;
The knowledge of the bees.
All a mystery.
I have lain out with the brown men
And know they are favored.
Nature whispered to them her secrets,
But passed me by.

They instructed my civilization.
Stately and full of wisdom
Was Hin-mah-too-yah-Laht-Kt;
Thunder rolling in the mountains;
Joseph, Chief of the Nez-Perces;
Who, in five battles from the Clearwater
To Bear Paw Mountains,
Made bloody protest against Perfidy and Power.
Ah-laht-ma-kaht, his brother,
Who led the young men in battle;
Tsootlem-mox-mox, Yellow Bull;
Cunning White Bird, a brown Odysseus,
And indomitable Too-hul-hul-soot,
High Priest, dignified; unafraid; inspired;
Standing half-naked in the Council Teepee,
Insisting in low musical gutturals,
With graceful gesture,
"The Earth is our Mother.
"From her we come;
"To her we return.
"She belongs to all.
"She has gathered into her bosom
"The bones of our ancestors.
"Their spirits will fight with us
"When we battle for our home
"Which is ours from the beginning.
"Who gave to the White Man
"Ownership of the Earth,
"Or what is his authority
"From the Great Spirit
"To tear babes from the nursing breast?
"It is contemptible to have much where others want."
And squat, slit-eyed Smokhallah,
Shaman of the Wenatchies, and Chelans,
Half-draped in a red blanket,
Haranguing his people to die
In brave fight on the bosom
Of the Mother who bore them.
Wily Sulk-tash-kosha, the Half Sun,

Chieftain, persuading submission.
"The White Men are more abundant
"Than the grass in the Springtime.
"They are without end and beyond number."

Where are those many-colored cyclones
Of painted and feathered horses
With naked riders, wearing eagle-feathers,
Brandishing rifles, bows, and lynx-skin quivers,
Gleaming through the yellow dust-cloud,
Galloping, circling, hallooing, whooping
To the War Council?

L

Just over there where yon purple peak,
Like a great amethyst, gems the brow of the Desert,
I sprawled flat in the bunch-grass, a target
For the just bullets of my brown brothers betrayed.
I was a soldier, and, at command,
Had gone out to kill and be killed.
This was not majestic.
The little gray gophers
Sat erect and laughed at me.
In that silent hour before the dawn,
When Nature drowses for a moment,
We swept like fire over the smoke-browned teepees;
Their conical tops peering above the willows.
We frightened the air with crackle of rifles,
Women's shrieks, children's screams,
Shrill yells of savages;
Curses of Christians.
The rifles chuckled continually.
A poor people who asked nothing but freedom,
Butchered in the dark.
The dawn would not linger,

Nor the slow-advancing day refuse to come.
The larks saluted the morn
As if there had been no murder.
In the accusing light of the remorseless Sun
It was not good to see brown boys and girls
Scattered about the grass in Death's repose;
On their sides, in reckless weariness.
On their backs, arms sprawled out carelessly,
Or drawn over their eyes, as if to shut out the light.
Nor pleasant to see the fearful gateway
In the just-budding maiden-bosom,
Whence startled Life had leaped to search the void.
Chubby babies, with a blue bullet-hole
In the innocent breast, the soft little belly.
And mothers whose bosoms ran blood with the milk.
They lay quiet in great dignity;
Their eyes staring at us indifferent;
Almost contemptuous.

LII

Broad as the front of the sea,
Rolling, heaving, advancing, swelling,
Behold a triumphant multitude.
It will break in thunder on the shore,
And the land shall be made clean.
Above the sea of gray faces
Writhe two great standards.
On one is written "Justice."
On the other "Freedom."
They are written in blood.
Onward the tide surges, mounting upward;
Men with pale faces;
Women with despairful eyes,
And little children who have never laughed.
The banners of their poverty

Dance like demons,
And the tramp of their feet
Is the ponderous throb of an engine
Without a master.
They are coming
From mines, mills, and factories;
From slimy slums of cities;
From dark and dangerous caverns of the earth;
From narrow, dripping tunnels of darkness;
From clamorous, devouring penitentiaries of industry;
From white-hot hells of furnaces;
From the mind-maddening laughter of machines,
And the devouring cruelty of cities.
Their banners grimace against the dawn,
And the rags of their misery jump with glee.
Behind them, hobbling, grinning, leering,
Scramble the misshapen spawn of Civilization.
As leaves upon the floor of the November forest
They cover the earth, and like the rustle of leaves
Is their breathing:
"Revolution! Revolution!"

They are not going down into the pits.
They are not marching to the factories.
They are not going to the furnaces.
I know they will not turn back
More than the centuries turn not back.
More than the relentless rivers turn not back.
More than the waves turn not back
Which dash the great ship upon the rocks
And churn her bones savagely.
Death sits in the eyes of the imminent host.
They have accepted the challenge
And are pressing forward, ready to die and to kill.
Their breasts are naked.
They have beaten their picks into swords,
Their saws into knives.
Their eyes are fixed.
They are willing to die.
Death is their drummer;

Drumming upon the unknown graves
Of the oppressed.
Like knapsacks on their backs,
Bowing them over,
Is the untold suffering of the centuries.
They are heavy with ages of martyrdom;
The unimagined, patient Poor
Whose blood has forever welled up
About the knees of Oppression.

Revolution, dark and brooding angel;
Only ministrant who lifts up the bruised head;
Nurse who wipes the blood from martyr lips
And gives life-giving waters to those who thirst;
Saviour and Preserver;
Helper and Deliverer;
Your hands are gilt with crimson.
Your feet are the strong feet of a runner.
Your head is crowned with a crown of thorns,
And precious drops drip down
Your resolute face.
Dread Angel of the Awful Presence,
Open and set the captives free.
Dark, silent, loving, cruel, and merciful One,
Hold yourself not aloof.
You are our hope;
Our only redeemer.
Come, with thunder and with lightning,
That the air may be clear.
Come, with deluge and tempest,
That the Earth may be purified.
Come, with agony and bloody rain,
That Life may be made anew.
Pitch headlong from the cloudy battlements
And with heavenly fire utterly destroy
This distorted and misshapen world,
That another may rise in beauty,
And the little children be born into joy.

LIV

When August noons are hot, good it is to lie
Under an oak or spreading maple, in dry weeds
And grass that, dying, tell of sunburnt summer,
Loosing the soul toward a fellowship
With the unseen wanderer who snatches up
A handful of dust and playfully,
With a child's gesture, whirls it upward.
Good it is to look into the blue,
Between the shading leaves that shift and move;
And looking, dream and muse and speculate
What is the sky?—What is Infinity?
And what this kind, old mother-nurse who bears
Us tenderly until the evening, when she locks
Our eyelids down in a great peace and folds
Us into sleep—What is a weed?—a tree?—an ant?
What is a dust-whirl?
Perhaps, the finely powdered brain and skull
Of one who long ago in a most ancient time
Nursed at the breast awhile, lay in the mother lap
And looked into the sky—looking—wondering.
Perhaps I—who now am tossed in tireless arms,
Will, as a whirl of yellow dust, hold for a moment
The speculative eye of one who then will muse,
As I now do "What is the sky, and space
And life and death and what the purpose
Or no-purpose of a yellow dust whirl?"
So loafing in the dying grass along
A country road we only hear at first
The bark of distant dogs—a colt's shrill neigh
Or bellowing of bulls, pawing the dirt
Into the faces of their fellow prisoners,
The patient sheep. But when deep silence
Has attuned our ears to finer things, we hear
The little voices of the leaves and grass;
Katydids and locusts, crickets and grasshoppers
And the rumble of the burglar bumble-bee, plush-coated,
Searching blackberry blossoms and wild asters.
So when you rest upon the dusty way of life

Your summer peace will be disturbed by bark of Presidents,
The grunt of politicians and the bellowing
Of Congressmen who violently paw the dust into the eyes
Of sheep locked in a pasture long gone dry.
But sure as frost will follow, six weeks from
The katydid's shrill monody, you presently will hear
That great, stupendous, awful word—"A Statesman."
Then lay your ear close to the grass and as
You heard the cricket's violin beneath
The bark of dogs and bellowing of bulls,
You certainly will hear beneath the elocution,
A fine, thin, mocking, ribald laughter.
The Devil and his merry imps waking
Hell's roof and rafters with their dearest jest,
A Statesman—The State's man—
Never the People's man—The man who hatches war.
Young men—young women—there could be no war
If you would think—It is great toil to think.
It makes the tired soul sweat.
The sweat of the soul is salt.
It keeps life sweet.
Statesmen delight to drug you with that
Anodyne which leads you drowsily to Lethe.
"The People rule"—The People never ruled.
What is to rule ? To take by force—to break
By force a people to a Master's will.
To cheat the people with a cheating Law—
That is to rule—the people never ruled—
And yet for every flock there must be leaders.
Nature abhors monotony,
Continually she labors in the alcoves of
Her mystery for the eternal different
And the always new;
She holds two master keys, divine—
Birth—and Death.
One hangs continually fresh garlands;
The other sweeps the withered out.
In those cathedrals of the Titans, where the sun
Himself creeps secretly to worship, one sequoia giant

Pillars up the sky beyond the rest, and yet he holds
No privilege by Law of sun or rain or air;
The great field equal and the struggle free.

When steadily the wedge of honker-geese
Splits the night sky from south to north,
A captain leads—but not for self—and when
Like Jove—he wearies of his combat with the air
And falls into the general line—another
Takes his place with the same urge—
The equal benefit of all.
A bison herd has leaders—
Bulls, with mighty shoulder-humps, and massive heads
And patriarchal beards—foretops that screen
The fiery eyes, forever watchful.
When wide-spread, scarlet nostrils snuff the taint
Of wolf or man upon the wind, then massive heads
Are lowered and the up-curved horns of ebony
Front every danger; guardians of cows and calves.
These have no privileged pastures, no monopoly of waterfalls
And foamy streams and do not send young bulls
To fight while they, with silk-robed cows,
Wallow voluptuous in the cool, soft mud.
I have known peoples without "State" or "Statesmen";
And without gallows, jails, palaces, police or slums;
No poverty nor crime—none dreamed a man,
Above the cunning, grey coyote-thief,
Could have a wish to steal the common heritage
And cheat his brother into slavery,
Minting the weary, drudging life to coin
And to crime.
These were a people nursed at Freedom's breast so that
They could not guess at slavery but watched the hawk
Wheel in the air—and gazed into the face
Of every man in proud equality, as eagles stare
Against the sun from mountain crags.
The food of life, a general gift to all
From the great mother, partitioned by the chief;
He equal with each child—and fronting death
To keep the birthright of the child,

Not governor by force—but by the custom of
The tribe giving counsel and decision in a father's tone.
No forced obedience, but the disobedient was
An outlaw from the tribe—and such there never were.
Each owned what he himself had made—or she had made—
Blanket or bag, bow, basket, spear or tepee or canoe.
A commonwealth—Equality the guide and men and women
    free.
What need of jails—police or penitentiaries?
A simple people, whose smoked tepee tops scarce thrust
Above the willows, where the rippling little river ran.
No sky-assailing towers—no railroads, banks, no radios,
Except the blackbird's whistle and the crane's high call;
In every thought and act all free; from basket cradle
Swinging on a willow bough or branch of juniper
To the unmarked grave where the wind played with
The grass and Nature stooped a moment but
Refused to mourn.
The pine trees were their brothers and the cuckoo-owls
Their cousins; clouds their messengers. The winds
Ran from afar to bring them news. The rivers
Spoke to them in that blurred tongue of unseen spirits
And the hidden dead. The lava cliffs unrolled
To them pictures of the great travail, before
Man was—before the rivers were or any sea;
When all the world was flame and mountains blazed
As torches and the rivers were of fire.
Freely they gave and freely took without humility,
And, unafraid, they wrapped their souls about them
And lay down upon the mother-breast, so close,
They heard the beating of the cosmic heart:
Knowing that they were kin to all—and all
Were kin to them—and life—not property,
The destiny of Man.
Their houses, flitting as dry leaves in Autumn wind
Were frail to let the stars come in: and to them came
Freedom, Equality and Justice; to lie upon the black
    bear-robes
Spread soft before the central fire, whose thin

Blue smoke went straight up to the gods.
A happy people. I have heard their songs and flutes—
Their chants and drums—their stories, laughter and
Their weeping—a happy people—accepting the great mystery
Without rebellion, as the juniper of many winters accepts it
And the larkspur of one melting spring accepts it;
As the beautiful doe with spotted fawn accepts it
And the beaver, which is cunning to dam up the rivers
In the meadows where tall, shivering aspen grow.
Very clear are the round, brown eyes
Of the beaver—full of wisdom.
A happy people, knowing a loving mother
Has provided more than enough for her children.
Glad are the days when the sun returns
Into the north, bringing a promise of plenty;
When salmon begin to leap in the rivers
And wickiups of willow are hastily built
Along the bank where the rapids toss
And like silver arrows the salmon desperately dart
Toward clear fountains and gravelly beds
Where they were born. All build a wing dam
To guide the shining ones into a narrow channel,
To meet, as all must meet, their fate,
Entangling nets and piercing spears.
Then is the red flesh split and spread on drying racks;
Sheets of flame when the sun shines through.
Bright are the evening fires that toast the salmon;
And sweet the half burnt head—Winter forgotten.
Now the children bathe in the river and run on the shore,
Shooting with arrows. Bear comes down to the fishing.
At the end of the running the chief divides the catch
With just equality. Was it not all the gift of the mother?
Did not all build the dam? Or when the Enormous Sea
Offers Earth's children a gift and sends
Through its bays a torrent of herring,
Eager to spawn on the sea weed—
Bark huts are built near the shingle and cedar boughs
Anchored in shallows until well loaded
With pearly eggs, heavily they are lifted,

Masses of opalescent spoil, dripping from the sea.
Feasts of salt-sea morsels; abundant harvest,
Smoked and dried and packed in parflêche bags
For the lean and hungry days when the sun refuses his love.
Now trout vault for the gauzy wings above
Dark quiet pools and slip into the willow traps.
Green things grow and juicy—young tender nettles,
Dock just sprouting,
Thistle shoots, mustard, wild onion, Indian lettuce.
The golden chariot rolls its pageant;
Wild carrots, couse and the sweet camas bulbs
Whose pure cerulean lilies pave with sky the meadows.
Fruits and seeds and meat, blackberries, strawberries,
Huckleberries, loved by foxes and by bears;
Wild cherries and wild plums; amethysts from desert hills.
Wokus—the rich seeds of the lotus lily
Of Klamath marshes and the high lagoons.
Ducks and geese which followed the sun to the south,
Have come to these protecting swamps and raised their
    broods.
And long-shanked cranes.
Porcupines are fat; grouse have ceased from drumming,
And lead their busy speckled young.
Sharp-eyed boys with an unerring throw
Stone fool-hens from the tufted pines;
Abundance everywhere, even to bursting.
And as the grudging One steals near,
Wider and wider the mother spreads her arms.
The lordly ones come lower in the hills;
Haughty elk and dainty stepping deer,
And antelope fleet over the desert.
Now is much feasting—festal time of the whole year.
Continually the hunters come, bearing great burdens,
Fat carcasses swinging on poles between two carriers.
Joints hiss upon the coals, and bubble, pots,
Boiling the heads and shanks; cutlets, stuck
Before the blaze on willow wands, drip fatty juice.
The sticky toadstools sought beneath the pines
By greedy elk and bear, toast succulently, with

Good smell of roasted nuts.
The winter store of meat is jerked and packed,
As hard and black as ebony, and the grave chief,
 With the solemnity befitting one who deals with life
And justice, makes apportionment. Always the hide
To him who struck the quarry first.
But presently the mountains lock their doors—
Let fall the barriers and silence comes
As comes the snow. No thing stirs.
Even rabbits have found wings and the small
Grey crow comes closer, begging its share.
And so the long dark nights, the short dark days,
Winter—so slow the melting days which break
The chains—the Sun delays his love.
Long—long—too long the Mother lies
Locked in hard icy arms—past hope, too long.
The children hunger and the men grow lean.
Gone is the meat and small the store of roots
And it is good to chew the inner bark
Of the black pine to ease sharp hunger.
The chief sends out the hunters—in three bands—
To dare the mountains and meet Death
Along those snowy parapets where elk and deer
Have made their yards—and stand against
The fiercest fear of all, the grey wolf pack.
Each hunter has a double handful of dried roots—
No more—the rest is fate.
Three days—and nothing heard—and four—and five.
Still nothing—Starvation sits beside the fire.
Then through the evening dusk, a far, faint call
That tells the hunters have returned, and bringing game.
Five bucks—three does—a cougar and an elk
He had pulled down—Where are the others ?
These thought that they would be the last, but they are first.
The chief allots, and the tired hunters
Who have eaten liver, heart, kidneys and marrow-gut,
Lie by the fire, their task well done.
Morsels are snatched, burning the lips,
And once again the belly-skin is stretched.

The wrinkled, grey shaman, by children feared,
And feared by squaws and men, tightens his drum
And chants reproaches to the angry sun—and prayer.
The moon walks through the pine tops and the children hear
How came the sun and moon and stars and how
The Indians first got fire.
A simple people with no gallows and no jails.

INTRODUCTION TO *Maia*

Maia IS THE MOST LAVISHLY designed and expensively printed of all
C. E. S. Wood's books. Printed at F. W. Baltes in an edition of 186
copies, *Maia* features ten plates by Wood's friend, the painter
Alfred Brennan. Two of the plates (reproduced on page 253) are
quite flattering portraits of Erskine and Sara, making them look
like figures out of Greek mythology. The book is thirteen and a
half inches tall and nine and a half inches wide, folio size, and
bound in linen and boards. The typeface is Priory Text, a black
letter type that is elegant and suggestive but difficult for the
modern reader. It was, however, one of Wood's favorites, possibly
because of its ornate richness and its medieval, Biblical authority.
Each page is embossed with a design of twin dolphins. The deluxe
paper is cream colored, thick and untrimmed.

A sonnet sequence that follows the seasons, *Maia* intersperses
sonnets with prose meditations and short lyrics. Two of Sara's
poems appear and the frontispiece of a couple watching a sunrise
is Wood's own. Several epigraphs, printed in a large point size and
in a cleaner typeface, possibly Janson or Caslon, carry these
words: "The reader must also be a poet," "Life is not in the years,
but in the living," and "Poetry is everywhere." The colophon
credits "scrivener Kitty Beck" and "A. L. B." (Alfred Brennan) for
"decorations and types," and John Julius Johnck, a printer who
was working with Baltes at the time and would go on to a fine
career as a printer and book designer.

MAIA

XLVII

Thrice-blessed are we, my lover with grey eyes,
  To dwell within this peach-perfumed spot,
Far from the paltry turbulence and lies.
  Here, narrow superstitions are forgot;
We live our life as Nature willed we should,
  In full abandon of the wholly free;
Knowing that untaught longings are all good,
  The soul-blown seed from far eternity.
The scarlet dogwood strips her beauty bare,
  But the dark pine stands clad for winter snow;
Shall every weed perceive its proper care
  And not the spirit its true welfare know?
Better than all Man's blighting, blind control,
The unchecked blossoms of the God-born soul.

LXV

Winter, big, brawny wrestler of the year,
  Watching subdued above Spring's bridal-bed
Until her first faint waking signs appear,
  Garlands of buds about her lovely head.
How masterful you are, strong, naked one,
  Brown in your lustihood, and in your train
Dance all the sisterhood of Earth and Sun,
  In silver weavings of the sweet, slant rain.
I like your reckless brawlings through the land,
  Your burly buffets and rough challenges;
I'll boldly take your wet and dripping hand
  To try a bout where grinning satyrs press;
Or watch you lying on Earth's bosom, cold,
Whispering to coax the jonquil cups of gold.

LXVIII

From freedom comes our growth and all our good.
  I know how deep your soul has hungered it,
Just to be free in a bound, stupid, rude
  And too intrusive world. To, musing, sit
Weaving the fabric of your fantasy;
  Joying in creation-lust. Creator thou;
Rich in the rustless ores of poesy;
  Slaking your soul-thirst in the nectared Now.
As humming-birds the honeysuckle suck,
  We will rejoice in rains which make the flowers;
From thistles we'll the purple blossoms pluck,
  Toss garlands on the free, unfettered hours.
So you shall find from sordid bonds release,
And in my arms the sure and perfect peace.

XXI

Put up your lips, O sun-parched Earth, and drink
    The cool, bright draught sucked from the old, salt Sea.
Fill full your brooks and fountains to the brink,
    To cheer when Summer burns too grievously.
Winds tear and tumble the distracted trees;
    Hoarse as the sea through the bent branches roar;
But now, with gentle hissing through the leaves,
    The sky-flung drops in whispering music pour;
Then a gold rift proclaims the storm is done,
    And Earth, all dripping, stands with shining feet;
Her million jewels flashing back the sun,
    While silenced birds renew their joy complete.
I would heart-ease quickly might follow pain,
As song of birds comes after summer rain.

WOOD'S LONG LAW CAREER is distinguished by its unusual diversity. He had wealthy and powerful clients such as the New York international banking firm of Lazard Freres, the Charles Ladd Estate, and the North West Electric Company, but he also defended Margaret Sanger, Emma Goldman, and Marie Equi. This last case, although he lost it, called forth one of Erskine's most eloquent and original briefs, one that displays his persuasive combination of legal skills, resourcefulness, and knowledge of the classics.

Marie Equi was a Portland physician, sympathetic to socialism and the I.W.W., although a member of neither, and unalterably opposed to militarism and World War I. In a letter to U.S. Attorney General A. Mitchell Palmer in the spring of 1919, Wood describes Dr. Equi as "an Italian . . . of exceeding sympathy for suffering and poor humanity" who had been highly commended for splendid service in San Francisco during the 1906 earthquake and fire. Early in 1918, however, Dr. Equi was arrested, jailed, and convicted in Portland for speaking out against the war and for demonstrating in the front of a patriotic parade. The case was carried to the United States Circuit Court of Appeals, Ninth District in San Francisco, to be heard on the 29th of May, 1919.

The brief that Wood filed on her behalf brought him recognition beyond Oregon. For example, U. S. Senator Homer Bone of Washington regarded it as "one of the finest bits of briefing I had ever seen because of your forthright approach to the problem of individual rights under the Constitution." According to Wood's eldest son, Erskine, his father's whole defense of Dr. Equi was that her conviction was "in violation of her constitutional right of free speech, and realizing that the precedents cited by the prosecution were against him, he turned to Rabelais." Despite the brief's virtues, it could not prevail against the persistence of wartime hysteria and Dr. Equi's appeal was denied. In 1920, she served ten months of a three-year sentence in San Quentin. She died in 1952, a forgotten woman.

from Free Speech and the Constitution in the War

Of what uses are authorities except as they exemplify the philosophy of the law, whose foundation is truth? To pile up cases and proudly point to the height of the pile, or to accept them with bated breath as the Revealed Word, though they are the utterance of mere men of like passions and limitations as ourselves who happen to be clothed for the moment in silk gowns and legalized power, is to surrender reason to superstition, to bow before the oracle, unquestioning the human priest who sits behind the screen. This superstitious following of the larger body of cases regardless of their reasoning is no better than the judicial method of Justice Bridlegoose, who defended himself against the charge of rendering a corrupt decision:

> *My Lords, I listen to the proctors and advocates of the one side patiently and then to the proctors and advocates of the other side patiently, just as your lordships do; then I retire to my chambers, where I have a great brass scales—the Scales of Justice. Into one pan I place all the bills, petitions, complaints and demurrers whatsoever, prepared by the solicitors, proctors, counsellors, notaries and prothonotaries of the one side, and into the other pan I place all the answers, replies, cross-bills and counter-pleadings whatsoever prepared by the solicitors, proctors, counsellors, notaries, and prothonotaries for the parties of the other side; just as your lordships do, and to whichever side weighs down the scales, I give my decision, just as your lordships do. If by chance the Scales of Justice should hang evenly balanced, then I appeal to God; just as your lordships do—and I place the dice in the box and shake first for the one side, then for the other, and to whichever side receives the highest throw I give my decision; just as your lordships do. For forty years, my lords, this has been my just and unalterable practice, which has given satisfaction until now, and I am at a loss to understand the failure of justice in this case unless it be that, as by the growing infirmities of age my eyesight has become dimmed, I mistook a deuce for a trey.*

It was the sacrifice of justice to distorted and garbled theory, and to the exigencies of the moment; the surrender of judges to royal wishes and to the demands of governments pleading "Necessity" which produced this, the bitterest and wittiest satire on the courts.

We shall presently quote from some of the authorities on which the Government relies in this case, cited in its brief, and we shall ask if they do not wholly violate the philosophy, the history and the precedents of the law as to free speech. We shall ask if Star Chamber or any other tyranny for the suppression of freedom of thought, speech and conscience could not and would not have cheerfully adopted these very utterances as quite sufficient for its purposes. Of what use to cite authorities on our side? The authorities to which we and the judges of this bench were bred as illustrating the steady march of the law toward unrestrained, unpunished speech in opposition to government, toward the protection of the life and liberty of innocent persons, have been blown away like autumn leaves by false and ridiculous subterfuge and sophistical logic born out of the passions of war. The noble edifice in which we were all reared, Bench and Bar, and which we were taught to defend as the Temple of Justice, founded in the eternities and to which all those persecuted by tyranny might flee, has been bombed and we walk about in its ruins; but let us poke a little among the ruins and see if we can find the old foundations.

The Bill of Rights of the United States Constitution was not the offhand, sudden production of Thomas Jefferson and Thomas Paine; but merely worded the maxims of Liberty wrung from the centuries by the noblest of all soldiery, the brave men, deserted and slain on scaffold and in dungeon, who gave up life that the future might have life; the rebels against the Lord's Anointed, who died to make men free. The Bill of Rights in our Constitution is only the verbal record of centuries of resistance to the suppressions and restrictions of governments who always are the majority, in the sense of wielding organized power against unorganized helplessness. These constitutional protections are in actual fact always for the weaker, and either they must protect these weaker, whether few or many, or in time they will assert themselves in armed rebellion.

Tyrannies were and are always against a minority; a strong coercive power, *force majeure* legalized against an unorganized, unofficial lot of individuals. It makes no difference if the government be an absolute monarch with the unorganized masses of the people secretly against him; organized government is always stronger in its physical force than any group of individuals. Government has always stood for "the will of the people" in the sense that the people by their silence consented to the tyranny; by their acquiescence they supported the government. It has always been the lonely few who fought, protested, went to execution or prison cell for freedom. History has clearly taught that if these few do not get free speech by constitutional protection they will get it some other way. So the unwritten British Constitution and our written one in their essence are the bulwark of the few, or the *weaker*, even if *many;* the unwelcome, the friendless, the isolated few; in advance of their time agitating for the new thing, for still further change, that children may be born into a greater measure of happiness. Man has always agitated and probably will agitate till the end of time; the conception of freedom is as infinite as Time.

The great popular majority never needs constitutional protection. Their license is always in their numbers and the popularity of their views. Their tyranny over the minority may be greater and more savage than that of any autocrat. We want to emphasize that the Constitution of the United States protects—no, it does not protect, but it was intended to protect—free speech against the tyranny of either the few over the many or the many over the few; to safeguard against all tyranny by superior force and all suppression from any *force majeure* whatever. Once more, for it is important, the first amendment in its concrete human application, was intended to be the shield for the *weak, unpopular few.* This is the teaching of its historical evolution. This is its basic philosophy. This is the reason for its existence. Any court that permits it to fail of this high purpose has raped the Goddess of Liberty.

Fourth Stage
(1920-1944)

This fourth stage, stretching over two decades, was the longest in C. E. S. Wood's writing career. He was at last able to put the practice of law in Portland behind him and look for a place where he and Sara might make writing their chief concern. After spending several years in San Francisco and the first eight months of 1924 in Europe, they decided to build the house in Los Gatos that was their home as long as he lived.

Between 1920 and 1940, the United States, along with the rest of the world, underwent rapid and dramatic changes. The era was set off by two world wars and bisected by the Great Depression. The twenties saw the Palmer raids against alien radicals, including Emma Goldman, the revival of the Ku Klux Klan, and the execution of Sacco and Vanzetti in 1927. Nicola Sacco and Bartolomeo Vanzetti, Italian anarchists, were arrested, tried, convicted of murder, and sentenced to death in New York in 1920. Liberals and radicals in the U.S. and abroad charged that they had been tried for their radical views, and the case became a *cause célèbre*. The Depression decade of the 1930s saw the repeal of prohibition, the passage of Franklin D. Roosevelt's alphabet soup of reform bills, and the outbreak of war in Europe with Germany's invasion of Poland in the fall of 1939.

The reactionary temper of the 1920s provided convenient targets for Erskine's satiric *Heavenly Discourse*, brought out by the radical Vanguard Press in 1927. Two years later that same press published a third edition of *The Poet in the Desert*, in which Erskine added passages that gave the poem a more radical tone. Vanguard Press hoped to equal the popularity of *Heavenly Discourse* with Wood's *Too Much Government* (1931) and *Earthly Discourse* (1933), though neither came near to doing so.

From 1925 until Erskine died in 1944, life at The Cats was a rich mix of the privacy to write that the two poets coveted so much, an involvement in national and international causes, and the joy of entertaining a variety of friends.

Examples of the extent and variety of activities at Los Gatos abound. On the local scene, Erskine spoke and wrote and contributed cash to support Tom Mooney, the radical San Francisco labor leader imprisoned in San Quentin for the alleged bombing of a Preparedness Day parade in 1916. His conviction was a patent frame-up but he was not pardoned until 1939 by California Governor Culbert Olson. Max Hayek, a Viennese Jew and German translator of Walt Whitman, Rabindranath Tagore (East Indian poet and philosopher), and *The Poet in the Desert*, sought Wood's help in fleeing Hitler's Germany. The Woods offered him asylum at The Cats, enlisted help from their friends, and contributed money to the San Francisco Committee for Emigrés that enabled Hayek to escape via Cuba late in 1938.

A substantial part of Erskine's energy over the years went into letter writing. He kept up a voluminous correspondence with the American painter J. Alden Weir, and maintained somewhat less extended exchanges with William Rose Benét, poet and editor of *Saturday Review of Literature*; with Corinne Roosevelt Robinson, Teddy Roosevelt's sister; and with Mark Van Doren, poet and professor of literature at Columbia University.

In this fourth stage Wood consolidated his reputation in American letters and published or republished those works upon which his literary standing rests: *A Book of Tales, The Poet in the Desert, Heavenly Discourse,* and *Poems from the Ranges.*

Wood's remarkable health held until 1935 and his personal vision and magnetism combined with his literary production to impress a number of people that here was a writer of real stature. An editor who had disliked Wood in the past, Colonel Hofer of *The Lariat*, proposed in 1925 in *Overland Monthly and Out West* that Erskine was a good candidate for national poet laureate.

It is in this period that many of Erskine's literary friendships were formed—Jeffers, Steinbeck, Taggard, Rose Benét, Van Doren, Steffens. Erskine and Sara's devotion to literature, to making a gracious home, and to each other impressed and delighted those who knew them. After many years, Wood was living as he had wished and it showed in the energy with which he wrote and contributed to the literary and political life of the time.

Clearly, the last two decades of Erskine's life were golden years made doubly precious because they were shared with Sara who, over and above her devotion to him, was able to establish herself as a California poet of some distinction.

THIS IS A PORTION of a loving and witty will-in-verse that Erskine wrote to his children and grandchildren. Dated, "The Metolius River, Jefferson County, Oregon, July 1, 1921," it is another manifestation of his gift for occasional poetry. Here, Wood bequeaths various aspects of the family's summer retreat at Camp Sherman according to his sense of each child's character.

FROM THE TESTAMENT OF CHARLES ERSKINE SCOTT WOOD

In the names of all the Pagan gods,
I, Charles Erskine Scott Wood,
The sole and single of that name,
Knowing seventy years of ill and good,
Unknown to that junk dealer, Fame,
Though in my youth I, stupid, fought,
Wearing the livery of the State,
Whose might is by the richest bought—
A bully which protects the great;
And served that prostitute, the Law,
Whose favors are for rich and strong;
And now, white-headed, last I draw
My pen to write a twilight song;
But not for Fame.—I write these words
In the pine woods, where mountain balm
Sweetens the air and many birds
Twitter unto the forest calm
Each his own song,—careless if he be heard—
Make now my last sure will and testament
For that dear and up-sprouting brood,
Those grandchildren, in hut and tent,
Who share with me this solitude
And whom I must too shortly leave.
Good-bys at seventy are uncertain things.
The gods delight poor mortals to deceive
And Time flies in the dusk on owlish wings.

To NANCY HONEYMAN, around whose face,
Slender and sad, cling long curls dark,
I leave the peace and quiet of this place:
The tall pines, which in solemn park
And shadowy aisles, red pillars stand;
And when with folly she is grey,
Will still be here, stretching strong hands
To welcome her who has been long away.
To her I give some certain beds of mine
Where soft on pine-leaves many an hour I lay,
My back against a kindly comrade pine,
And watched the chipmunks on the logs at play.
To her, also, I make a good bequest
Of the people of the woods, the wide-eyed deer,
Burly black bears, squirrels and the rest,
Especially this chipmunk, who with neither fear
Nor reverence now at me squeaks and jibes
From my own log, jerking his little tail.
I mean the one with black and yellow stripes
Along his sides. Nor let this giving fail.

Erskine with members of his family at Camp Sherman, circa 1928

To "Buzzy," David Erskine Honeyman,
Of the quick smile, I freely give the flowers,
And that's a treasure for the great god Pan.
Blue lupines, orchids, pale, which after showers,
Each holds a moonstone at its stem,
Blue penstemon, red cardinals and bright
Indian paintbrush, and the diadem
Of cool, damp spots, the Mt. Hood lilies, white;
Wild peonies, and by the river's brim
Yellow snap-dragons. All the flowers and weeds
Unknown, or low, or tall, I give to him;
But not the grasses, herbs or fruits or seeds.
These I except; one who owns the wild flowers
Has all the brightest of the long year's hours.
To him I give the nectar in the cups,
And draughts of that mad-making nectar,Truth.
Bitter it is, but of it all gods sup.
Also to him, that comic fellow,Youth,
With morning-glory clown-cap, harlequin
Suit of poppies, lilies, sunflowers, blue
Larkspur and wings of cobweb, thin.
Take care of them; they easy are torn through.

To Erskine Biddle Wood, called Erskinson,
I give all trout in the Metolius,
The pretty dottings their bright sides upon,
And the red streak;—the sudden splash and fuss
When quick they show a golden-gleaming side;
As swift they dart through the green waters cool,
The big ones who majestic, sullen hide
Each in his own dark ever-boiling pool.
Especially I give to him that monster one
He hooked at Horseshoe Bend and for an hour,
A long hour by the watch and by the sun,
Valiant fought, praying the gods for power
To land him, and that Daddy would but come.
But who can hold or stay the hand of Fate?
When conquered, only gasping, sudden gone
By the mere lifting of his giant weight.
So sink we in the pool Oblivion

By our own weight.—To stout-heart ERSKINSON
I do bequeath this trout and his estate.
The round-eyed beaver unto him, also
I give, shy vassals of the river,—cunning folk,
Engineers who dam the river flow,
Hew trees and dig canals. If they but spoke,
They would be wise as us;—could shoot and vote.
The grey-haired Moon who, since this round World's
    birth,
Has climbed Green Ridge, sees us and sees the beaver
As coldly she looks down on our dark earth.
I wonder which she loves, and which the River.
I give him mornings on the river-bank,
Song of the river when the new sun shines
On the ripples, and the grass with dew is dank
Also the solemn discourse of the pines,
At evening when the melting shadows fall
And Peace sits on the bank with folded wings;
The birds all chirruping a good-night call,
And deep in dusk a yellow warbler sings.
The river-deeps, grey as his honest eyes,
I give to him. They run for many a mile,
And none can know, or guess, what in them lies;
And silver shallows, sweet as his grave smile;
And as appurtenant to this, my gift,
I give the salmon-flies that to the breeze
Of June their gauzy sails uplift;
The caddis and the gnats, all such as these;
And the overhanging banks so lush and brave;
But not the evening primrose, or candles white
Of the big-leaf. These I have given DAVE.
The river is for ERSKINSON's delight.

The fourth stage of Wood's career brought him a measure of fame, probably for the right reason. C. E. S. Wood was a very witty man. Alfred Powers, author of *History of Oregon Literature*, called him "the merriest of men" and a brilliant conversationalist. He also had a sharp eye for hypocrisy and pretense and sharpened that eye throughout his life. It is not surprising that as he matured his talent for satire would flower. His Christmas pieces and his "Impressions" column in *Pacific Monthly* bristled on occasion with invective and irony, combining a rollicking sense of humor with a refined sense of social justice.

Wood's satirical side blossomed in response to the First World War. In 1914, possibly at the suggestion of John Reed, Max Eastman, an editor of the effervescently radical new magazine, *The Masses*, asked Wood for something humorous. Moved by rage, Wood responded with a series of dialogues, a form he had experimented with in "Impressions," a form not alien to the legal profession, and one that showed his reverence for the Socratic method.

As a satirist, Wood was rough and tumble, relying on parody, irony, and burlesque. Satire tries to break down petrified beliefs, oppressive proprieties, and stereotypical sentiments in order to promote the free flow of human relations. "Freedom, freedom, always freedom," God says in *Heavenly Discourse*, "then let us see what will come of it."

Two things are necessary for satire: a sense of the absurd and an object of attack. In the conservative social orthodoxies of patriotism, prudery, bigotry, censorship, dogmatic Christianity, and organized religion, Wood found hardened credences needful of dismantling by the engines of satire. In such types as munitions makers, KKK leaders, bigots, and censors, and characters like Billy Sunday, Anthony Comstock, Teddy Roosevelt, and William Randolph Hearst, Wood located the absurd through the instrument of parody. Both *Heavenly Discourse* and *Earthly Discourse* make liberal and hilarious use of parody and burlesque, though the former is more slapstick, more rough-hewn and Juvenalian. Wood's use of parody is one of the most engaging and barbed aspects of his satirical style. The objects of Wood's satirical attacks hoist themselves with their own petard, dangling from their foibles, giving readers some cleansing guffaws.

The central irony of *Heavenly Discourse* is that the setting is a heaven in which a benevolently irritable God is not particularly interested in earth, "that little pill." The universe is so large and magnificent and functioning so beautifully according to the laws of freedom that earth's travails seem childish, petulant, infinitesimal, and vainglorious to the God of *Heavenly Discourse.*

The basic structure of *Heavenly Discourse,* therefore, is ironic. The earth and her agents (who get to heaven but are often not treated as they would expect) see things one way, but God and his host of philosophers, writers, political figures, social reformers— Voltaire, Thomas Paine, Rabelais, Robert Ingersoll, Mark Twain, Socrates, to name a few—see things in quite another. There are also various angels, led by St. Peter, who seems rather befuddled since God has relieved him of his gate-keeping duties. Satan shows up, promoting war, greed, and idolatry, gleeful at the mendacity of humanity, and God tolerates him, saying, "I must admit the devil relieves the monotony." The same God and the same Satan appear in several of the dialogues in *Earthly Discourse,* but the setting is no longer heaven, which mutes the power of the satire.

Some of the discourses are quite topical. One is called "England's General Strike" and another ("The Monkeys Complain") deals with the Scopes trial; many contain characters and allusions contemporary readers might find hard to place, such as Elihu Root, Anthony Comstock, and Wayne Wheeler. However, Wood's vital sense of parody allows the reader to recognize an interfering politician, a moral prig, and an evangelical prohibitionist, identifiable and enduring stereotypes in most societies.

One of the most mirthful features of Wood's satire is his use of the verbal tempest, a cataract of words, sometimes a series of epithets, sometimes an effusion of praise. In *Heavenly Discourse,* Wood often gives these to Rabelais, who strings together a long, succulent list of wines or beers or viands to defend them from a Puritan or warmonger.

The satire in *Heavenly Discourse* (1927) and *Earthly Discourse* (1937) recalls Menippus and Lucian of the Roman era. Used by Voltaire in *Candide,* Rabelais in *Gargantua and Pantagruel,* and Twain in *"1601"* and *Letters from the Earth,* this type of satire is constructed around dialogues in which various types of people make ridiculous their own points of view.

Heavenly Discourse, C. E. S. Wood's most popular work, had its origin in the fall of 1914 with a witty attack on the war in Europe called "A Heavenly Dialogue" published in *The Masses,* and written in response to editor Max Eastman's request. He and co-editor John Reed liked the satire and asked for more. Erskine complied, stipulating only that the word *discourse* be used instead of *dialogue* in subsequent conversations. Wood wrote nine more satiric discourses, all of them consistent with *The Masses'* masthead that trumpeted its pledge to print "what is too naked or true for a money-making press," before the government suppressed the magazine in 1917 for alleged interference with the war effort.

About eight years after the demise of *The Masses,* at the urging of friends, Wood revised and added to the satiric discourses until he had forty. In 1927, Jacob Baker, editor of Vanguard Press, a radical New York publishing house, brought out a fifty-cent edition of 3,000 under the title *Heavenly Discourse.* In an introduction, Floyd Dell, a former editor of *The Masses,* called the satires "in their wit and truth and imagination the expression of a large and noble mind" and "a lofty and sensitive spirit." He went on to place Erskine "in the great tradition of Aristophanes, Lucian, Rabelais, Swift, Mark Twain, Anatole France, and Bernard Shaw."

The first edition sold out almost overnight and the book soon became Vanguard Press's best seller. In 1944, a few months after the author's death, *Heavenly Discourse* went into its 25th printing and shortly thereafter, in the fall of 1945, Penguin Books bought reprint rights from Vanguard. Writing to William Rose Benét on that occasion, Wood's widow Sara remembered seeing Penguin books on little bookstalls on the Seine with Erskine in 1924 and hearing him say, "This is the way to educate the people, cheap editions of good books. . . the masses should have books like these,"—"and now his *Heavenly Discourse* is one of them."

Erskine was not surprised at the success of his satire for, while he admitted that much of *Heavenly Discourse* dealt with episodes or figures no longer current, he recognized an enduring need to ridicule war and prudery and intolerance. He knew, too, that although some would find the discourse heavy-handed, there was an audience among the young, the rebellious, and the unconventional that would relish raucous satire fashioned to bludgeon rather than pierce. Horace Gregory, writing in *New Republic* (January 1, 1930), hailed *Heavenly Discourse* as "the best example of rough and tumble journalistic satire ever published in this country."

Heavenly Discourse carries as frontispiece a portrait of the author by Hugo Gellert, a New York artist who favored radical reform. As the story goes, a printer, in a hurry to meet a deadline, phoned the Vanguard editorial office demanding Erskine's picture for the frontispiece. "You have it," the publisher answered. We sent it with the copy." "Well, it's not here," snapped the printer. "The only picture we have is one of God." There were also eight illustrations by cartoonist, Art Young, each cut catching the spirit of the text. Wood wrote publisher Jacob Baker: "Proofs just received and my wife and I laughed ourselves sore over Art's imagination and humor."

Wood has fun with his characters—Noah, the drunken mariner who prefers wine after his experience with water; Rabelais, incessantly bemoaning the loss of his mortal gullet; Satan, petitioning Omniscience for a contract to permit him to light and move the stars, certain that he can generate enough power in hell to run the universe; God himself, his patience tried almost beyond endurance, mutters, "I'll be damned," and then realizes that, of course, he can't be. Nor was the humor always within the discourse, as when a woman customer asked a San Francisco book dealer, in a phrase of unconscious redundancy, where she might find "Celestial Intercourse."

Wood was pleased to learn of the kinds of readers *Heavenly Discourse* was winning. The largest sales in 1928 came from the Hobo Bookstore on San Francisco's Market Street. A cafe on Telegraph Avenue in Berkeley kept a short stack of the book at the cash register. Professor of history Huntley Dupre of Miami College, Oxford, Ohio, wrote that, after he read his class some selections from *Heavenly Discourse*, 13 students asked for the book at once, 30 more the next day, and then 8 more. He thought Erskine would be happy to know "there are some who could not themselves make their weapons but who are glad to use those you forge for them."

When all is said, for at least a generation, *Heavenly Discourse* proved to be an effective vehicle to project its author's hatred of war, his disdain for sham, and his passion for freedom, not to mention his sense of humor.

Introduction to "Marriage"

This discourse, first printed in *The Masses* in 1915, was in large part responsible for the removal of the January number from New York City news stands because in the discourse Jesus asks God: "Father, were you and mother ever married?"

Marriage

[*God and Jesus are strolling through the universe, stepping from star to star.*]

Jesus: Father, how small the earth is in the infinity of space, among stars, bewildering in magnitude.

God: Yes. A speck. Why are you so fond of it?

Jesus: I don't know. Because they crucified me, I guess.

God: Well, yes, I can understand that.

Jesus: We love where we forgive, and we never forget where we have suffered.

God: No, I suppose not. I never suffered.

Jesus: Didn't you suffer when Aaron set up the golden calf?

God: No. I made him suffer.

Jesus: Father, am I the only son you ever had?

God: No, my son. I have had many sons, but you are the only son I ever had by a Jewess.

Jesus: Father, were you and mother ever married?

God: Ever what?

Jesus: Married. Holy matrimony. Holy wedlock.

God: Holy smoke! what are you talking about?

Jesus: On earth when a man and a woman love and want to unite their lives, they have first to get leave or license from somebody— then they have to stand before a priest or some other man and say something, and he tells them all right they may love. They are married. But when you are married, it is for forever and you can never go apart, even though you grow out of love and are very unhappy.

GOD: My son, your earth-visits are beginning to affect your mind.

JESUS: I don't say this. But they say it is your law.

GOD: Who says so?

JESUS: The priests and the county clerk.

GOD: When you want to know my law come to me—or look around you. You don't see or hear this foolishness anywhere else, do you?

JESUS: No, only where there are men and priests.

GOD: My laws are universal. Your mother and I loved each other and you were born as flowers are born.

JESUS: Then I am a bastard?

GOD: What do you mean?

JESUS: On earth, if the father and mother are not married, the child is a bastard. And I was born on earth.

GOD: You don't seem to be able to get away from that perfectly absurd earth.

JESUS: No, it's not that, but now in the midst of this war to end war, they want to get more babies for soldiers in the next war and there will be a lot of poor little innocent bastards. The Church—

GOD: Don't mention it. We have nothing to do with it.

JESUS: And the State—

GOD: What's that?

JESUS: The rich few who govern the people.

GOD: O, gods?

JESUS: Yes, in a way. The Church and the State, in order to have more men for more wars, are urging a lot of young men and women to take out permission papers for leave to love and have babies.

GOD: That's marriage?

JESUS: Yes.

GOD: Holy matrimony?

JESUS: Yes.

GOD: What makes it holy?

JESUS: The love of the pair for each other.

GOD: What has the Church or the State to do with that?

JESUS: Nothing. But as I was saying, the Church and the State urged the young people to get babies; certificates, I mean, so that they could get more babies for more wars.

GOD: Couldn't they get any babies without this certificate?

JESUS: Certainly, and that's the trouble. A lot of young people are doing it, but the children will be bastards.

GOD: Won't they be just as good babies?

JESUS: Yes.

GOD: Did the babies insist on certificates?

JESUS: No.

GOD: Won't they make just as good soldiers and mothers of soldiers? The boys can be killed just the same?

JESUS: O, yes.

GOD: Then what's the trouble?

JESUS: I don't know. Only, if the parents are not legally married, the babies are bastards.

GOD: So they punish the babies? Is it marked on them?

JESUS: No.

GOD: Does it hurt their health?

JESUS: No, Father, but Christians look down on them. They say such births are not lawful.

GOD: Christians look down on most everything that is loving and sensible. Has this loving and pairing without permission been going on very long?

JESUS: Ever since creation.

GOD: My! My! How awful!

JESUS: Father, you are mocking.

GOD: I have to—in order not to send an affliction on your stupid, silly pismires and blot them out. But they will do that themselves. Why not kill the unlawfuls as soon as born? Why let them be born?

JESUS: O, the State and the Church can use them; but the idea is this: the parents are rebels, in a way. They didn't have leave from Church and State to get these babies.

GOD: Well, I'll be—no, of course, I couldn't be. Listen. Won't these babies grow up to be men and women?

JESUS: Yes. But the Church and the State will call them bastards. They'll be forever disgraced.

GOD: Who? The Church and the State?

JESUS: No, the babies.

GOD: Are you disgraced?

JESUS: No, Father. I am your beloved son.

GOD: My beloved son. Who was never smirched by Church or State. Leave to love. Let us go home. Your talk has made me just a little tired. I can endure anything but stupidity. My law is—The stupid shall pass away.

INTRODUCTION TO "BILLY SUNDAY MEETS GOD"

HERE WOOD USES Billy Sunday as the central figure in an attack on Protestant evangelism. William A. Sunday (1863-1935) was born in Iowa and moved to Chicago in the 1880s to play major league baseball. In 1886, at a Chicago street revivalist meeting, Sunday came to Christ and went on to become a famous evangelical preacher in the tradition of Charles Finney, Dwight Moody and, more recently, Billy Graham. Wood ridicules Sunday as an ignorant, fanatical buffoon.

Other characters, already in heaven, who figure in the discourse and are the antithesis of Sunday include George Eliot (Mary Ann Evans, 1819-1880), distinguished English novelist who rebelled against her evangelical upbringing and renounced religion totally; and Robert Ingersoll (1833-1899) son of a Congregationalist minister, who became an attorney and a free thinker. Ingersoll was a superb orator and was widely known as "the great agnostic." Herman Morgenstern, keeper of a saloon, and Margaret Hartwell, mother of an illegitimate child, were Erskine's inventions, as was the heaven of the African Medicine Men.

Billy Sunday Meets God

Scene 1

[The outer battlements of Heaven, near the Earthly Gate, the battlements glittering with angels and archangels; the gate surrounded by guards, their wings restlessly flashing. St. Peter and a group of angels removed some distance back on an eminence. The gate opens a slight crack and the soul of Billy Sunday comes in.]

St. Peter: Michael, I thought the gate opened. Did something come in?

Michael: No, nothing.

St. Peter: Didn't the gate open?

Michael: Infinitesimally. The smallest soul in the universe couldn't have got in.

St. Peter: Certainly, something seems coming this way.

Michael: Is there a heaven for monkeys?

St. Peter: Oh, yes; but this isn't their gate.

Michael: Well, it's a monkey. Got in by mistake. That's what the gate opened for.

Raphael: I don't think it's a monkey. See it roll over and over.

Gabriel: It's like nothing on earth or in heaven.

George Eliot: Or the waters under the earth.

St. Peter: I can distinctly hear it bellowing.

Michael: It is frothing at the mouth.

George Eliot: Perhaps it is an idiot.

St. Peter: Well, it is now running toward us very fast, tossing arms and legs. We shall soon know.

[Billy Sunday's soul runs up, breathless. Puts out his hand to St. Peter.]

Billy Sunday: Well, old Pal. Here I am at last. Knocked the ball over the fence. Home run. Beat the Devil to the plate. The dirty, stinking, brimstone scab. He got his filthy claws on me, but I swiped him one in the guts that made him kiss that putrid hoof of his and forget his mother. Where's the kid?

St. Peter: Who?

Billy Sunday: Your boy Jesus.

St. Peter: I am Peter.

BILLY SUNDAY: Oh! I thought you was God. That's one on me. Where is God? Didn't he know I was coming? Me and him's been chums. Thick as thieves. For years. Pardners. I sent up more souls than anybody since that guy, Peter the Hermit. Bet I just about filled up this old caboose. Prospered at it, too. Talk about muzzling the ox. You can't muzzle me. I ain't no ox. I'm a bull, that's what I am. And I can make any bull of Bashan look like a Jersey heifer. I've been sending a stream of souls up here, like they was played out of a fire nozzle and at a discount, too. Bargain-counter rates. Trot out a gang of my souls, Pete, heifers and all. They'll want to see the fellow that umpired the game for them. Ain't none of my souls in this bunch?

ST. PETER: What is your name?

BILLY SUNDAY: Who? Me?

ST. PETER: Yes.

BILLY SUNDAY: My name?

ST. PETER: Yes.

BILLY SUNDAY: Don't you know me?

St. Peter: No.

BILLY SUNDAY: Ain't this heaven?

ST. PETER: It was.

BILLY SUNDAY: Oh, Ballyhoo. Take me up to the boss.

ST. PETER: Who?

BILLY SUNDAY: Take me up to the Old Man. He'll know me. This is ridiculous. I'll bet I've stocked this place. I'll bet you couldn't swing an arm, right paw or south paw, without hitting a soul I've sold his ticket to. While you fellers have been sitting around on clouds, drawing bellyache out of harps, I've been putting pep and ginger into the work. Going right down to hell and kicking the rotten cowardly Devil on his stinking tail and dragging souls out of the brimstone by their hair, and them in the baldheaded row by the slack of their breeches. Take me up to God. He'll know me. I ain't got no time to waste on porters and gatekeepers.

GEORGE ELIOT: Crazy!

MICHAEL: I don't understand him.

RAPHAEL: There's a mistake. He doesn't belong here.

ST. PETER: Gabriel, take him to the Throne.

BILLY SUNDAY: Did you fall guys ever get left? Pete is on to his job.

[*Puts his thumb to his nose and wiggles his fingers at the angels. Goes out with Gabriel.*]

Scene 2

[*God is on the throne of the universe. Jesus is standing beside him and millions of angels shine on either hand. Gabriel and Billy Sunday approach.*]

GOD: What is it, Gabriel?

GABRIEL: Peter sent me with this. We don't know what it is.

BILLY SUNDAY: It's me, God. Your pardner, Billy Sunday. You know my holler. I'll bet I've shook that throne a thousand times and made the Devil run like a yellow cur with a tin can and a bunch of firecrackers to his tail. I fought the old Brimstone Belcher to the finish, but I had to take the count at last, and here I am. Where is your wife and my brother, Jesus?

GOD: Jesus, is this your brother?

JESUS: I do not know him.

BILLY SUNDAY: Why, I have introduced you and your father to some of the biggest audiences you ever had. Glory! Glory! The Devil is turning poor sinners on his fork in the fires of hell. Too late for them, not too late for you. Come to Jesus! Come to Jesus! Glory! Glory! Salvation is free. God has got his foot on the Devil's neck, holding him while you can jump into heaven. Be quick! Jesus holds open the gate. Come to Jesus! Glory! Glory! Don't wait a minute. Come to Jesus now! Now! Right now! . . . That's the stuff. Recognize it?

GOD: No. Terrible. I never heard of you.

BILLY SUNDAY: Why, this place must be jammed with souls I sent here.

GOD: No. Not one.

BILLY SUNDAY: Not one?

GOD: Are there any, my son?

JESUS: Not one.

BILLY SUNDAY: Where are they?

GOD: I don't know. I never heard of you.

BILLY SUNDAY: Are you sure this is heaven and that you are God?

GOD: No. Not sure I am God—but this is heaven.

BILLY SUNDAY: Well, I want to tell you right here if this place isn't packed with my souls like a circus-tent on the fourth of July, it isn't the old, reliable, genuine heaven we were brought up to. Someone's been asleep at the switch.

GOD: This is heaven, and none of your souls are here.

BILLY SUNDAY: They must be somewhere.

GOD: Not necessarily. The cosmos is so very large and fanatics are so infinitely small.

BILLY SUNDAY: Well, something is wrong. I must have got into the wrong pew. Aren't you Jesus of Nazareth in Galilee—that was?

JESUS: Yes.

BILLY SUNDAY: Well, I've been calling you my brother ever since I began to hate Satan, as loud as I could holler.

JESUS: My brothers neither hate nor holler. They are the pure in heart, quiet, without malice, whose law is love.

BILLY SUNDAY: I guess there is some mistake. Is there any other heaven?

GOD: Many of them. There is one for African savages who shout and howl and jump around as you did just now. Maybe you will find your friends there.

BILLY SUNDAY: Why, there is Herman Morgenstern. I sent him to hell. He kept a family beer garden on Fourth Avenue in New York, that cesspool of sin. I sent him and the whole rotten, putrid, stinking, cowardly bunch of saloon-keepers lower than hell. They are so low down they will need an airship to reach hell. What is he doing here?

JESUS: I liked him. He was a gentle, charitable soul.

BILLY SUNDAY: But kept a beer saloon.

JESUS: I lived with publicans and sinners.

BILLY SUNDAY: And there is Margaret Hartwell. She had an illegitimate child. She sold her body. She was a harlot. I sent her to hell. How did she get here?

JESUS: I liked her. The one with her is Mary Magdalen.

BILLY SUNDAY: She sold her body.

JESUS: Who sold her body?

BILLY SUNDAY: She did, Margaret Hartwell.

276

JESUS: Are you sure? Did you ever think that your friends, the captains of industry, the money changers, the rulers of society, and the church that steals my name to serve them, sold her body?

BILLY SUNDAY: Oh, you are wrong there. The rich, powerful people are my best friends.

JESUS: It is easier for a camel to go through a needle's eye than for a rich man to enter into heaven.

BILLY SUNDAY: They pay liberally, I teach their slaves to put their trust in God and the hereafter, patiently submitting to the masters now. I was booked two years ahead when I cashed in.

GOD: When you what?

BILLY SUNDAY: Cashed in. Hopped the twig. Croaked. Died.

GOD: Gabriel, what is that bad smell?

GABRIEL: I don't know. I have noticed it ever since this got in.

GOD: See if anything is wrong with the sewer to hell.

[*Gabriel goes out.*]

BILLY SUNDAY: Who is that big angel?

GOD: That's Bob Ingersoll. He fought superstition all his life.

BILLY SUNDAY: Oh, let me get out of here. This is not heaven. Not a soul here I know, and harlots, saloonkeepers, infidels; a rotten, putrid, dirty, hell-begotten—

GOD: Don't jump so. Remember, you are dead.

BILLY SUNDAY: —sin-livered, soul-stinking bunch! I fought them all my life and when I died—

GOD: Will you be quiet? You are foaming at the mouth.

BOB INGERSOLL: I know his kind. A half hysterical, half hypocritical, altogether egotistical mountebank.

BILLY SUNDAY: When I died I said to my wife: "Nell, send for the butcher and have him skin my hide and tan it into a drumhead and have a man go around beating the drum and saying, 'Billy Sunday still lives and he will fight Satan and the dirty, rotten, stinking bunch of wine-sellers, gamblers, harlots, till they are in hell, where they belong. For Jesus' sake'."

JESUS: Stop! Do you know my earthly life, my earthly death? I forbid you my name.

[*Gabriel comes in.*]

GOD: What is it?

GABRIEL: The sewer is all right. It is this soul.

GOD: I thought so. There is no stench so terrible as that of a putrid soul.

GABRIEL: I noticed it when I was bringing him up, but did not think any soul could smell so bad.

BOB INGERSOLL: He has used "rotten," "putrid," "stinking" so often that it has struck in.

GOD: Gabriel, you know those pits where the sulphur fumes come up from the old hell?

GABRIEL: Yes, Lord.

GOD: Take him over there. Clean him, bleach him, fumigate him, and drop him down into that heaven where the African Medicine Men are.

INTRODUCTION TO "'T.R.' ENTERS HEAVEN"

IN ONE OF HIS MOST HILARIOUS DISCOURSES, Wood lampoons Teddy Roosevelt, who charges into heaven, terrorizing even Satan, who is paying God a visit. Erskine portrays Roosevelt as a frenetic militarist, eager to arm the angels and get heaven into the war to end all wars. In an impassioned, poetic monologue Rabelais urges Roosevelt—who wants to annihilate German militarism with a greater militarism of his own—to spare "in the name of the gullet, if not of Christianity," something of the plenitude of food and drink that is particularly German. Wood, of course, knew Roosevelt and approved of his trust-busting and conservation policies, but he could not abide what he considered to be the former president's jingoism.

"T.R." Enters Heaven

[*God is on his throne. Voltaire, Rabelais, Ingersoll, and others are near the throne.*]

[*St. Peter, Gabriel, Raphael, the Devil, and a host rush in, panic-stricken.*]

St. Peter: Save yourself, Lord. Save yourself. Something has got in.

Gabriel: It broke down the gate.

Raphael: It is coming. Save yourself.

God: Is it the Devil?

Satan: No, no. I am here. Hide me. Omnipotence, I ask protection.

God: Who is it?

Ingersoll: What a roaring.

Voltaire [*To Rabelais*]: My friend, I guess heaven has come to an end.

Rabelais: That does not trouble me.

Satan: O, that roar. Hide me. I never thought he'd get in here. Hide me. I know him.

God: Who is this thing of terror?

Satan: Yes. That's him. T. R. T. R. Don't you know him? T. R.?
[*Satan's teeth chatter.*]

God: Never heard of him.

Satan: Never heard of Teddy? O, God!

God: No, I never heard of him. Stop shivering.

Satan: Oh! Oh! Surely you know the Colonel.

God: Never heard of him, I tell you. But what a frightful uproar. Is it an army?

St. Peter: No. Just him. Just him. But, O, God—

[*Enter T. R. He holds out his hand to God.*]

T. R.: Dee-lighted. Dee-lighted, I am sure. I have heard of you.

God: Indeed.

T. R.: Possibly we have met somewhere?

God: No, I think not.

T. R.: Were you ever in Washington, D. C.?

God: Never.

T. R.: Well, there is certainly something familiar about you. Don't rise.

GOD: Take my seat.

T. R.: Thanks awfully. [*Sits down.*] Now, where is Michael?

GOD: He is away in a new star called the Orb of Brotherly Love.

T. R.: Why, that's our earth.

GOD: No. This is different.

T. R.: Well, who is commander-in-chief here? It drives me crazy to sit quiet this way. Who is commander-in-chief ?

GOD: We have no commander-in-chief.

T. R.: Who leads your armies ?

GOD: We have no armies.

T. R.: What? No armies? I don't believe it. How do you get on? How will you defend yourself? Well, who is head of your organization?

GOD: We have no organization.

T. R.: No organization? No armies? Well, it's a mighty good thing I came. How on earth—I mean, how in heaven—are you going to get into this war without an army, and how are you going to levy taxes and conscript the angels without an organization?

GOD: But we are not going into any war.

T.R.: Not going into the war! Do you seriously tell me that you are not going into this great war to end war and for freedom and democracy and world peace? Have I died in vain only to come to a heaven of cowards, dastards, poltroons, contemptible, white-livered, white-feathered, chicken-hearted slackers? Have you no patriotism, no sense of national honor, dignity or democracy? Have you no common brotherhood, no Christian unity?

[*Gabriel and the Battered Soul of the Pacifist enter. The Battered Soul has been put together, but wobbles in spots.*]

Listen to me. You certainly are going into this war. I'll raise a division myself or I'll raise hell and I'll show you what the fighting spirit is. We are going into this war. Do you understand?

VOLTAIRE: *Voila les dents.*

RABELAIS: *Sang de Dieu.*

T.R. [*To Gabriel*]: What is your name?

GABRIEL: My name is Gabriel.

T.R.: O, yes, Gabriel; trumpeter. I remember. Dee-lighted, I am sure. Go out at once and organize a publicity bureau. Make a proclamation that a T.R. Club must be started in every precinct.

Recruiting offices must be opened all over heaven. Proclaim and also post notices that Colonel Roosevelt will in person lead an army of angels against the Huns in the great cause of Christianity and democracy, and expects every angel with a drop of red blood in his veins to volunteer, and if any dirty, sneaking, white-feathered slacker refuses to do his bit—[*the Battered Soul falls into a fit*]. Well, well. What's the matter here?

GABRIEL: This poor Battered Soul has just fallen in a fit.

GOD: Revive him.

[*Battered Soul revives and Gabriel lifts him up.*]

What is the matter?

BATTERED SOUL: O, dear God, every time I hear those words I fall into a fit.

GOD: What words?

BATTERED SOUL: "Do his bit."

GOD: But you can't afford to fall in a fit for all the silly words you hear.

T.R.: Silly! Silly! Those modest, beautiful, patriotic, eloquent, noble words silly? I tell you that every man must either do his country, his bit, or somebody. Gabriel, have all the white-winged angels dyed red, white, and blue—no, red and blue. I won't have a white-feathered one in my whole army. Make 'em red. No, not red—that's Bolshevik. Make 'em blue—I don't like it, but it can't be helped. Make 'em blue.

GABRIEL: My commands come from God.

T.R.: Sure. Don't you hear me? I'm going to take over to Germany —yes, to the whole world, to the whole universe, my honor, my patriotism, my loyalty, my policies, my democracy, my Christianity, myself.

VOLTAIRE: *Ciel! les dents.*

RABELAIS: *La voix.*

VOLTAIRE: Might I humbly suggest it has been brought to us here that the Germans claim a world *Kultur* and a democracy also? Indeed, as I look down upon them, it seems to me if they would only unhorse their spurred riders, they have the foundation for a better society than yours: no slums; no poverty; no hopeless old age.

T.R.: I'll unhorse their spurred riders for them.

VOLTAIRE: Perhaps. But don't you think every people should unhorse its own riders? A revolution from the outside? No, impossible. A people must make its own revolution.

T.R.: Sir, I tell you I shall annihilate them. What the world needs is the democracy of America, of New York, of Ludlow, of Paterson, of Lawrence, of Bayonne, of Passaic, of the Solid South, united with the splendid democracy of England, of Ireland, of India, of Africa, of Egypt. I shall annihilate this German militarism with a more thorough militarism of my own.

RABELAIS: *Pardon. Pardon, Monsieur.* Spare something. In the name of the gullet, if not of Christianity, spare the delicious Strasbourg paté; the leberwurst; the Westphalia hams. Ah, those excellent Westphalian thirst-provokers. Spare the Bismarck herring; kielerspratten, sardellen, sausages. Heaven, the sausages, with rye bread—the bread of the people, and beer—the drink of the people: pale amber Pilsner and dark, topaz Münchner. Slayers of throat-parching thirsts; one envies the giraffe his neck. Beer, the liquid bread of the ancient Egyptians; foaming nectar, smelling of the Bohemian hop-yards where the sun shines in September on festooned vines; the air aromatic with golden pollen blown from the pendant hops. Jewels on the neck of a tall, blonde, voluptuous Gretchen. Hops are medicinal, sir. A golden gift from golden-crowned Ceres. Medicinal. I am a physician and tell you so. I beg you spare beer. And do not speak of annihilating the golden sweat from those sunny slopes of the Rhine, the Moselle. O, the long-necked bottles of liquid sunshine, gift of the antique twisted vines, centuries rooted in good German soil. Johannesberger, Steinberger, Hochheimer, Liebfraunmilch—are we not poetical under our arbor? The milk of Venus. And our good Doctor Berncastler. The Steinwein, Riesling, and Weisling. Not bottled drunkenness and combat, sir, but bottled friendship, good comradeship, songs, handclasps, weddings, christenings, feastings, the sap of good old Mother Earth. The sacrament of love and brotherhood. Yes, sir, and of religion. The golden blood of the great Dionysus. O, those oaken tuns of the Rhine. I, a Frenchman, sir, would hasten peace and return to earth if I might lie under their aureate shower. Spare something of Germany, sir. And there is music and medicine, science and drama, and blonde Gretchens, sir. I, a Frenchman, plead that you leave us something of Germany.

T.R.: Who are you?

RABELAIS: *Pardon, Monsieur.* François Rabelais. Let me say with proud humility, one of the makers of France.

T.R.: O, I know you; an obscene old drunkard.

RABELAIS: *Pardon.* A humorist. Never drunk, except with my own fancies.

T.R.: A lecherous old scoundrel.

RABELAIS: *Pardon encore.* Never lecherous. All merely humor. Scoundrel—Ah—*peut-être—chacun à son gout.*

T.R.: I say you are obscene.

RABELAIS: *Hélas,* there is nothing so obscene as war.

T.R.: You are a drunkard.

RABELAIS: *Ma foi.* Are you perhaps also a humorist? There is no drunkenness like to war; nothing so foolish—so useless. What has it ever settled? What has it ever brought that was worth the price? The supreme stupidity of man is war—the game whose pawns are the young men. When did ever a people make war? When did ever a people want war till they were first made drunken by the masters? War, the supreme stupidity; the drunkenness of all drunkenness!

T.R.: I, myself, am temperate in all things.

RABELAIS: In *all* things? In *all* things?

T.R.: Yes, sir; in all things and at all times.

GOD: How we deceive ourselves. [*To Gabriel, who leads T.R. away.*] Gabriel, let him look at Alexander, Hannibal, Caesar, Napoleon, the great soldiers who each and all made a failure of fighting.

[*Satan comes out from his hiding behind God and St. Peter. Jesus comes in.*]

SATAN: I breathe again.

GOD: Let us all meditate in the hush of this sudden quiet, invoking from the universe—peace. Peace, the great builder; the great healer; the plow that turns furrows of civilization for the rain of love.

JESUS: Unless this come the peoples shall surely perish.

This delightful discourse casts doubts on the efficacy of
Protestant prayer and suggests that sometimes supplicants get
more than they bargain for. Erskine makes Aquarius a comic
figure, not overly bright and lacking in discretion, and has fun
with the double entendre of Aquarius "making water" over the
Atlantic Ocean.

Denver Prays for Rain

[*God holds a new star in his hand; turning it slowly, carefully,
examining it. Around him are angels and archangels. Gabriel and
Hermes in attendance.*]

God: Hermes, what is that awful buzzing in the radio?

Hermes: God Almighty, I will see.

God: Gabriel, have one of the electricians look into it—Volta,
Steinmetz, Franklin—somebody.

Gabriel: Yes, Lord.

Hermes: I can't make head or tail of it; just a lot of groaning and
buzzing.

God: Gabriel, see if you can understand it.

Hermes: It reminds me of a pair of bellows Hephaestus once had at
his forge—whines, groans, sighs, sobs, squeaks, and nothing but
wind.

Gabriel: I know. It's a prayer.

Hermes: That's what I said. Nothing but wind.

God: A prayer? From the earth, of course?

Gabriel: From the earth.

God: Of course. Is this the earth sabbath?

Gabriel: No, Lord.

God: Then why on earth are they praying?

Gabriel: They are in trouble.

God: O yes—they do also pray when they are in trouble. What's the
matter?

GABRIEL: They want rain.

GOD: Who wants rain?

GABRIEL: Denver, Colorado, United States, Earth.

GOD: Why do they bother me for every little local, petty, particular want? Don't they understand that I have a whole universe on my hands? They mean nothing to me—

GABRIEL: No. They only think of themselves.

GOD: Well, I have to admit that is one of my laws. Where is Aquarius?

HERMES: I don't know. Out on his job, I guess.

GOD: Call him—quickly.

[*Hermes goes out. St. Peter comes in.*]

Peter, you are the very person I want to see. Who started this habit of praying to me for picnic weather, crop weather, haying weather—for babies, automobiles, new pants—and successful jelly? Do your people think I have nothing to do but run a department store for their benefit?

ST. PETER: Why, people always prayed and offered up sacrifice, didn't they?

GOD: Yes. For really big things—to win a war or something like that— but these little foolish local troubles—Denver wants rain.

ST. PETER: Jesus told us to ask.

GOD: But there is reason in all things. He didn't mean you to ask for jam on your bread or more coal in the cellar or more wine.

ST. PETER: More wine? Excuse me, Omniscience. No one today would think of praying for wine.

GOD: Why not? If for water?

ST. PETER: It would be wicked.

GOD: What would be wicked?

ST. PETER: To pray for wine. Besides it would be simpler to see a bootlegger.

GOD: A bootlegger? Ah, yes. I remember. Someone said Jesus was one at Cana. Well, Peter, if your church is responsible for this prayer habit, stop it. Ah, there is Aquarius.

[*Aquarius comes in with his watering pot.*]

AQUARIUS: Here I am, Lord.

GOD: Where were you?

AQUARIUS: Watering the Atlantic Ocean.

GOD: Is that necessary?

AQUARIUS: No, but I felt like it.

GOD: Why don't you water—what's the place?

GABRIEL: Denver, Colorado, United States, Earth.

GOD: Yes, that. Why not water that? They are howling—I mean, praying—for rain, and you watering the Atlantic.

AQUARIUS: The Atlantic is on my circuit. You told me to water when I felt like it. When I get over the Atlantic I feel like watering. I think it's the water that does it—so much water.

GOD: Well, for my sake, hurry over to Denver, Colorado, United States, Earth, and feel like watering there. Give them plenty.

AQUARIUS: My pot's nearly empty.

GOD: I will fill it. Go on—hurry. Give Denver plenty of water. Water it so I never hear from it again.

AQUARIUS: I'll do my best but this pot is pretty old and—

GOD: O hurry up! You are always grumbling.

[*Aquarius goes out.*]

One of Art Young's inspired illustrations for Heavenly Discourse.

AQUARIUS ANSWERS A PRAYER

GOD: Did you ever see such a literal, stupid, obstinate old fellow in your life? And I have to trust watering the earth to him. Peter, give your attention, your personal attention, to your church. If it is responsible for praying every time somebody wants rain or sun or something, stop it.

ST. PETER: I don't think it is my church. We are well organized and don't bother you much. It's those other fellows—Methodists. They are ignorant people; Baptists. Ha! It's the Baptists—they are strong on water. It would be just like them to water their prayers.

GOD: O, by myself, there goes that radio again. Gabriel, see what it is; that simply cannot be a prayer.

GABRIEL: Yes, it is, Lord. It's a prayer.

GOD: A prayer? That a prayer?

GABRIEL: Yes, Omniscience. A prayer.

GOD: Sounds more like a riot. Well, what is it now?

GABRIEL: It's from Denver, Colorado, United States, Earth.

GOD: O for my sake. Tell Aquarius to hurry up.

GABRIEL: Yes, Lord—wait—Lord, wait—no—they say it is pouring torrents. They want you to stop it.

GOD: Want me to stop it? By myself, do they think I have nothing to do but dance attendance on them?

GABRIEL: They say it is another deluge.

GOD: Where's Noah? Where is Noah? Somebody find Noah.

GABRIEL: The rivers have flooded, dams burst, houses washed away, fields covered with mud, crops ruined, and still it pours in sheets.

GOD: Confound that stupid Aquarius. He has no discretion. Hermes, tell Aquarius to stop. Hurry, Hermes, hurry. I certainly will have to find another water-carrrier with more discretion.

HERMES: Instantly, Lord.

GOD: First they pray for rain, then they pray to stop the rain. Impudence. Do they think I have nothing to do but watch Denver, Colorado, U. S. A., Earth?

GABRIEL: Now a fight is going on. Two Reverends, when the rain began, each laid claim to having produced it by prayer; now the people want to lynch them.

GOD: What's that?

GABRIEL: I don't know, Omniscience. I think it is Christian.

GOD: Whatever it is I hope they do it. Go on.

GABRIEL: And each now declares the flood is the other's fault. One pounds his pulpit—

GOD: What's that?

GABRIEL: I don't know. I just give it as the radio gives it.

GOD: Yes. Well?

GABRIEL: One pounds his pulpit and shouts: "Enough, Lord, enough." And the other bangs his fist on the Bible and shouts: "Lord, this is ridiculous." Boats are in the streets.

GOD: Send Noah. I tell you they need a sailor.

HERMES: He has stopped.

GOD: Who? Noah?

HERMES: No, Aquarius.

GOD: Well, it's time. Never mind about Noah.

HERMES: Here comes Aquarius, Lord; he wants to see you.

GOD: What does he want?

HERMES: He wants to talk to you about his job. He says he doesn't understand it.

GOD: I should say he didn't, but he'll have to keep it.

HERMES: He says he can't please everybody.

GOD: Neither can I. Now don't disturb me. I want to examine this star. There goes that infernal radio again. What is it now? More prayer?

GABRIEL: Not exactly. The Denver Power and Light Company want to thank you through the Reverend Jenkins Undershot for the recent abundant rains.

GOD: Huh! Glad somebody's pleased. Disconnect that radio.

[*All go out.*]

Judging from his manuscripts, drama greatly interested C. E. S. Wood. He wrote much more of it than he published or that ever reached the stage. Except for private performances, most likely in his own home, Wood had only one play produced: *Odysseus*, which was staged in San Francisco in 1923.

Evidently, Wood wrote drama for his own pleasure and that of his friends. His correspondence with W. W. Catlin, investor, poet, and supporter of Emma Goldman, contains discussions of a play called "Rufus Augustus Superbus, Emperor of Rome." Though there was much consideration of mounting a production of this comic opera, it lies in manuscript in the Huntington Library, along with over twenty other unpublished plays. Listing some of them gives the reader an idea of Wood's interests and enthusiasms: "Bacchus," "Kit Marlowe," "The Ogre Who Reformed," "Romeo and the Movies," "Thora, the White Throated," "When Time Stood Still in Arcady."

Testimony to Wood's interest in drama is his pamphlet, "An Appeal for a Dramatic School for San Francisco," which argues that wealthy San Franciscans should support a dramatic school because a city becomes truly great through its support of the arts. Characteristically, he writes:

> *The time will come when our industrial princes will see they owe it to the society from which they have drawn their wealth to value also those spiritual things of that society which, though they do not pay, are the real things of life, the enduring things.*

Wood's essentially unrecognized passion for the theater testifies to his versatility and to his belief that the enduring things of life do not pay.

Introduction to "Circe, A Drama with a Prologue"

Wood's drama takes as its starting point the episode in Homer's *Odyssey* in which the enchantress Circe turns Odysseus's men to swine. Odysseus, helped by Hermes, resists her charms and convinces her to return his men to human form. She helps him visit Hades, and she tells him what perils he will meet when he sets sail again. Wood's *Circe* explores the year Odysseus spends on Circe's isle, which is given only a few sentences in Homer. Circe, who is immortal, falls in love with Odysseus, coming to realize the power of human love. After he has sailed away, she calls death down upon herself, unable to bear for eternity the loss of mortal love. Themis, daughter of Uranus and Gaea, had oracular powers and was the protector of hospitality and the oppressed.

Interestingly enough, the theme of mortal love being superior to immortality appears in *A Book of Tales*, Wood's first book. The final tale, "The Tale of Shshauni and Susshupkin," written by Wood, tells of how, after many trials, Shshauni reaches the "immortal land," but returns to this world because eternity would be "endless pain" without his beloved Susshupkin.

CIRCE, A DRAMA WITH A PROLOGUE

FROM ACT IV, SCENE 1

ODYSSEUS: Beloved. You must have sent yourself before yourself. I was communing with you in my soul.

CIRCE: Do you love me, Odysseus?

ODYSSEUS: Do I love you, Beloved? There was a brook in Ithaca which glanced and ran, breaking the sun into a myriad sparks, laughing merrily in its tune. Then, a river, it warbled to its banks and last swept broadly to the waiting sea. I drank at its fountain and bathed in its clear pools, but could not swim against its later tide. So you refresh me, bathe me, bear me on. Circe,—of the thousand, thousand lights and depths,—I'll love you unto death.

CIRCE: Oh, no. Death is through with you. I have kissed immortality between your lips. Your eyes shall never dim, nor voice grow thin. No ache of age shall creep into your bones, nor fear into your heart, and Time, that unrespective thief, shall lay no carving finger on your brow. You and I shall live unchanged while at our feet the world, a village pageantry, flows on.

ODYSSEUS: How often when Achilles passed, my eyes have followed him and led my thought to envy of his sire in Thetis' arms. I hoped some goddess would woo me to her immortality. My love is reverent to you.

CIRCE: I want not reverence. I'd be loved as women are. O Eros, leveler, binding heaven to earth. Odysseus, do you love me?

ODYSSEUS: I love you. I—

CIRCE: Stop! Say that again,—I love you. Only that. It is the sum of all. If true, it is enough. If false, it is too much.

ODYSSEUS: I love you.

CIRCE: Words cannot better it, nor add a grain to its full freight. It never can grow stale. Say it in endless repetition till the endless end of days.

ODYSSEUS: I love you.

Enter Themis.

THEMIS: Circe, beware of Love and Death. Of Love, beware. Beware! Beware!

CIRCE: See, Themis, see! How proud I am to be a prisoner to Love.

THEMIS: Of Love and Death beware. Beware! Beware!

Themis goes out.

ODYSSEUS: We may smile at Themis, poor melancholy ghost. We shall love into the dusk of Time. Try all the peaks and depths. Perhaps hang breathless over some bold man who dares the gods. Strange, strange to me it is to think the years will countless pile but not abate my lustihood.

CIRCE: Oh, not a hair. Cheated Time will look upon a love which never can grow dim. Now this instant I will make a bridal-feast, shall send old Time a-singing down his path. My father's self shall stop to look.

Circe lifts her arm and a host of sprites fly in.

[*To a sprite.*] Wingcap, weave for me a moonbeam-robe with happy thoughts caught in the web.

Sprite goes out.

[*To another.*] Slide on a sunshaft to Africa's hot sands. Bring thence the fire that lights a tigress's topaz eyes.

[*To Odysseus.*] Shall I, with jealous claw rend the air which dares to woo your cheek? No, no. We'll have no mortal mildew on immortal love.

Sprite goes out.

[*To another sprite.*] Airy Psyche, make me a mantle of the wings of gemmed blue butterflies with studs of gold-green beetles.

Sprite goes out.

[*To another sprite.*] Starflame, build me a coronet of lantern-flies to grace my hair. So shall my lover find me in the dark.

Sprite goes out.

[*To Melpomene.*] Quick, quick, to Morpheus, Melpomene. Beg for me splendid dreams beyond the utmost building of our waking hours. Let music be divinely heard. Away! Away! Distill happiness as dew. Bid the wind come laden with plundering of mignonette, magnolias, lemon-blooms, the fresh and fragrant mint and aromatic beds of basil. Let the air sparkle with the song of birds. Bedeck the sward with flowers,—the flowers with dewdrops, and every dewdrop mirror to a joy.

Melpomene goes out.

My love, I will awake your mind to fair conception of the gods and lift you up to bright celestial fires, immortal fields. Look how the watchful East hangs on her wall a lamp. Strike once again, amid this hush, that sweetest blow upon my heart—

ODYSSEUS: I love you. Lover, I love you. O Circe. I think my destiny is yoked to some far-shining star, so much in silence of the night my soul yearns upward to the over-sparkling mystery. Naught which is stranger to my fate could draw me so.

CIRCE: I'll show you lights shall make the stars seem pale and I will whisper in your ear a tale shall live beyond this present time, so men will say, a myriad ages hence,—"Odysseus, he whom Circe loved. Circe, the baneful goddess; Circe of the wicked wiles. Circe, daughter of the Sun; and how Love conquered her. Circe and all her arsenal, captive unto Love."

End of Act IV

Odysseus, THE ONLY ONE of Wood's plays ever produced for the stage, was performed at the School of the Arts of the Theatre in San Francisco and directed by Maurice Browne and Ellen Van Volkenburg. It was accompanied by incidental music played on primitive instruments and presented on a bare stage with a sheet of canvas daubed with patches of blue and sea-green as a backdrop.

In this brief play with three characters and two choruses—one of men and the other of maidens—Wood offers an aged Odysseus who is tired of war, wishing his sword had been a sickle. We include it in its entirety.

ODYSSEUS, A PLAY IN ONE ACT

Persons of the Play

ODYSSEUS

ARCHOMEN (a youth of Ithaca)

DICTYS (a youth of Thebes)

MEN OF ITHACA

MAIDENS OF ITHACA

Prelude

music

Scene I

[*The ocean beach. Lines of surf. Beyond, the blue expanse of ocean.*]

[*Archomen and Dictys come in.*]

ARCHOMEN: There he is. There! close to the foam-arches (*Archomen points)*; alone and looks afar; beyond the waves. He holds a staff.

DICTYS: Is that indeed Odysseus?

ARCHOMEN: That is Odysseus.

DICTYS: He stands straight as the staff he holds and overpowers the ocean. And that one I see is the Odysseus who with Agamemnon and Achilles fought at Troy. O Zeus!

ARCHOMEN: That is the man. He knew Ajax—Telemon, Agamemnon,

Nestor, Menelaus. All the heroes and the demigods. There stands the one who burst the walls of Ilium and widowed Hecuba.

DICTYS: He whom I see there pleaded with Achilles, talked with Ajax. Saw Priam on the walls and knew Helen.

ARCHOMEN: He knew Helen; daughter of Zeus. He looked upon that radiant brow; those perfect lips. He is very old!

DICTYS: O how old he is. And is Penelope alive?

ARCHOMEN: Penelope is dead long, long ago. Telemachus is dead. They all are dead. He has outlived them all.

DICTYS: The gods have kept him. Archomen, scarce can I believe that I now truly look on that Odysseus who led the hosts all through the endless siege of Troy; Odysseus, whom Calypso loved. Our cities tell of him; the rhapsodists chant his wide wanderings; breathless escapes and strange home-coming, guided by Athene. And I look on that very Man. O.

ARCHOMEN: Look on him well. He may be gone tomorrow; as at evening we see rose-breasted swallows; making the eaves alive—but next morning none—silence.

DICTYS: But there he is. O may we speak with him?

ARCHOMEN: Assuredly we may; but will he answer? Ah, I do not know. Sometimes he speaks with silent looks as if he were not here. I think he lives more with the dead.

DICTYS: Quick: Let us go to him. I'd rather speak with him and touch his living hand than have the world-persuading gold of mighty Midas.

ARCHOMEN: Come. Let us have speech with him and hear the very voice of that loud war cry which scattered Trojan warriors as sheep are scattered by the bear.

[*They go out.*]

Scene II

[*Another part of the same sea beach. Odysseus is standing close to the foam-circles, left by the highest waves. He looks out over the sea, a staff in his hand, a sword girt to his side.*]

ODYSSEUS: Eternal brawler; forever clutching. Is there no satisfying? I stand where young Odysseus stood, sailing for Troy. I bathe my feet, as then, in the soft foam. It runs the same. Foam-lipped wolf, you are not changed; not in one snarl, one growl, one leap; but where those youthful limbs, taut as a bowstring? Ha! shrunk to this. Those clear eyes not second to the eagle's, clouded and blurred, and that young face now fallen to this wrinkled mask. Ye cruel gods, where has gone the reckless mind which nothing feared and questioned all? Why this change and not the change? Why not the end? Calypso, have your kisses done this thing to me? Denied me rest. Left me to wither, not to fall. A stranger in a stranger world. Alone. Alone as if I were the last on earth; forgotten by the gods.

Circe, has your sorcery done me this curse? To linger, linger, not to go? I am as one who through the vista of a forest sees the light he cannot come to. I stand where stood the multitude that dim, far day; I see out there the shining sails they saw when young Odysseus winged to join the Argive fleet.

Was I of kin to him? He seems a stranger to me, told in a tale.

Of all that host, not one, not one. Great Agamemnon but a memory, Priam and Hector and Achilles ghosts; rose-lipped Helen for whose goddess face mad thousands died; ashes, ashes and forgot. Not one. O for so long; not one. My boy Telemachus gone before me. Gone before me—gods; and is that just?

Hush, incessant quarreler. Stop. Stop your brawl. Can you not a moment cease your savage roar? So many times you put your fingers on my throat; always they slipped. Shall I now let you freely take what you so often clutched at? O gentle, sweet Nausicaa, who harbored me naked from this wrath; where are you, gentle, sweet Nausicaa? Is that your soul out there? And do you beckon me? My white winged one?

[*Archomen and Dictys approach.*]

ARCHOMEN: Reverend King—

ODYSSEUS: Are kings still reverend?

ARCHOMEN: Most humbly we salute you, great Odysseus. And may we speak with you?

ODYSSEUS: Say on, young Archomen. Youth has a kingship may speak anywhere.

ARCHOMEN: Here is young Theban Dictys. He has left his home and dared the treacherous One to look on you.

ODYSSEUS: So? So? He is welcome. Very welcome. Are no old men in Thebes?

DICTYS: O godlike hero, on the whole earth is but one Odysseus.

ODYSSEUS: Poor barren Earth, or should I say most fortunate?

DICTYS: Fortunate she has Odysseus, poor in that she has but one.

ODYSSEUS: Ah ha. Your tongue will take you far. I had a clever tongue when I was young. You notice I am old; or did you notice it? or would you call me old? Perhaps you'd say that I was young.

DICTYS: O let me kiss but the robe's hem of him the gods preserve so long.

ODYSSEUS: So you do notice I am old? Ah, yes. You notice that. And would you have a jewel from an old, old man?

DICTYS: I tremble, King Odysseus. A handful of this sand would be jewels infinite from you. You are immortal to me.

ODYSSEUS: Zeus!—I seem like to be, and turn to a grasshopper. Here is a jewel for you—Let your tongue speak truth. It will be profitable to you—I did not do it. Men are such fools. O I could make a lie seem very truth. I am an old man now. You have a courtly tongue. Stick to the truth, young boy. It is more profitable.

DICTYS: Great King; was not your Trojan wooden horse a lie?

ODYSSEUS: No. No. Horses do not lie. I was the liar—I was the master liar of them all. And I, the master liar, say train your young tongue to truth. There is a jewel for you from an old man—who has seen some things. Yes. Has seen some things; and done some things. Yes, done some things. Ha. Children. Children. How contemptible it was: childish and contemptible.

ARCHOMEN: Dictys would touch your hand, O great Odysseus.

DICTYS: Yes, I would touch the hand that has clasped Nestor's; all the heroes.

ODYSSEUS: They are all dead. I would clasp the hand of what's to come. Your name is—?

[*He takes the hand of Dictys.*]

DICTYS: My name is Dictys; and my father, Argesilaus, is a merchant of Thebes.

ODYSSEUS: So? Is he dead?

DICTYS: No, King Odysseus. He is old but he still lives.

ODYSSEUS: Give him my sympathy. Give him my sympathy. I say give him my sympathy.

ARCHOMEN: May Dictys hold your sword?

ODYSSEUS: The others have grown too heavy. This was forged for me at Troy by Cecrops, a swart Cretan, broad shouldered. It is all iron. It slew Phorbas and many more. And to what end? Tell me—I now am old. Say to what end? I wear it for my vanity. A boy could take it from me; yes—And yet I live. Is it not shameful? Here. Take it.

[*Hands Dictys his sword.*]

DICTYS: When I shall see my folk again, and all the men of Thebes, I then can say I—this very Dictys who now stands before you—I have held the sword of King Odysseus—warm from off his thigh.

ODYSSEUS: I would it were a sickle. Keep it. Take it with you. Show it to them. Tell them it has many slain. Tell them I would it were a sickle.

DICTYS: Mine? Great King. And do you give it to me?

ODYSSEUS: Yes. Yours, yours—I would it were a sickle. Take it not so deeply. I but give what I've no use for.

DICTYS: I will out-treasure it beyond my life. My father shall create a temple to it—He is rich.

ODYSSEUS: O, is he rich? Then let him build a temple to it—that is just. It served the rich. And shall again.

DICTYS: O, Thebes shall guard it as a gift from the true gods—great hero—demigod—I take it as a gift from the great gods. [*He kneels.*]

ODYSSEUS: Foolish gods! I would it were a sickle.

[*Dictys rises.*]

ARCHOMEN: Noble and gracious Conqueror of the world! Tell us of Helen.

[*Odysseus looks afar and makes no answer.*]

See. He answers us with silence. Come. As I told you, he is not with us; he is with the dead.

DICTYS: Let us walk backward as from a fane. Let my eyes feed until the last.

[*They go out.*]

ODYSSEUS: Helen. Yes, you were beautiful. Many were slain for you and great spoil taken. You were very beautiful, most beautiful. Let my time-weighted mind think not of her. Gentle Nausicaa, dove-voiced Nausicaa. Nausicaa of curving arms; so gentle and so kind. Her brow an ivory wall where watch-fires burned, her lips the heavenly gates, and her heart: Love's fountain overflowing. Look! The maidens have come down to bathe. I see them dance upon the shining sand, beautiful birds. Their bodies flash and gleam in the sun. I have rejoiced in the white bodies of women, but I am an old man now; old; very old, and know Love lingers not in Aphrodite's bed, but with winged Psyche in the high secret places of heaven. Hark. Their laughter mocks the cry of gulls. I am old; a dry stalk of anise by the road, a skeleton of summer, sharing not in spring. The walls of Troy are dust; our fleet a story in the ear. And I alone. Alone. Deserted! I will not endure it. Her white hand beckons me. Poseidon—Ancient One—you outlive us all—you always triumph. I bid you freely take what you so often snatched at. Is that a gull's wing or the hand of my Nausicaa? Nausicaa—Gentle Nausicaa—I come; Nausicaa. I come.

[Music.]

[Odysseus walks out into the sea and disappears in the tumultuous waves. Archomen, Dictys, and others come in.]

PEOPLE OF ITHACA: Where is the King? Where is our hero? Where Odysseus?

ARCHOMEN: He was here. Dictys and I here talked with him just now. Look. Look. His staff. His staff.

[Archomen reverently lifts the staff and holds it against his breast.]

DICTYS: The gods have taken him.

[Music.]

[Archomen now holds the staff upright with one hand. Dictys approaches Archomen, and together they hold the staff. Men of Ithaca and maids of Ithaca slowly come towards Archomen and Dictys but pause at a little distance. Dictys now releases his grasp upon the staff and falls away a little. Archomen turns toward the people and very slowly uplifts the staff.]

[Music pauses.]

ARCHOMEN: The gods have taken him.

[Dictys turns to the sea and bows very low; his arms drooping. Music. All follow the example of Dictys. Archomen, holding high the staff, moves slowly off; Dictys follows him, and the people follow Dictys.]

Slow Curtain.

Music continues for a time.

Poems from the Ranges, published in 1929, comprises twenty-two lyrics, mostly rhymed, set in Wood's beloved eastern Oregon Desert. These lyrics render a region—Harney Valley, Blitzen Oasis, Steens Mountain, Alvord Desert—depicting its beauties and dangers, rhythms and images, its way of life. It is as good a book of lyrics presenting a place as has been written by a Northwest poet.

Published by Lantern Press and printed at the Grabhorn Press in San Francisco, *Poems from the Ranges* is an exquisite example of fine-press printing. The frontispiece, designed and cut in wood by Ray Boynton, is an adaptation of his mosaic in the courtyard of The Cats. The text is letterpressed in Deepdene Roman, a typeface created in 1917 by the great American typographer, Frederic Goudy. The book was printed in a numbered edition of five hundred copies, fifty on handmade paper and signed by the author.

Poems from the Ranges received little critical notice, though some of the pieces, "First Snow" in particular, earned a good deal of praise. In the *Northwest Literary Review* (1935), Verne Bright called it, "The finest lyric ever written on this west coast." Several of the poems appeared in *Poetry: A Magazine of Verse* in 1924.

Some fifty years later, two of the poems were reprinted in the anthology *The Best Loved Poems of the American West*, published by Doubleday (1980). *Poems from the Ranges* is a neglected classic—a profound evocation of a place in time and a profoundly beautiful specimen of book making.

Wood in eastern Oregon, circa 1897.

First Snow

The cows are bawling in the mountains.
The snowflakes fall.
They are leaving the pools and pebbled fountains.
Troubled, they bawl.
They are winding down the mountain's shoulders
Through the open pines,
The wild-rose thickets, and the granite boulders
In broken lines.
Each calf trots close beside its mother
And so they go,
Bawling and calling to one another
About the snow.

Billy Craddock in Rome

O, the swallows and the swallows
Against the sky of Rome;
And my heart follows
Away back home
To the P Ranch on the Blitzen
And the swallows in the air.
Take me back into the desert,
To the big, wide quiet there.
The irrigation-ditches, the slender poplar-spire
Lifting to sunrise and sunset
A shaft of golden fire,
And wind across the alfalfa field,
Where hums the honey hive.
I am sick of Christs on crosses
And not a Christ alive.
I am sick of men in petticoats
And everywhere a bell;
Let me hear the brown sage-thrasher's note,

The bubbles, shakes, and trills that float
Where the sagebrush-billows swell.

I am sick of painted corpses;
O, the stars above the hills,
The neighing of wild horses
Where naked starlight spills;
The breath of dawn that blows so cool
Upon a sleeper's face;
The gallop of the sunrise,
A stallion in a race.
No candle-smoke nor images;
No perfume in a prayer.
Only the listening desert
And the unbreathed desert air.

I am sick of herds of churches
And the foolish tales they tell.
The ranches, O, the ranches,
And a good, clean chance at Hell.
O what to me, by day or night,
Is old Peter's wart of a dome?
Squaw-Butte can knock it out of sight,
Away back home.

The Blitzen Oasis After Rain

Every leaf glistens; the whole world glitters;
Lombardy poplars, rustling with a silken rustle,
Drip from pointed leaves gold-flashing sundrops.
Each sudden gust shakes down a sparkling shower,
A bright rehearsal of the thunderstorm.
Small birds, silenced, now begin to twitter,
Swallows dart again, tracking the crooked mazes of the
    air,
Shuttles of the air, skimming the pool,

And on the steaming door of the blacksmith shop
A yellowhammer beats his sharp, reverberant tattoo.
The wind runs along the willows,
Footing them to paths of silver.
From drenched alfalfa fields, a honey smell:
Aromatic odors, blown from all the brave
And bitter weeds that dare the desert—
Greasewood, sagebrush, rabbit-brush, deathweed,
    wormwood,
Bitter and fragrant.

Against the black horizon lightning darts;
Thunder grumbles sullenly afar,
A mad old bull, cast out, defeated.
Beyond the irrigation ditch,
Beyond the line of cottonwoods,
Beyond the barbed-wire fence,
Out in the still unslaked, defiant waste,
A sagebrush thrasher bubbles up his joy.

THE CATTLE CAMP—NIGHT

Bring sagebrush—bitter-smelling sagebrush,
Bitter and spicy sweet:
Desert weed to desert fire,
Flame tongues twisting high and higher,
While softly the horses' feet
Pound and crush the desert dust.
Tales of women—bitter and spicy sweet;
Oaths, cigarettes, and ribald songs of lust;
Croak of an old sage-cock.
Down from the upper dark a nightjar's cry
Drops like a plummet; the wall of lava rock
Towers like a fortress frowning on the sky.
One by one the cattle fold their knees.

A wakeful cow grumbles deep and low,
Age-old jungle sound of age-old woe.
Night lets fall her veil of mysteries.
Tinkle of spurs—the night guard.
Arcturus, great bear warden, torchlike, sweeps
Upon his watch; the lake is myriad-starred.
The cow camp sleeps.
A cuckoo-owl sobs sadly and is still.
Beyond the outer ramparts of the dark,
Unhappy, pained, and shrill,
Coyotes bark.

INTRODUCTION TO "THE SUN RETURNS FROM HIS SOUTH-WANDERING"

THIS CHRISTMAS PIECE, perhaps the last Wood sent out, was written
in collaboration with Sara. The poem is headed by a wood cut of
Ray Boynton's mosaic from the patio of The Cats (also used on the
label of their "Princess" wine), showing two naked lovers holding
out their hands to catch the manna of heaven. The poem is a
pagan paean to the winter solstice, a leitmotif in Wood's later
Christmas pieces.

THE SUN RETURNS FROM HIS SOUTH-WANDERING

The Sun returns; O let us welcome him.
He will mantle his Earth in veils of green
And enamel her with blossoms
Challenging the rainbow.
He will bring golden fields, sweet fruits
And will bestow abundant harvests.
The grape shall hang her bunches between the leaves
As a mother's breasts, heavy, full of milk.
Father of Light, Father of Warmth, Father of Life,

Without you, Nothing; Icy Darkness; Impenetrable Death.
For a time you left with us only the stars,
Pin-prick pictures on the night,
But now, through the Northern Gate, you march
Triumphant. Your children clap their hands,
Well knowing you will sparkle the air with buds
And with singing of birds.
Love will awake at your coming.
Father of Life, forget not your Daughter.
Forget not your Sister. Forget not your Spouse.
Forget not her children.
Make our year to spin beauty, season unto season;
Beauty and Joy season unto season.
O Father, prepare us a cradle,
Prepare us for slumber
And for a symbol, we will burn candles.

INTRODUCTION TO "EARTHLY DISCOURSE"

JIM HENLE, EDITOR OF VANGUARD PRESS in New York, was delighted in the spring of 1935 when C. E. S. Wood informed him he was thinking of writing some more satiric dialogues. Collectively these would be called *Earthly Discourse* and would target public figures and situations current in the 1930s, along with an attack on an 1803 Supreme Court decision.

Earthly Discourse, an obvious companion piece to *Heavenly Discourse,* was published in 1937. It comprised eleven dialogues of very uneven length. God is on earth for a visit. St. Peter and Satan appear from time to time, but the other characters are either figures from the 1930s—Hearst, Hitler, Edward VIII of England, Mrs. Simpson, the woman for whom he gave up his throne—or fictitious creatures—Miss Featherthroat, Bishop Pussyfoote, Bob Uppercut, and the like. Most of *Earthly Discourse* lacks the spontaneity and brevity of its heavenly forerunner that Erskine claimed "wrote itself."

For Wood "The Supreme Court and the Constitution" was the backbone of the work. Its 213 pages constitute two-thirds of the book and read like a rather elaborate and extended lawyer's brief. In 1803, through John Marshall's decision in Marbury *vs* Madison, the U. S. Supreme Court assumed the right of judicial review of legislation passed by Congress. Wood was convinced that nowhere in the Constitution was such power granted to the court.

The next longest discourse of 50 pages, "King Cophetua and the Beggar Maid," is a four-act play that deals approvingly with Edward VIII's abdication from the throne of England to marry Mrs. Simpson, an American and a divorcée. Publisher William Randolph Hearst comes under fire in several dialogues for abusing his power, especially in "Satan and the Publisher." God appears now and then but the setting throughout is on earth. "Swastika" is a condemnation of Aryan anti-semitism in Hitler's Germany. Themes found in *Heavenly Discourse* reappear, as in "Censor and Censure" and Christ is tarred and feathered in "Santa Rosa." "The Congress of the Frogs" imitates Aristophanes to mock representative democracy and the Supreme Court.

INTRODUCTION TO "THE SINS OF THE FATHERS"

THE SETTING IS THE SUPREME COURT. Angelo Herndon, a black "member in good standing of the chain gang of the sovereign state of Georgia," is before the bar speaking for himself and eight fellow blacks unjustly jailed for inciting to riot and organizing a labor union. Wood employs an effective chorus of voices to carry his ironic message in a manner reminiscent of Vachel Lindsay. Wood also laments the absence of a woman on the court.

THE SINS OF THE FATHERS

[*The courtroom of the Supreme Court of the United States. The members of the Court—The Chief Justice and eight Associate Justices— enter in procession, headed by The Chief Justice and followed by The Clerk of the Court with The Court Journal under his arm.*]

[*The Justices are robed in voluminous, balloon-sleeved, black silk robes. The Clerk stops at his desk on the right of "The Bench." The Chief Justice and four Associate Justices ascend to the dais where is "The Bench"—nine great overstuffed leather chairs. The Chief Justice stops in front of the middle chair and the first four Justices in front of the first four chairs and face the courtroom and remain standing. The other four Justices pass around at the back, ascend the dais, and stand respectively in front of the four remaining chairs, facing outward. At back, ghosts of Washington, Jefferson, Madison.*]

THE CLERK: Hear ye, hear ye, hear ye. The Honorable the Supreme Court of the United States is now in session. All those having business before it will draw near and give their attention. God bless the United States and its Honorable Supreme Court.

A LAWYER: Only those who know the career of the Supreme Court and its steadily reactionary "property" decisions, five to four, can appreciate what a terrible drain this demand puts on God.

ANOTHER LAWYER: So easily do we become accustomed to comedy or tragedy by constant repetition.

> *Vice is a monster of such frightful mien,*
> *As to be hated needs but to be seen;*
> *Yet seen too oft, familiar with its face,*
> *We first endure, then pity, then embrace.*

A LAWYER: I think Pope says "her face." But to the disgrace of the country, there is not a woman on the Supreme Bench.

[*A procession of Negroes, men and women, enters.*]

ANGELO HERNDON: God bless the United States and the Supreme Court.

THE CHIEF JUSTICE: Who are you?

ANGELO HERNDON: My name is Angelo Herndon. I am a member, in good standing, of the chain gang of the Sovereign State of Georgia.

THE GHOST OF WASHINGTON: Georgia! A penal colony.

THE GHOST OF MADISON: Georgia! Settled by convicts.

THE GHOST OF JEFFERSON: Georgia! Champion of Slavery in the Constitutional Convention.

[*They look at each other.*]

THE CHIEF JUSTICE: What do you want?

ANGELO HERNDON: Justice.

THE CHIEF JUSTICE: Why do you come here?

ANGELO HERNDON: I do not know where to go. I am lost in the wilderness.

THE CHIEF JUSTICE: You are in the Georgia chain gang?

ANGELO HERNDON: Yes, Judge.

THE CHIEF JUSTICE: What was your offense?

ANGELO HERNDON: I am a Negro.

THE CHIEF JUSTICE: I mean, of what crime are you guilty?

ANGELO HERNDON: My great-grandfather was kidnaped from Africa and sold into Georgia as a slave.

THE GHOST OF WASHINGTON: Georgia! Slavery.

THE GHOST OF MADISON: Georgia! Convicts.

THE GHOST OF JEFFERSON: Georgia! A penal colony. [*The three ghosts look at each other.*]

THE GHOST OF WASHINGTON: I was President of our Constitutional Convention and we all felt that slavery was inconsistent with the vital principle of the new republic we were founding: freedom.

THE GHOST OF JEFFERSON: I wrote the Declaration of Independence, and slavery gave the lie to every word and phrase of that proclamation: our appeal to the world.

THE GHOST OF MADISON: Every state represented in the Constitutional Convention, except South Carolina, North Carolina, and Georgia, wanted to abolish slavery as utterly inconsistent with the principles of our Revolution, and, as an economic program, suicidal in its final results, commercially and morally. But South Carolina said she needed Negro slave labor for her rice swamps; North Carolina said she would not desert her sister state, and Georgia, which was settled by convicts exported from England, said she wanted slaves to work for the master class. We could not do without their votes, so we submitted.

THE GHOST OF WASHINGTON: We compromised with a provision that there should be no fresh importations after the year 1807. The states wedded to slavery thought by that time they would be well stocked with slaves, and the supply could be kept up by domestic breeding. Virginia and the Northern States thought the evident bad economics and inhumanity of the institution would cause a voluntary surrender, as had happened in the North.

THE GHOST OF JEFFERSON: A cancer in the body politic—a curse upon the generations.

THE CHIEF JUSTICE: Which still curses us.

[*A baritone Voice from the Negroes intones.*]

VOICE: He visits the sins of the fathers upon the children unto the third and fourth generation.

The third and fourth generation.

The third and fourth generation.

And more—and more

Until the awful end. The end, the end.

[*A tenor Voice.*]

VOICE: O Lord God, we are lost in the wilderness.

O Lord God, we are lost in the wilderness.

We are lost in the wilderness,

The wilderness.

[A *soprano Voice.*]

VOICE: Open your sky, Lord, and come down.

Come down,

Come down. . . .

Open your sky, Lord, and come down.

[*A baritone Voice.*]

VOICE: Vengeance is mine. I will repay, saith the Lord.

I will repay, saith the Lord.

Saith the Lord,

Saith the Lord.

CHORUS: O Lord God, we are lost in the wilderness.

We are lost in the wilderness.

We are lost in the wilderness.

Open your sky, Lord, and come down.

Open your sky, Lord, and come down.

THE CHIEF JUSTICE: Who are these people?

ANGELO HERNDON: This is the Brown Choir, Judge, of the First Colored Baptist Church of Atlanta, Georgia.

THE CHIEF JUSTICE: What did you say you were convicted of?

ANGELO HERNDON: Of inciting the slaves to rise.

THE CHIEF JUSTICE: What? Are you crazy? What did you say?

ANGELO HERNDON: Of inciting the slaves to rise.

THE CHIEF JUSTICE: What do you mean?

ANGELO HERNDON: You see, Judge, there was an old slave law in Georgia, of the time before the Civil War. It said anyone inciting the slaves to rise against their masters could be punished with death or life imprisonment, or a term of years. Of course, this law was supposed to be repealed by the Civil War and the abolition of slavery. It was forgotten and was considered repealed.

THE CHIEF JUSTICE: It certainly was. It was repealed by the Civil War.

ANGELO HERNDON: Yes, Judge, but I went down to Georgia and started to organize a labor union among the colored workers.

THE CHIEF JUSTICE: You had a perfect right to do that. That was free speech. Well?

ANGELO HERNDON: Well, the police and a mob broke into my room and found some Communist literature there.

THE CHIEF JUSTICE: You had a right to have it. That was free press. Well?

ANGELO HERNDON: So I was arrested and tried under that old slave law and was convicted and sentenced to twenty years in the chain gang.

THE CHIEF JUSTICE: That is infamous.

SOPRANO VOICE: O God, we are lost in the wilderness.

Open your sky, Lord, and come down.

BARITONE VOICE: Vengeance is mine. I will repay, saith the Lord. . . .

CLERK: Order! Order in the Court!

[*He raps with his gavel.*]

THE CHIEF JUSTICE: Let them sing, that's free speech, too. The Lord may come down, and he'll certainly insist on free speech.

ANGELO HERNDON: You see, Judge, the Fourteenth Amendment was passed, especially, to give the colored people some protection in the South. But you gentlemen have twisted "due process of law" into protecting property which the colored people never did have. But I read in the papers that some of you said the New York law fixing a minimum limit for wages and a maximum limit for working hours, for women and children, was unconstitutional, because it robbed the employer of his money without due process of law, and deprived the women and children of their freedom of contract. But you and Judge Stone and a minority dissented. Judge Stone said this anxious protection of the women was "grim irony." So I thought it might be grim irony to say the colored person in the South has had "due process of law," when only naked forms have been followed and the Spirit and intent violated so that a trial is no better than a lynching. Twenty years in the chain gang is a long time, Judge, really a lifetime, and I am out on bail now, so I thought I'd come and talk to you. I am lost in the wilderness.

SOPRANO VOICE: O Lord God, we are lost in the wilderness.

We are lost in the wilderness, Lost in the wilderness.

BARITONE AND SOPRANO VOICES: Open your sky,

Lord, and come down.

BARITONE: Twelve white men in the jury box.

SOPRANO: Open your sky, Lord, and look down.

BARITONE: Twelve white men and not one brown.

BASSO: Not a chance. Not a chance.

SOPRANO: Open your sky, Lord, and look down.

BARITONE: Nine brown boys in the prisoners' dock.

SOPRANO: Open your sky, Lord, and look down.

BARITONE: Nine boys jailed by bar and lock,

Nine boys brown.

BASSO: Not a chance. Not a chance.

SOPRANO: Open your sky, Lord, and look down.

BARITONE: One white judge on the judgment seat;

One white judge and all complete.

BASSO: Not a chance. Not a chance.

SOPRANO: Open your sky, Lord, and look down.

CHORUS: Nine brown boys lift their hands on high

And cry with a lost child's piteous cry,

"Not a chance. Not a chance.

Lord God, help us or we die."

SOPRANO: Open your sky, Lord, and look down.

CHORUS: A blinding light fills the awful place;

Jesus walks on Galilee.

Heaven lies on His pitying face,

The Glory, the Power, and the majesty.

He lifts His arms in the blinding light

And lo, the brown boys all are white.

Gentle as Love His arms sink down:

The men in the jury box now are brown.

He shows His nail-pierced palms and feet

And sits Him down in the Judgment Seat.

THE CHIEF JUSTICE: Mr. Clerk, adjourn the Court.

THE CLERK: This Court is now adjourned.

[*The Court and The Clerk hurry out, the Judges crowding on one another's heels. As the Court goes out, the Chorus sings.*]

CHORUS: The wind is blowing from the South,

Alabama.

And bloody froth on the black boy's mouth,

Alabama.

The south wind has a smell not good,

Alabama.

The south wind brings a smell of blood,

Alabama.

Stand up, black boy. Do you know your sin?

Yes, Judge, the color of my skin,

Alabama.

You shall hang by your neck till you are dead.

Yes, Judge; and Christ for sinners bled.

Look in your heart, Judge. Look within.

My sin is the color of my skin.

Alabama.

By the neck. By the neck till you are dead.

Do you understand what I have said?
Don't stare at me with that awful grin.
No, Judge. In the noose I'll swing, I'll swing, I'll swing.
I'll swing for the color of my skin.
 O Alabama.
 What's that which hangs like a plummet of lead
 Against the moon?—and a sun bloodred.
 It is a man whose soul has fled.
It will hang. It will swing till the dawning gray,
Of the last eternal Judgment Day.
 O Alabama.
 Georgia,
 Georgia,
 Alabama.

[*The Chorus goes slowly out, singing.*]

Introduction to "Sonnets to Sappho"

THIS BOOK IS A SONNET SEQUENCE dedicated to Sappho, the great
Greek poet, one of Wood's names for Sara. It contains this
dedication, "to the onlie Begetter of these insuing sonnets: SBF,
wife, lover, companion." This, the last book Wood published,
reflects his sadness at his diminished potency and his unfaltering
devotion, in the face of death, to Sara and sensual beauty. Printed
in 1939 by the Grabhorn brothers, it is another lovely example of
the bookmaker's art.

Sonnets to Sappho

XXX

Have you forgot the wintry nights, pitch-black,
When you fed fat the torch—a heavenly ray
To light me to your bed? I did not stay
For javelins of rain nor tempest wrack.
My thoughts like laden bees are winging back
With nectar of the honeyed hours I lay
Warm by your side, forgotten the hard way;
Now weeds are growing in the love-worn track.
How beautiful the fluent snake-like twist
Of your girl-body when you wound your braid;
And where your rope of amber beads was laid
Is smell of myrrh, and here your amethyst
Which pulsed against the golden throat I kissed:
So rich in love—I was of Death afraid.

Introduction to "Collected Poems"

FIVE YEARS AFTER WOOD'S DEATH, Vanguard Press published *The Collected Poems of Charles Erskine Scott Wood*. Sara provided a thoughtful foreword, explaining Wood's life and philosophy. The poet and anthologist, William Rose Benét, wrote a sensitive introduction in which he compares Wood to Whitman and calls *The Poet in the Desert* "one of our greatest national poems." The book received warm reviews focusing as much on Wood's character as on the poetry. Rolfe Humphries, in *The Nation*, wrote of Wood's "power to see, delight in the seen, capacity to bring back the richness and the color, the sensuous quality of experience." *The Library Journal* described him as "a legendary figure." In *The Saturday Review of Literature*, Gustav Davidson sees Wood as a "pagan enemy of shame. . . who was like one of the major prophets of old judging his own time," and asserts that "a place must be made for Charles Erskine Scott Wood beside the bards of America who laid their lives and their gifts, in full and incorruptible measure, on the altar of song."

Collected Poems is organized into seven sections. The first features 16 of the 22 poems in *Poems from the Ranges*. Sara writes in her foreword that *Poems from the Ranges* had appeared "in a limited, expensive Grabhorn printing" and had "consequently small circulation." Sections VI and VII contain *Odysseus* and the 1918 version of *The Poet in the Desert*. Sections II, III, IV, and V collect his lyrics and some longer poems. From section II, "To Lincoln Steffens (a poem to him and seven poems about things he understood)," we reprint "Vagabond's Song." Section III is named "The Labors of Man and Beast," from which we take "Antonio Ploughs" and "Thick-Necked Horses," one of Wood's finest poems of praise, and "Goats," a lovely piece written out of his travels in Sicily. From section IV, "As Year and Day Turn," we take "Summer," and "Sun Worshiper." From "Aspects of Love," section V, we reprint "What Shall I Say of You," a poem dedicated to Sara, "Diana," and "A Day in April," a fine example of the way Wood often mixed Eros and the natural world.

Sara points out in her foreword that Wood did not consider publication terribly important. He loved a beautiful book but the publication of individual poems in magazines came about only when his work was requested. Only three of the lyrics in the collection had previously appeared in magazines ("Goats" in *The Nation* in 1926, "Antonio Ploughs" in *The Liberator* in 1923, and "Summer" in *The San Franciscan* in 1928). Wood reprinted "Summer" and "What Shall I Say of You" in *Selected Poems* (1937), a small handsomely printed collection of poems by Sara and himself. "Goats" was also featured in *Braithwaite's Anthology of Magazine Verse for 1926 and Yearbook of American Poetry,* edited by William Stanley Braithwaite.

It is interesting that so many of Wood's lyrics, including many of his finest, were not published in his lifetime, appearing for the first time in *Collected Poems* in 1949.

VAGABONDS' SONG

I will sing a song to the loafers of the world,
The vagabonds, the bards, tellers of great tales,
Children of the stars,
Feeding on the grain which falls from heaven;
Sweetness in the eyes,
Madness in the brain,
Favorites of the Gods,
Strolling down Eternity, singing songs.
Bow down ye dull and money-grubbing souls
Before the ghosts which want no statues.

I will make a song to the loafers of the world.
I will sing a song to the immortal vagrants,
Dew upon their eyelids,
Morning on their brow.
They drink the tears of the moon
And kiss the lips of sybils.
They watch the bright-armed ones
Who soothe impatient streams
To a low-warbled melody.
Or on the mountain-peaks, with the wild goats,
Listen to great voices.
They meet Pan on samphire-scented paths
And lie with him beneath a chestnut,
He busy with his often-fingered pipes.

I will sing a song to the loafers of the world
Who have ploughed the sky,
Sown to the foamy furrows,
And reaped the immortal corn.
The circle of the Unguessed World is theirs.
Where were Odysseus, Aeneas, Robin Hood,
Arthur, Tristram, Haroun, the Orthodox,
But for the loafers,
Makers of Sagas and of Vegas?
O where were Scotland but for scapegrace Bobbie Burns,
Or France without her outlaw Villon,
Fame's darling thief, immortal wastrel?
I will place a wreath of pine upon the brow

Of Whitman, that rugged mountain, rough with boulders,
Giving cool and freshening springs to those athirst,
Bard of man's brotherhood,
Singer of his own time and of all time,
Seer of daily things made great,
Poet of a hoped democracy:
Man clasping hand with man, all free,
All equal in the tall equality
Of common manhood:
America's gray Homer,
Magnificent old loafer.
The gods are loafers.

Aliens

Guiseppe Morosino; harvester of the Sea,
Brown as a cod's back, or ribbon of floating kelp;
"Papa" the children called him,
"Papa Guiseppe."
Hair silver like a herring, or smelt,
Half-owner of the "Donna Giulia,"
All owner of young donna Giulia,
The beautiful madonna, soon to be one.
She smiled upon her man; her Giuseppe,
Brown with the brine, fragrant of the sea,
Strong as the rocks, gentle as a summer tide.
Better to her heart than boyish suitors
Who wondered at the match.
Addio, sposo mio—Addio, carissima mia—
Donna Giulia returned to her kitchen singing,
"Ma contree 'tiss of dee,
"Sweeta land of Leebartee."
The wind was right, and right the tide,
The fishing banks were ripe for harvest;
Rock cod, sea bass, striped bass; sand dabs,
Rex sole, mackerel, and skate.

Slipping from out the seine into the hold
A bright quicksilver stream;
Dark backs, white bellies, silver sides.
Silver for Giulia and the baby soon to be.
Giuseppe rolled down Taylor Street
With singing heart and sea-like sway,
Swinging his demijohn of good red wine;
A bag of onions, bread and cheese.
Fisherman's Wharf, and there the saucy "Donna Giulia";
Blue as the sky and a broad white stripe.
Matteo Augustino, grizzled, too, and brown,
Giuseppe's partner, there awaited him;
More sparkle in his eyes than common with
The men who face the treacherous All-Devouring One.
Hola, Matteo. Hola, Giuseppe.
The things are stowed. The demijohn of wine;
The seine, a brown heap on the bow;
The lines with baited hooks
Hung in a glistening circle on an iron ring.
Two prohibition agents in plain clothes
Asked Giuseppe if he would not sell
A little wine. "No. No. He would be gone
Three days; he might be blown to sea.
He had no wine to sell."
"Only a drink." "Why, certainly a drink."
They offered money. "No. No. What! For a drink of wine!"

Our Judas Government insisted
"Just for good luck."
"O well—good luck."
These Americans are curious but they love Liberty.
He took the Judas piece of silver and the Government
    arrested him.
Giuseppe stared—he did not understand.
"The 'Donna Giulia' taken? He must go to jail?"
A knot of swarthy fishermen pressed close;
"Giuseppe was arrested for the wine?"
"That could not be."
"Wine was the gift of God."
Power-bloated minions of the "Government,"
Our great, good "Government,"

Seized suddenly the frightened Giuseppe,
Who shook them off as a great dog
Shakes off water drops. He drew
His fishing knife—Some rapid shots
And Giuseppe's body crumpled on the wharf.
The Law had spoken—Law omnipotent,
Of Christ's fanatics who would burn a witch.
Donna Giulia, big with the child to come,
Sang in her kitchen, happily
"Ma contree, 'tiss of dee,
"Sweeta land of Leebartee."
And they were bringing home her murdered man.

Antonio Ploughs

Antonio ploughs and fat the furrows fall,
For cabbages and cauliflower and beans.
Antonio ploughs, and chants a challenge call
To his black stallion—Ercolé.
Ho, Ercolé. Ho, Ercolé.
Ho, Ercolé. Do you perhaps remember
The day you cleaned the stable of a king?
Augeus was his name. You cleaned his stable.
Ho, Ercolé. That was a good day's labor.
Plough deep. Plough deep, my Ercolé, and I will sing.
Plough deep, Ho, Ercolé,
For cabbages and cauliflower and beans.
Ho, Ercolé. Perhaps you do remember,
When for another king you reaped the grain
In Sicily and heard the song of reapers,
Now I will sing you such another strain.
Plough deep. Plough deep and shame the lazy sleepers.
Plough deep. Plough deep, my Ercolé.
Ho, Ercolé. Ho, Ercolé.
Those were old days, and these are other scenes.

Plough deep, my Ercolé. Plough deep and deeper.
For cabbages and cauliflower and beans.

THICK-NECKED HORSES

God, I love a horse.
The nervous, floating antelopes of turf
And course who charge the goal as surf
The shore; spent in a mile their hearts' resources;
But best I love the strong, grave, resolute work horses.
Buttocks, mountain broad and necks whose arch
Is massive as a cape curved to the sea and knees
Firm as a derrick, bushy fetlocks, legs like trees.
Majestic, solemn, slow, the rhythm of their march:
Nature's own, when powerfully the load
They draw on even street or rugged country road.

Calm, wide foreheads; plumy, heavy manes;
On the broad front perhaps a shining star;
Clear quiet eyes which always patient are
Though the whip crack and slap impatient reins:
And when they strain against a heavy hill,
Their silken nostrils open as a flower;
A tulip, red, and so, with valiant will,
They storm the fortress, unflinching, brave in power;
Great haunches wrinkling—rippled satin, bright;
Man such a pigmy to their generous might.
Obedient to a word, a shout, a sign; or left or right
They back—stand over—lift; and no disputes,

And if it be a well accustomed haul
The driver may doze on—they do it all.
Who would not love the gentle, noble brutes?
I pull them grass and as you may suppose
My cheek gets welcome from a velvet nose.

GOATS

What I liked best in Sicily
Was not great smoking Aetna, nor the fanes
Of old Greek gods, noble in majesty
Of death;—but the early fresh-milk trains;
Coming from hills where borage leaves hold dew
And the sky-born flowers of lapis blue
Are wet with Night; trains of whimsical
Black, brown, and spotted grave she-goats
With stare indifferent and quizzical:
Furry tassels dangling at their throats.
Nonchalantly they saunter into town,
Biting, this way and that, the wayside weed
With dainty, lip-selecting, goaty greed,
Skipping lightly to a crumbling wall
Or house top, looking humorously down
To mock, with wag of beard, the herder's call.
Through narrow streets they pass from door to door,
And full of sympathy for motherhood,
Fill frothing bowls for babies of the poor,
From bulging udders, soft and round and good.
By the dripping fountain of the public square
Women wait for them, chatting while
White jets are squirted into bottle-necks; a stair
Up to a sick man one, in leisure style,
Climbs, grinning back with sly, satiric guile.
Their duty done, they lie down in shadow-place
Against a wall, chewing their sidewise cud;
Till presently, with pretty, mincing pace,
Back to the mountain and the tumbling flood.

A Thought

It is a very simple thing
To lie beneath a tree
And hear the larks and linnets sing;
Why is this given me
And not to every living thing
That would be glad and free?

Summer

Sing a song of Summer—of leafy, sheafy Summer,
Coming from cool mountains to walk the dusty way;
Her petticoat upgathered, filled full with woodland
    fragrance:
Tasseled pine, madroña, wild grape and bay.
She lifts brown arms to the piled celestial masses,
Invoking their blessing: shadow and showers.
She wades waist-deep the wind-billowed meadows
Where grasshoppers fiddle the brittle hours.

Birds have sunk deep now in deep wood sancturaries
But goldfinches glean the fencerow seed:
Thistle, dock, wild lettuce, and ripe blackberries
Which Summer offers to their vagrant need.

Sing a song of Summer—leafy, sheafy Summer,
Grass in her hair, her smock much torn
By sharp sweet-briar as she rides the rustling harvest
Of well-bound sheaves to the wheat stack borne
On creaking old wagons with high-piled load
The mouth-drooling oxen heedless of the goad.

Hot noons by the wayside among purple asters,
Goldenrod shaking yellow plumes now;
Drooping-eyed, she dozes, nodding, nodding.

Stroking the ear of a cud-chewing cow;
By a ditch with her seven pink piglets,
Summer-drunk and snoring, sleeps a heavy-dugged sow.

O sing a song of Summer. I have often seen her
Where the hawk's shadow runs on the bouldered steep;
Under an oak, seeking sweet seclusion,
Around her couched the new-fleeced sheep
Bleating softly to the sun-burnt One;
Oxen far below in the broad yoke swaying,
Their dust a cloud shining golden in the sun.

And I have seen her naked with the colts beneath the
    willows;
A dark pool lisping toward a beach of sand;
A green heron posing on one leg, stately
Among the shining ripples where the slender rushes
    stand.
Sing a song of Summer: a bumblebee's low thunder
And wings of butterflies throughout the land.

Sun Worshiper

Naked, bare as I was born,
In the sun I love to lie;
Under the bank of yellow rocks;
And watch the wings that dot the sky.
Birds are gathering into flocks,
August is outworn.
Over me caressing creep
Unseen fingers, Sun and Wind.
Soft sun-fingers plough me deep,
And make me ripe and amber-skinned.
I smell the heat tang of ball-sage.
Summer turns another page.

WHAT SHALL I SAY OF YOU?

What shall I say of you
Whose smile ripples love
As this impetuous stream
Ripples the sunbeam,
Capturing the blue plumes of lupin
Gracefully leaning over?
You brought me life.
You brought me love,
Held carefully between your hands
That its fullness be not spilled,
The dewy cup still beaded with morning.

You offered it as a child gives an apple,
Shyly, hesitantly, hoping it will be taken.
You brought me all.
Keeping nothing back,
Exalting me poet—poet and lover.
You were the poet;
Poet and priestess
Who, reverent, approaches the altar
Seeing the dream-eyed god who awaits her;
The sybil who goes into the mists of the mountain
To meet the hidden one she serves,
Hearing everywhere the voice of the god
In the mysterious, circumambient murmur.

You melted your life into mine,
Wholly, completely, perfectly,
Giving yourself to me
Without show or fuss,
As rivers meet and mingle in a deep canyon,
Where, far below, the eagles float small as sparrows,
And from the leaping torrent comes no sound.
You brought fire to the altar,
A living flame, undying, eternal;
Standing devoutly erect, hands raised,
White robed, white souled, immaculate,
You cast recklessly into the flame, incense

And the amber box of the incense.
You delivered all to the sacred flame,
As beckoned the gods whom you worshiped.

Perhaps all gods are only the image
Of the priestess devout who approaches the altar;
Who wistfully walks to the edge of the pool
That is stirred by the god she seeks and sees
In the dark, mysterious depths,
A serious, beautiful, illumined face
With eager, questioning eyes
Which sinks at her going.
When you go the god of me sinks,
O pure and passionate priestess.

DIANA

I set my back against a beechen heel.
There was an earthy smell of bark and moss.
As a lazy boy grumbles, the fretful little brook
Scolded; a squirrel gave his pretty tail a toss
And I bethought me this would be a nook
To which a dryad or a nymph might steal;
The beech trees drawing close to shelter her,
From some young cowherd, frightened lest he stir.
A dry branch cracked, two snipe leaped in the air,
The bushes shook and from their curtain stepped
A girl just shaped to dewy maidenhood.
She, on a rock (below which, tranquil, slept,
A pool, dark green and deep) a moment pensive stood,
Then higher coiled her ruddy ropes of hair,
And gazed, Narcissus-like, into the pool
Which coaxing held up arms inviting cool.
With a young doe's shy and timid confidence,
She looked about, and cautiously emerged

From her imprisonings (a slim new moon
Creeping from a silver cloud). The ripples surged
About her belly, beautiful and bright as summer noon.
Long time she splashed in playful innocence
And glittering rainbow drops in showers
Fell on the overleaning grass and flowers;
In the sun upon the water-polished rock she lay.
I thought the sun to kiss her should be glad.
Shaking some drops from every glistening tress
She stroked herself awhile, pensive and sad,
Drew her dull husk over her loveliness,
As the moon, grown sick of her lone empty place,
Hides on a hill her pale, despairing face,
And through the wistful bushes took her way.
The place was very empty with her gone.
I felt my brow—remembering Actaeon.

A Day in April

I never shall forget the day in April
When from the rough wind we found such sunny shelter
In a dense grove of eucalyptus at Laguna.

Above us tree tops swayed; and dark blue nightshade
Flowered along the path by which we entered—
Silver-stemmed bush-mallow screened us,
And pungent wormwood, excellently bitter.

In center of the grove, as slim as naked maidens,
Three sapling eucalyptus trees swayed slow and graceful,
Elegant as dancers circling an altar,
Swinging in slow rhythm lovely tresses.

A pair of hummingbirds above us mated—
Love-meeting of two gemmed and jeweled fairies.
Purple finches twittered to the evening,
And we built from some stones a simple altar.

We burned dry eucalyptus leaves and wormwood,
And brought the wild, blue hyacinths and nightshade;
Offerings to the Immortal One, relentless;
The ever-conquering, soft, seductive wrestler,
Who smiling came from out the evening shadow
And threw us gently on a bed of leaves.

INTRODUCTION TO "IF ANY WOULD FOR ME BUILD A TRUE BIER"

IT IS DIFFICULT TO DATE this poem, though it appeared in 1918 as number LXXIX in *Sonnets*. This is the poem Sara followed when she sowed Wood's ashes in the oak grove at The Cats.

IF ANY WOULD FOR ME BUILD A TRUE BIER

If any would for me build a true bier,
    Bring my dumb ashes to a pleasant spot
And scatter them without despairing tear
    About a young oak. So by time forgot
I shall be joyous in the strong oak's veins
    And laugh from out his leaves to the blue sky,
Rejoice in summer sun and winter rains
    And know perhaps a gentler ecstasy
Than this life gives. Birds frolic in the boughs
    And breezes play. And so the seasons pass.
Lovers I know will come to kiss their vows
    And lie awhile upon the whispering grass.
And some who knew me may come here to give
A petal of the heart while yet they live.